THE RUSSIAN TRANSFORMATION
Political, Sociological, and Psychological Aspects

Edited by Betty Glad and Eric Shiraev

St. Martin's Press
New York

ISBN 0-312-21566-5

Library of Congress Cataloging-in-Publication Data

1. post-communism—Russia (Fedration) 2. Russia (Fedration)—Social
conditions—1991– 3. Russia (Fedration)—Politics and government—1991–
4. Soviet Union—Politics and government—1985–1991 5. Communism—
Soviet Union. I. Glad, Betty. II. Shiraev, Eric, 1960–
HN530.2.A8r868   1999
306'.0947—dc21   99–13575
                                                                                        CIP

Design by Binghamton Valley Composition

First published: July 1999

10   9   8   7   6   5   4   3   2   1

Acknowledgements

As coeditors of The Russian Transformation, we are heavily indebted to Patricia Karl, a research associate in the Richard L. Walker Institute of International Studies at the University of South Carolina. Not only did she edit an early version of the manuscript, she made many useful substantive suggestions for its improvement.

Betty Glad was also assisted in her contributions to this volume by research assistants provided by the University of South Carolina. These included Oksana Syrchikova, Mariye Anastasiou, Daniel Crabtree and Maricelly Assuncao. She is also personally indebted to three exchange student she host-parented during the completion of this work. Not only did these three young students make her life richer, they helped in other ways. Dennis Litoshick from Minsk provided many insights into Russian culture and psyche. Andrei Lozovik from Chelyabinsk wrote background papers on the Russian economy. Petter Frizell from Norway and Andrei Lozovik cheerfully aided in the final spelling and footnote checks.

We gratefully acknowledge the helpful advice of Peter Reddaway, Lee Sigelman, and Vlad Zubok, and the support of the Department of Political Science at George Washington University. Special thanks to Allan Wittacker at National Defense University and Richard Dobson at USIA for valuable suggestions during the initial stages of our work on this book.

Contents

Part III: Popular Adaptations

Part IV: Conclusions

Introduction

Betty Glad with Patricia Karl

In this work on the Soviet/Russian transformation we delineate three broad categories of issues critical to the development and direction of reform. In part I we address the question of leadership as a catalyst in the Soviet transition. In part II we look at the broader political, institutional, economic, and sociological changes that were introduced by the new leadership. The carryover of patterns from the Soviet past to the new Russia will be noted where relevant. In part III the contributors analyze popular adaptations to these institutional changes. Gordon Smith, in "The Psychological Dimensions of the Transition" (chapter 8), delineates six historical phases in terms of the leadership/public reactions to the tasks that must be undertaken. The emphasis in the remaining chapters in this section will be on popular adaptations to changes in phases three through five. Particular subjects addressed include overall attitudinal changes towards governmental institutions, generational differences in those attitudes, the impact of new political parties on political attitudes, changes in gender role perceptions, pop music as a reflection of value changes, and Russian attitudes towards the West.

Political scientists have often assumed that totalitarian regimes could not produce transitional leaders committed to democratic reforms and values. Hannah Arendt, in *Totalitarianism* (1969), argues that these regimes are so corrupt that people who come to power are opportunists whose main goal is to maintain their positions within the political hierarchy. Yet Mikhail Gorbachev, Eduard Shevardnadze, and Boris Yeltsin—persons socialized in such a system—arrived on the Soviet political scene in the mid-80s with commitments to reform it. In chapter 1, Glad and Shiraev argue that Gorbachev could have decided to maintain his status and position as general secretary, tinkering with a few minor reforms. But with the introduction of his perestroika, glasnost, and "new thinking" policies he opened up the system with consequences he did not always anticipate. His goal was the reform of the Soviet Union and communism, not its demise. It was his very commitment to the Marxist ideals that had enabled him to come to power and to take the major institutions in Soviet society—the Communist Party and the military—with him in his first steps toward reform. At first Gorbachev as general secretary was able to remove several old-line Stalin traditionalists from leadership positions in the Communist Party. But in attempting simultaneous efforts at social, economic, and political reforms Gorbachev undertook an especially difficult task. The opposition to his policies grew. By 1990, most of Gorbachev's supporters had left his team. He failed to build an alternative political base and was left in a politically isolated position.

In chapter 2, Glad and Shiraev explore the background and psychological characteristics that provide some explanation for Gorbachev's motivations. Familial, school, and party influences contributed to the creation of Mikhail Gorbachev as a good Soviet citizen, a relatively happy young man who loved his country; internalized the communist values; and developed the skills, strength, and abilities to excel in it. Gradually, however, he began to see discrepancies between official dogma and his own experiences. His education in the law faculty at Moscow University gave him a broader perspective on the world than would be the case for many of his peers. Gorbachev was also a product of the post-Stalinist thaw. The revelations of the horrors and purges of the Stalinist period at the Twentieth Party Congress in 1956, and Khrushchev's denunciation of Stalin's cult of personality at the Twenty-second Party Congress, led to Gorbachev's commitment to attempt reforms within the system. This political adaptation guided him to a strategy of finding safe arenas where he could try some reforms, but remain true to his own beliefs and protect his position within the party. As a leader he had qualities not often present in the Soviet political elite: charisma and a capacity for original thinking. Drawing upon some of these leadership tactics and skills, he was able to use the appointments process and persuasion to bring the Communist Party along with him, at least initially. But he had his vulnerabilities. Lacking a strategic plan, he settled for "motion." Used to keeping his own faith, he failed to reach out to maintain the loyalties of aides who might have stayed with him to the end. During the final months of his office, he compounded his problems by his inability to see that the Communist Party had deserted him. The attempted coup in the summer of 1991 not only took him by surprise, it also marked the end to the valiant campaign he had undertaken six and a half years earlier.

The other key architect of reform in the Soviet transition was Eduard Shevardnadze, Gorbachev's foreign minister. As Melvin Goodman shows in chapter 3, he was a brilliant and ruthless political infighter who promoted the principles of the new thinking that he and Gorbachev embraced. He believed that deep cuts in defense spending could pay for the new economic reform policies, that ideology should not be the basis of foreign relations, and that the Cold War competition with the United States was draining Soviet resources and isolating the country from foreign investments and technology. To accomplish these goals, he and Gorbachev would have to gain control of foreign and defense policy from the Communist Party and the military and seek a rapprochement with the United States. The methods employed along these lines are analyzed in this chapter. In some ways more farseeing than Gorbachev, he saw the changes taking place in Eastern Europe long before the Berlin Wall came down. In the end, Shevardnadze's disagreements with Gorbachev over the pace of reform, the use of force in the Baltics and Georgia, and the eroding political situation in the USSR led Shevardnadze to resign from the government. Two years later, as the new head of his native Republic of Georgia, then newly independent, he initially ruled by emergency decree and finally took Georgia into the Commonwealth of Independent States (CIS).

In part II the focus is on the new institutions and sociological structures created in the new Russia. As Glad points out in chapter 4, the same totalitarian system that produced Gorbachev and Shevardnadze incubated and propelled Yeltsin into the leadership of post-Soviet Russia. Boris Yeltsin, like Gorbachev, was a product of his psychological and sociological environment. His personality characteristics, however, suggest that even in the Soviet Union a variety of personality types may rise to the top of the political system. Reared in a harsh familial environment, he became a hardened, impulsive, and risk-taking man. During the early phases of the Russian transformation, his attacks on Gorbachev and his egocentric behavior led to his expulsion from the Politburo. A brilliant politician, he found a new political base in an increasingly discontented Russian public. After May 1990, he had official positions within the Russian Soviet Federative Socialist Republic (RSFR) from which he could make his bid for ultimate power. Utilizing the principles of sovereignty and of self-determination for Russia, he was able to undercut

Gorbachev, while at the same time contributing to the demise of the Soviet Union. At the helm of the new sovereign Russia, he undertook the task of creating new governmental and economic structures. In this process he played a central role in defining the Russian presidency as the key institution in the new political system (Elster 1998). Moving boldly ahead on his economic reforms, he privatized much of the economy, lifted price controls, and restructured the state farms and state-owned companies. Unfortunately, he was even less successful than Gorbachev had been in increasing the productivity of the Soviet economy. Production dropped, consumer prices jumped, inequalities in income grew, corruption increased, and organized crime had a field day. By the fall of l998, the Russian polity was faced with the most extreme economic crisis of his presidency, and Yeltsin's popularity had plummeted to a rating of 1 percent.

With the demise of the Soviet Union, the Russian Federation had to redefine itself as a nation. As Carol Barner-Barry points out in chapter 5, there were two possible orientations in this process. One grew out of the pro-democracy movement during the Gorbachev period and favored a civic nation based on citizenship and equal rights for all people residing on Russian soil, regardless of ethnic origin. The other movement emphasized the importance of ethnically based nationalism. In short, this group wanted ethnic identity (Russian) to be the cornerstone of the new state. In 1991, it was clear that the prevailing policymakers wanted a civic nation. The new Russian Federation was called Rossiisksaia Federatsiia. The solution to the national identity question, Barner-Barry suggests, is impeded by several structural problems. One is how to balance the demands of ethnic Russians with non-Russians. Another major structural problem is one of asymmetry in power-sharing between the center (Moscow) and the subunits of the federation. These structural problems grew and worsened under the leadership of Boris Yeltsin.

In chapter 6, Eric Shiraev elaborates on some of the themes introduced in chapter 5. He shows that the new political and economic elite in Russia has its roots in the middle levels of the Komsomol and the Communist Party. Privatization of state-owned enterprises resulted in members of the former Soviet nomenklature's occupying the top echelons of power and business where they could take financial advantage of old Soviet assets. The lack of control on these privatized properties opened up enormous opportunities for illegal personal gain for those in privileged positions. The result has been a concentration of power and property in the hands of a limited number of entrepreneurs and capital flight out of the country. The "New Russians" who could profit from the restructured business environment supported Yeltsin's reform policies. However, for those Russian citizens who were closed out of the free-market opportunities, life became financially devastating.

The rampant corruption in Russia today, as Bryan Kuns points out in chapter 7, can be traced back to decision-making practices in the former Soviet Union. Working within a centrally controlled and bureaucratically stifling environment, people got things done by cutting corners. Patronage circles based on family and social networks—clans, as it were—enabled managers to function with some degree of efficiency. Though there had always been corruption in the old Soviet system, the Communist Party provided constraints on the types and degrees of corruption, and limited the worst excesses. With the demise of a strong central government and a controlling political party under the new regime, corruption operates without restrictions. Privatization of governmental monopolies created opportunities for corruption on a massive scale, and the new democratic leaders formed alliances with the new economic leaders to buttress their positions in office and make some money for themselves. The government's inability to discipline key financial institutions and businesses has partially contributed to the financial crisis of the end of the 1990s. Kuns concludes the chapter by showing how an overly legalistic conception of corruption can obscure the nature of the power struggle currently underway in Russia.

In part III the popular adaptation to the institutional and sociological changes noted in part II are delineated from a variety of perspectives. In chapter 8, Gordon Smith relates leadership performance to popular attitudes, identifying six historical stages that one might expect in a difficult transition. In stage 1, a delegitimation of the old regime takes place. In stage 2, there is a mobilization of the leadership group for major changes. The process of decentralization and deinstitutionalization in stage 3 threatens the entrenched interests of the bureaucracy, creates economic hardships for the average citizen, and polarizes public opinion. Stage 4 of the transition is a period in which new institutions are built and fast, unrealistic reforms are undertaken. Stage 5 of the transition, which Russia now finds itself in, is characterized by the failure or inadequate performance of the new institutions. Cynicism, disillusionment, and a loss of support for reforms are the consequences (see Finifter & Mickiewicz 1992; Finifter 1996; Miller, Hesli, & Reisinger 1996). In stage 6, which at present is a mere possibility for Russia, a consolidation of the positive accomplishments takes place and the government moderates the pace of reform. In this stage the psychological state of the average Russian is emotional exhaustion.

In chapter 9, on attitudinal changes, Eric Shiraev delineates one of the biggest failures of the transition period. The government has been unable to influence attitudes and practices that would maintain public support for its policies. The breakup of the Soviet Union and the introduction of an uncontrollable free-market economy have resulted in public disillusionment, low political efficacy, and hopelessness about the future. It has also led to negative attitudes toward Yeltsin, the government, the "free market," and other institutions. People want order and stability, and greater equities in the distribution of wealth. All in all, as opinion polls show, most people are unhappy with the situation, but very few want to do anything about it.

As Shiraev and Glad show in chapter 10, many of the political divisions in Russia are based on the differing experiences of the generations. On the whole, those Russians who were socialized and came to their adult roles during the Communist regime (persons who are 60 or older) are the least receptive of the age groups to the policies of the reformers. This group is more likely to vote for the communists or nationalists and is more pessimistic about the future. Compared to the younger groups, senior citizens are more politically active, an indicator, perhaps, of their ties to the political opposition, which they see as reflecting their interests. The Brezhnev generation, people born before 1970, identify less with the Soviet regime than do their parents. They are aware of the problems in the transition, tend to focus on personal lives, and adapt to the changing system as necessary. Many people in this group are less interested in politics and more interested in transferring their skills to benefit from the political and economic changes. They vote less often than their parents do and more often compared to the younger generation. Russians 18 to 30 years old tend to be the most distinct supporters of Yeltsin. Socialized in a politically and culturally chaotic order, they lack the discipline and work ethic of the older generations. However, most of them, despite some radical trends, show little interest in politics and place emphasis on private activities instead.

The growth in the number of political parties and the Russian public's reaction to these new options is addressed by Mitina and Petrenko in chapter 11. Employing psycho-semantic surveys, the authors analyze the relationship between political parties' internal positions on issues (based on the answers of parties' members), the perception of nonmembers on the issues, and the dissonance or disconnect between the perceptions of the two groups. For a public not used to political party choices, the proliferation of parties with similar names and platforms is confusing and may not add to a transition to democratization.

The transition has also altered attitudes about gender roles. As Eric Shiraev indicates in chapter 12, Russian women have not benefited during the transition. In prerevolutionary Russian society, gender roles were patriarchal and paternalistic. Women were expected to suffer and sacrifice for others. Women made progress under the old Soviet system as their literacy levels rose. Political participation was promoted, in part through gender-based quotas, and women were encouraged to pursue traditionally male occupations. During the transition, Soviet quota policies were dropped, women's incomes declined, and discrimination and sexual harassment became somewhat more acceptable than they were in the 1980s. Some politicians openly stated that women did not belong in politics. The breakdown of the Soviet social services for women, coupled with economic hardships produced by the transition policies, have motivated Russian women to focus on local and family issues. There has been a growth of conservative political attitudes among women, who seem to want stability and order over the turmoil of the transition.

One of the most fascinating aspects of the transition is how it has affected popular youth culture. In chapter 13 Eric Shiraev and Sergei Danilov look at pop music as a mirror of the Russian transition. As shown in the chapter, the younger generation in Russia seems to have few emotional ties to Soviet-style cultural norms. The demise of government support for and censorship of the arts has meant that artists, to survive, have had to adapt to the new market forces. While there is more freedom in themes and styles of music, the relationships between artists and their capitalistic supporters offers other kinds of constraints. Popular music has become an attractive industry for organized crime, leading to money laundering, protection, and extortion. The new market-driven music also has meant competition among artists to attract large audiences. Performances, often containing vulgarity and sexist themes, flourish, as do songs romanticizing the criminal world. The authors show that in the mid-90s old Soviet tunes once again have become popular, glorifying aspects of the past. This trend is a reflection of the general public's disappointment with the societal changes and nostalgic feelings about the "safe and secure" past.

In chapter 14, Eric Shiraev suggests that the majority of Russians do not pay much attention to foreign-policy issues in their everyday lives, though most would like to see Russia as a great power. At the elite level, however, furious debates do take place. Three general categories of attitudes toward the West and the Unites States are identified. The national chauvinist orientation takes a negative view of Western policies and values. In the early 1990s, democratic reformers in the Yeltsin camp favored a partnership with the West. A smaller Eurasian group supports an independent Russian policy that would balance Russia's interest in Asia and Europe. Running throughout all these groups, however, there has been an ambivalence toward the West in general and a feeling that the United States in particular is ignoring Russian interests and treating post-Soviet Russia as a junior, inferior partner. The expansion of NATO, events in the former Yugoslavia, and the Russian economic crisis fueled these sentiments.

Andrei Melville, in the concluding chapter, analyzes the Soviet transition in a broader theoretical perspective. Each transition, as he suggests, has certain common features. But the Russian transformation may have special features that reflect particular conditions influenced by the Soviet past and the contemporary developments in Russia.

Part I

Political Leadership and the Initiation of Reforms

Chapter 1

The Reformer in Office

Betty Glad and Eric Shiraev

INTRODUCTION

Transformational leaders may often have difficulties maintaining the support of the very people they hope to serve. If the goal is a change not only in political institutions but also in the way people think and organize their economic and social lives, leaders' problems are apt to be overwhelming. As Gordon Smith notes in chapter 8, changes in the way people operate unleash not only hopes of a better future for many but also the fears and hatred of large groups of individuals whose values and interests are being challenged. The leaders who have imposed totalitarian or tyrannical regimes can deal with the backlash they experience through the use of terror, intimidation, and/or a relatively unconstrained use of state power to buy up support from strategically placed individuals and communities. But the leader committed to the development of democratic institutions through peaceful means faces a basic dilemma. The opposition must be constrained without the employment of political tactics that contradict the very goals being sought.[1]

In undertaking such a task, as one of the authors of this work has pointed out in a previous study (Glad 1996), the process of reform may be made somewhat easier if the leaders of the old and the new orders understand that they are in a cooperative enterprise. The leaders coming out of the old order must move carefully, carrying some of the entrenched forces with them. The representatives of the new order must keep up the pressures for change. But their demands must be made in ways that do not unduly exacerbate the anxieties of the entrenched forces. If a leader on either side fails in his or her task, a counteraction, possibly civil war, is apt to be the result.

But what kinds of persons are likely to undertake such difficult tasks? Transformational leaders with commitments to democratic values and the promotion of a cooperative world order do not often come to power in "totalitarian" regimes. Persons who rise to the top in such systems, it would seem, are apt to be particularly opportunistic, embracing as it were the need to lie and exercise cunning in the maintenance of the political apparatus they support. Indeed, Hannah Arendt in *Totalitarianism* (1968) suggests that the whole political system is so corrupt and self-sealing that there is little possibility for reform from within. In the totalitarian system, she argues, there is a "graduation of cynicism expressed in a hierarchy of contempt." Sympathizers in front organizations despise their uninitiated fellow citizens; the party members despise the gullibility of the fellow travelers; members of the party elites despise the lower levels of the party membership for their naiveté. For those at the very top of the governing circles, she argues, ideological clichés are simply devices to organize the masses, and leaders feel "no compunction about changing them according to the needs of circumstances if only the organizing principle is kept intact" (80–85).

Given Arendt's point of view, it is difficult to explain how Mikhail Gorbachev could come to power in the Soviet Union and even win some support for the far-reaching changes he introduced. In the first two chapters of this work we will offer explanations for these occurrences. In chapter 1 Gorbachev's efforts to transform the Soviet Union, as well as some of the obstacles he confronted, will be delineated. We will show that the representatives of the new order made choices that created difficulties for Gorbachev in his efforts to bring the Communist Party and other existing institutions down the reform path with him. In chapter 2 we will examine the socialization and psychological processes that contributed to Gorbachev's determination to reform the system all the while he was working his way through it.

In the process of our inquiry, the portrait of the totalitarian system presented by Arendt will be modified. As Gorbachev's own experiences make evident, within families and friendship groups some genuine relationships were developed. Direct experiences—such as the destructiveness of World War II and the horrors of forced collectivization—created realities that could not altogether be denied. Moreover, for persons such as Gorbachev, the Marxist ideals of equality and justice did have some power, providing as it were a standard against which the actual practices of those with power in the system could be judged.

THE INITIATIVES

Gorbachev, at least on the surface, is something of a puzzle. Clearly he was a skilled politician who conformed to the norms that every ambitious leader in the Soviet Union had to meet. He joined the Komsomol as a boy, was an organizer for that organization at the university, and joined the Communist Party. Returning to his native Stavropol district after his graduation from college, he secured the sponsors needed to work his way through the party hierarchy. His final rise to power was facilitated by patrons such as KGB chief Yury Andropov, ideology chief Mikhail Suslov, and foreign minister Andrei Gromyko.

Once in power he made it clear that he was a dedicated communist. His first major speech outlining his economic plans for the Soviet Union was delivered at the Smolny Institute where Lenin had his headquarters in 1917, during the Bolshevik revolution. In his book *Perestroika* (Restructuring), published in 1987, agricultural collectivization is justified "as a great historic act, the most important social change since 1917" (40). On his trips, when foreigners abroad tried to sell him on the superiority of the capitalist system, he cut the conversation short with comments to the effect that they could keep their system and he would keep his. As late as December 20, 1989, he told a session of the Congress of People's Deputies, "I am a communist, a convinced communist. For some that may be a fantasy. But for, me it is my main goal" (Doder & Branson 1990, 390).

Yet he was barely in office when he began to challenge the premises of the system in which he had been socialized. His perestroika policy, announced in May 1985 in a speech at the Smolny Institute, was an effort to revitalize the economy by rationalizing management, introducing incentives in the workplace, and decentralizing economic decision making. The waste and stagnation in the Soviet economy, he argued, necessitated a more efficient and rational system of administration. A month later he told the Central Committee of the Communist Party that the entire economy would have to be "retooled." Principles of cost accounting and a flexible price system would have to be introduced. The next year, in a speech at Krasnodar, Gorbachev called for the introduction of a market economy and limited private enterprise. He pointed to Lenin's New Economic Policy as a blueprint for his own plans (50, 8–0, 166).

Gorbachev's "new thinking" in the area of foreign policy, introduced during his first months in office, questioned some of the basic assumptions of the nuclear age. He argued that national security "can only be secured through general security" (Gorbachev 1985a, 1). There was "nothing inevitable" about continuing the confrontation with the United States; Gorbachev believed that the very phenomenon was an "anomaly" (Gorbachev 1985b, 1). However, the path to agreement had been made difficult by "super gladiators," attempts to secure a "deft blow," and "an extra point" in the "bout." Since time was growing late, it was "too great a luxury for the leaders of the Soviet Union and the United States to go to Geneva merely to get acquainted and then admire Lake Geneva" (Gorbachev 1985b).

Indeed, he offered other ideas about the nature of history that challenged the foundations of the Marxist-Leninist system. Thus he qualified the traditional Marxist notion that history guarantees the triumph of communism with the view that the international system would remain pluralist in the foreseeable future. Indeed, he argued that the Soviet regime was the source of new contradictions. Moreover, as he noted after an unprecedented visit with Pope John Paul II, he saw the world as having certain values with universal validity (Sheehy 1990, 220).[2]

His glasnost policy, introduced in 1986, was designed to free the Soviet people from external constraints so that the creative spirit could flourish in a variety of endeavors.[3] The precondition for the restructuring of the economy, as Gorbachev saw it, was to "wake up" those people who had "fallen asleep" and to ensure that everyone felt as if he or she were master of the country, of the enterprise, the office, or the institute. The social sciences, he noted, must be freed from the "scholastic theorization" and other forces that had driven out creativity (Gorbachev 1987, 29, 21). In culture, literature, and the arts "there appeared quite a few mediocre, faceless works that did not give anything to the mind or the heart" (A8). Many of these works, he suggested, did not address serious social or moral issues nor dealt with "true to life conditions" (*New York Times,* 28 January 1987). There is no one truth, he wrote in *Perestroika:* "[D]o not think that we have found the final truth which the others merely have to accept or reject. For us a new thinking is a process in the course of which we continue to learn and gain ever new experience" (Gorbachev 1987, 15–2). His emphasis, in short, on the need for spiritual rebirth through the process of democratization and the free exchange of ideas suggests that he was aware, in a way that Vladimir Lenin had not been, of the dangers of giving any one group a monopoly of power (see also Kull 1990). In an address to Soviet writers in June 1986, he bemoaned the absence of a "legal opposition" to the party by asking, "How can we control ourselves?" (Doder & Branson 1990, 77).

IMPLEMENTATION

Glasnost was implemented in a series of dramatic moves. Many previously "dangerous" books, novels, and movies were released to the public after 1985. Among them were works by Alexandr Solzhenitsyn, Andrei Sakharov, Anatoly Rybakov, and Tengiz Abuladze, to name just a few. After seeing the film *Repentance,* the story of life under an ostensibly mythical Georgian tyrant, Gorbachev told his aides to make enough copies of the film so that everyone in the country could see it (Gorbachev 1996, 20–7). In December 1986, Gorbachev personally ordered Andrei Sakharov's release from internal exile in Gorky. On October 5, 1987, Gorbachev became the first Soviet leader to publicly denounce Stalin. He called his crimes "enormous and unforgivable" (Doder & Branson 1990, 3, 172, 183). A party commission he appointed to review the purge trial of Nikolai Ivanovich Bukharin in the 1930s determined that it was a "gross violation of socialist legality" (Taubman 1988, 1).

The "new thinking" in foreign policy led to forward movement in the arms limitation talks. A series of offers suggesting that the Soviet Union would make concessions to achieve that result, plus top-level meetings between Gorbachev and Reagan in Geneva, Reykjavik, Washington, and Moscow, resulted in the signing of the INF (Intermediate Nuclear Forces) treaty and some forward movement on the limitation of intercontinental nuclear weapons. These meetings, when accompanied by the Soviet withdrawal from Afghanistan and the renunciation of the Brezhnev doctrine, substantially improved relations with the United States.

Perestroika would have its first impact on the Communist Party—as Gorbachev noted it must, in a Politburo meeting on July 26, 1986 (Chernyaev 1993, 91). Employing the same kinds of techniques that the men at the top of the Soviet system had long employed, Gorbachev started out with personnel changes. Boris Yeltsin was removed from the Politburo in February 1988. Gorbachev must have seen Yeltsin's impetuosity and commitment to drastic changes as anathema to his own efforts to bring the Communist Party down the reform route with him. Then obvious reactionaries at the top were replaced. By the fall of 1989, Politburo members Victor Chebrikov, Vladimir Shcherbitsky, and scores of Brezhnevite Central Committee members had been removed from their positions (Doder & Branson 1990, 386). By 1991 two-thirds of the Party apparatus at all levels and the entire membership of the Politburo had been replaced, along with three prime ministers and almost all members of the Presidium of the Council of Ministers (Chernyaev 1993, 63; Boldin 1994, 293).

Changes in party structures were introduced more slowly. First, Gorbachev promoted intraparty competition and took steps to separate the government from the Communist Party. Early in 1987, he secured the consent of the Communist Party for multi-candidate elections in the selection of party officials, factory management, and local government bodies (Taubman 1987a, 1; Taubman 1987b, A9; Keller 1987, A10). In addition, he put through measures to increase the power of local Soviets at the expense of the Communist Party and proposed the removal of the party from state economic management (Gorbachev 1996, 25–0). Following the All-Union Party Conference in the summer of 1988 and the Central Committee plenum of September 30, 1988, the Secretariat was restricted to deciding strictly intraparty issues (268). These changes, Gorbachev noted at a Politburo meeting on December 27, 1988, were designed to revitalize the Communist Party. "An atmosphere of party camaraderie and openness are being established . . . Strong people will be coming as a result of such a selection, this is what we need" (Politburo meeting transcript 1988).

Then Gorbachev led the party to accept a certain amount of inter-party competition and the creation of new political institutions. By June 1989 a new Soviet Congress had been created in which there was some real competition for elections to both of its bodies. Blocs were formed, and genuine, sometimes raucous, debates took place within their chambers. By mid-March of 1990, a presidency independent of direct party control was established with Gorbachev at the helm. He would hold the presidency for a five-year term, and the next time around the position would be filled through multi-candidate elections (Imse 1990, 1; Keller 1990a, 1). That same month the Communist Party reluctantly agreed to revoke Article VI of the Soviet constitution which had enshrined the Communist Party as the "leading and guiding force" in Soviet life (Gorbachev 1995a, 317). As Gorbachev noted at a meeting in Lithuania on March 13, he could accept the idea of multiparty electoral competition as long as the system was not artificially imposed. "We should not be afraid of it, the way the devil is of incense," he said (Fein 1990, 1; see also Associated Press 1989; Doder & Branson 1990, 408).

In addition, Gorbachev introduced institutional reforms in the Soviet military organization. He moved the Soviet Union from an offensive to a defensive strategic orientation and reduced the size of the army. (In December 1988 he announced his plans for a unilateral reduction of one-half million Soviet military personnel.) Men who seemed to share ideological perspectives close to his own were placed in top command positions. The retirement of Sergei Akhromeyev as chief of the General Staff of the army not long after Gorbachev's announcement of the proposed reduction of the army marked the removal from active duty of the last of the marshals of the Soviet Union. "This clean sweep of the most prestigious and strong personalities among the senior military elite," as one observer noted, "was a major step by Gorbachev, but one hardly noticed in the West" (Odom 1990, 58). In May 1989, Gorbachev revealed for the first time the size of the Soviet defense budget. It was about four times larger than had previously been acknowledged ("Gorbachev Reveals" 1989, 11).

At the economic level a few small-scale measures were introduced during the first two years of perestroika. Soviet producers were given the right to deal directly with the representatives of foreign companies. Pay scales were introduced that related remuneration more directly to individual productivity. A Law of Social Enterprise aimed to decentralize the economy by giving companies the right to buy directly from each other and to see a greater proportion of their output placed on the free market; the state itself was to be a customer, although a preferred one (Doder & Branson 1990, 82–90, 166, 239–40). In spring 1990, the Kremlin considered even more radical programs. Possibilities discussed included the disbanding of state industrial ministries and the development of a stock market. To assist people during the transition, programs such as unemployment insurance, job training, and other subsidies were also considered (Clines 1990a, 6).

UNINTENDED CONSEQUENCES

Perestroika did not bring about the economic revival it was designed to initiate. Partial reform measures proved to be worse, in some respects, than the command economy they were intended to replace. By 1989 the new private sector was unable to obtain supplies still under central control. Price reform did not occur, and inflation and the fear of inflation, previously unknown, led to panic buying, which in turn contributed to the scarcity of consumer goods in stores (Medvedev 1994, 39, 55). Wildcat strikes, fired by economic hardships, and the new doctrine of glasnost that legitimated such protests further undercut production (Keller 1989a, Desai 1989, Asiand 1989). The old, centralized economic system, after a series of unsuccessful attempts at radical improvement and acceleration, had fallen to pieces.

Glasnost, while it freed the human spirit, also had its downsides. The revelations of Joseph Stalin's crimes contributed to the delegitimation of the Soviet system at a time when there was no clear alternative set of values to replace it. People accustomed to being told what to do were not able to make an instant adaptation to the command that they should now be responsible, creative, and initiating individuals. Bereft of guidance from the center, local party officials became confused. They asked for advice but were told only to do what they thought was right (Ligachev 1996, 85). Even the public took offense at the lack of central direction. In 1988, during one of his discussions with an angry crowd on the streets of Sevastopol, Gorbachev directly encountered this dependence. "Who am I? A Czar? Or maybe Stalin? You want me to go from town to town saying: this is an apartment for you, this is pension for you, this is a decent salary for you, here I bring about order in your factory. And this is a thief, let's put him in jail. . . . No, you haven't understood the very core of perestroika if you demand something from me and if you wait permissions and treats from Moscow" (Chernyaev 1993, 230).

The new thinking, too, had foreign-policy consequences troubling to many Russians. The INF agreement between the USSR and the United States was seen by many in the Soviet Union as a deal that cut more deeply into Soviet strength than it did for the United States. The renunciation of the Brezhnev doctrine led to the disintegration of the Soviet empire in Eastern Europe as Poland, Hungary, Czechoslovakia, East Germany, Bulgaria, and Romania overthrew their Communist governments. Some replaced them with coalition governments; others rejected their ruling party outright. Following the fall of the Berlin Wall in October 1989, East Germany was officially reunited within the Western camp and the Warsaw Pact was disbanded. In any case, the communist bloc in Eastern Europe ceased to exist and the Soviets lost their buffer zone. The Cold War ended, but under terms that appeared to many in the Soviet Union to mark a victory for the West and total collapse of Moscow's geopolitical positions (Dobrynin 1995, 62–2)

The falling dominos did not end there. Calls for self-determination within the Union emerged. Initially, as in the Armenia-Azerbaijan dispute over Nagorno-Karabakh, the grievances began as ethnic rivalries. But shortly thereafter, secessionist movements emerged in several of the other republics. On December 28, 1989, Lithuania registered the first noncommunist political party in the Soviet Union, and Latvia voted to abolish the Party's "leading role." Though Gorbachev declared such actions illegitimate, in March 1990 the republics of Georgia, Lithuania, and Estonia declared formal independence from the USSR. Their actions were followed by Latvia in May and Moldavia in June.

In 1990, five years after Gorbachev first introduced his reforms, the Politburo published its assessment of the overall situation in the country: "People are upset with lack of stability in the society. Crisis continues in the economy. There is a hard financial situation. [We see] the overall decline of discipline and order. The crime is flourishing" (*Materialy Politburo*, 12 March, 1990).

As the polity seemed to be flying apart around him, Gorbachev became the target of popular frustrations. Results of a poll published in the popular weekly *Argumenty i Facty* in autumn 1989 indicated that Gorbachev was not among the top ten most popular figures in the Supreme Soviet (Doder & Branson 1990, 391). At the May Day ceremony in 1990, many people near the reviewing stand jeered the governmental officials and waved flags expressing sentiments such as "Down with Gorbachev" and "72 Years to Nowhere" (Keller 1990b; Keller 1989b; Coleman 1990, 29). By spring 1991, Gorbachev's approval rating had dropped to below 14 percent (Brumberg 1991, 54).

Yet for a moment at the Twenty-eighth Communist Party of the Soviet Union (CPSU) Congress in the summer of 1990 it seemed that the worst of times for the Soviet Union might have passed. Gorbachev seemed to have won control of the party as a vehicle for change. He was reelected general secretary of the Communist Party in the first publicly contested election for the post, and the leader of the party traditionalists, Yegor Ligachev, was defeated in his bid for the role of deputy leader. Moreover, the most obvious obstructionist members of the party leadership, including half the Politburo, had been dropped from the list of candidates for the Central Committee. The party, in short, seemed poised to do what the liberal editor of the *Moscow News,* Yegor Yakovlev, said it must do. It seemed to be in the midst of a transformation to a "younger

and more leftist party . . . to lead the country forward to more serious
reforms" ("Gorbachev Appeals for Unity" 1990; see also Gorbachev
1996, 36–1; Clines 1990c; Keller 1990c).

THE DENOUEMENT

Gorbachev's victory at the Twenty-eighth Communist Party Congress was
very short-lived. At the final session of the conference, the "populist"
leader Boris Yeltsin announced that he was leaving the Communist Party.
In a thinly veiled slap at Gorbachev, Yeltsin declared, "as the highest
elected figure in the Republic (of the RSFSR), I can only subordinate
myself to the will of the people." Making an ostentatious exit out of the
hall, he walked slowly as if expecting others to follow him. Though Gorbachev suggests that no one else followed Yeltsin down the aisle, newspaper reports indicate that several other members of the democratic
platform left the party at the time, including the mayors of Leningrad and
Moscow. Gorbachev's frustration at this turn of events was only slightly
concealed. In an emotionless voice he said, "that ends the process logi-
cally" ("Congress of the Dead" 1990, 30; Dobbs 1990, A15; Gorbachev
1996, 3–2). Gorbachev, in short, had won at least temporary control of a
party that had lost much of its vital spirit.

For some time Yeltsin had been challenging Gorbachev. Earlier, as
Moscow's party chief he had marched around the city, a camera following
him, contrasting his own disdain for party perks to the relish other party
leaders had for them. In the Politburo meeting of October 21, 1987,
Yeltsin suggested that a cult of personality was forming around Gor-
bachev, thereby tacitly comparing this general secretary to Stalin.[4] When
Gorbachev and his allies responded with attacks on Yeltsin's adventure-
some and egocentric ways, there was no turning back. By 1989, Yeltsin
was beginning to position himself as an alternative leader to Gorbachev.
Traveling to the United States in September as a private individual,
Yeltsin pressed until he secured a short visit with a reluctant President
Bush. And from podiums all over the United States he criticized Gorbachev's perestroika, marveled at the "wonders of capitalism," and
declared that the Baltic republics should be able to determine their own
futures (Morrison 1991, 10–5, 108).

Elected as the leader of the Russian Supreme Soviet in May 1990,
Yeltsin proceeded to employ the principles of "sovereignty" and "self-
determination" to undermine Gorbachev at the center. In June 1990, for

example, he pushed through the congress of the Russian Republic the Declaration of State Sovereignty, which asserted the primacy of Russian over Soviet laws and the right of Russia to the Soviet-controlled natural resources on the republic territory. The Shatalin plan for economic reform that Yeltsin pushed in the fall of 1990 would have extended the principle of economic sovereignty to all the other republics. The national government would retain only the control of defense, the money supply, scientific and space research, and communications and transportation (Morrison 1991, 14–5).

Though Yeltsin was his main antagonist, Gorbachev did not find much support from other reform leaders. Failing to see the political constraints under which he was acting, they showered him with demands for instant change. Most argued that only a quick and dramatic move toward a free market would save the economy. Some leaders questioned Gorbachev's endeavors to hold the Union together and characterized his attempts to exercise authority as indications of nascent dictatorial tendencies. Several democrats insisted that Gorbachev relinquish the post of general secretary. Some urged him to resign from the party altogether (Clines 1990b). But they also wanted him to strip the apparatchiks of their power and vest all authority in a democratically elected parliament (Izyumov 1990, 27). Even Andrei Sakharov, who was one of the really serious reformers, urged him to drastically restrict the authority of the KGB and provide for popular presidential elections (Dobbs 1997, 25–8). In short, the demands most of the democrats placed on Gorbachev suggest that they saw him as a kind of czar, a leader who, through the exercise of his individual powers, could bring about a revolution through the mere exertion of his will.

It is not surprising, then, that except for Sakharov and one or two others, none of the democrats offered realistic plans for securing the dramatic changes they sought. Nor did they construct the political foundations that might have provided Gorbachev with alternatives to his reliance on the Communist Party. To the contrary, the fluidity of the political system in which they were operating whetted political appetites, and for a while it seemed that almost any politician of note was forming his own political party. By 1991, there were hundreds of "political parties" in the Soviet Union, and none of them, except the Communists, had a large or all-Union membership (Yuriev 1992). In short, as Eduard Shevardnadze noted, "the democrats have always been too disorganized to give Gorbachev the support he needed." Their pleas for collaboration, moreover, have "always been accompanied by innuendoes and abrasive comments which Gorbachev must have found insulting" (Brumberg 1991, 56; see also Clines 1990b).

Not only did the democrats not provide Gorbachev with the support he needed, their demands for radical change made it more difficult for Gorbachev to bring the Communist Party traditionalists along with him on the path of reform. "My enemies are on the right," Gorbachev remarked bitterly on one occasion, "but the ammunition is provided by the left" (Doder & Branson 1990, 276).

Still, as long as these radical democrats remained in the Communist Party they strengthened Gorbachev's hand, enabling him to position himself as a centrist, a responsible leader devoted to reform but opposed to the trashing of all that had been good in the Soviet system. With their departure from the Communist Party in the summer of 1990, Gorbachev was isolated within a party that lost all impetus for reform (Medvedev 1994, 44, 105, 133). As Gorbachev remarked in frustration after one private meeting with regional party secretaries, these "Bastards! Besides their privileges and power they do not need anything!" He was left, in short, with a "scabby crazy dog" that, if unleashed, would crush perestroika (Chernyaev 1993, 242, 356).

Isolated within the Communist Party, Gorbachev moved to the right in the winter of 1991. In November, he flatly rejected the Shatalin-Yavlinsky plan that he had formerly endorsed. In December, he elevated Communist Party traditionalists to prominent posts in the government. With the resignation of Eduard Shevardnadze as foreign minister shortly thereafter, Gorbachev lost his last major reformer in the government. Gathering up power in the presidential office, he issued decrees that, at least on paper, substantially cut into the Supreme Soviet's legislative function. He also pushed through Supreme Soviet resolutions endowing the president with emergency powers, and threatened to impose direct presidential rule on turbulent regions of the nation (Mikheyev 1992, 113).

The powers of the military, police, and KGB were also increased. On November 27, Gorbachev's hand-picked defense minister, Marshal Dmitri Yazov, announced in a televised statement "a Presidential order sanctioning the use of force to combat a 'breakdown' of order in the USSR." In December, Vladimir Krychkov, head of the KGB, announced that the KGB would protect law and order and block all force trying to tear the Union apart. Warning against acceptance of Western aid, Krychkov claimed that the assistance was being used to subvert Russia. One presidential decree established a joint army-police patrol for enforcement of law and order. Another directed local governments to preserve supplies for the military. Another authorized the KGB and the military to enter any establishment suspected of speculative activities in order to inspect its books. Then, in early January 1991, troops were sent into Vilnius and Riga to repress secessionist moves there.

Throughout this whole process, Gorbachev came under concerted attacks from the right.[5] In a meeting with military officers in early November 1990, Gorbachev was accused of allowing the persecution of Communists and making one-sided concessions to the West. In February 1991, Ivan Polozkov, the first secretary of the Russian Republic's Communist Party, castigated Gorbachev for "giving priority to planet-wide values rather than class interests" (Brumberg 1991, 53). In April 1991, the leaders of the hard-line Soyuz group of deputies from the Supreme Soviet of the USSR called for Gorbachev's removal from power and the establishment of an immediate state of emergency with the suspension of the activity of all political parties. At the meeting of the Central Committee of the Communist Party four days later, Gorbachev faced so many criticisms along the above lines that he offered to resign. Pulling back from the possible schism that such an action could create, the hard-liners beat a quick retreat. Indeed, at the plenary session the members voted to invite representatives of other political parties to talks leading to the possibility of some kind of coalition government (53).

Even the Orthodox Church created pressures on Gorbachev from the right. On December 22, 1990, the Russian patriarch, Aleksy II, joined several nationalists and reactionaries in a letter published in *Sovetskaya Rossia* demanding that Gorbachev declare a state of emergency so that the country would not fall prey to a dictatorship of "anti-popular and anti-socialist" forces (56).

In the meantime, Yeltsin on the "left" was doing his bit to further undermine Gorbachev and the central government. In February 1991, he called for Gorbachev's resignation as president of the Soviet Union, blaming him for the economic hardships the Soviet people were experiencing (Morrison 1991, 23–2). In several other steps, he showed his disdain for authority at the center. Thus he called for the army to disobey Gorbachev's orders, and signed an agreement with the chairman of the Georgian parliament (a reactionary and ultranationalistic body) to establish joint police and army patrols in the territory of the former South Ossetian region. He took these steps unilaterally, without the consent or knowledge of even the Russian Supreme Soviet. On a trip to France in April, he urged France and the European Parliament to bypass Soviet authorities to deal directly with the Russian Republic. His suggestion was refused (Brumberg 1991, 53, 58).

As the Soviet Union seemed on the verge of disintegration, Yeltsin pulled back. On April 23, 1991, at Novo-Ogarevo, he joined Gorbachev and eight other leaders of the republics in the initiation of negotiations to replace the Soviet Union with a loose confederation.[6] The goal was to establish a constitution for a new union of the Soviet republics in which all of the officials would be elected (Morrison 1991, 25–6, 27–3).

The details of the coup attempt in August 1991 and its aftermath will be developed in the next chapter. Suffice it to say at this point that the coup attempt thoroughly discredited the Communist Party and destroyed Gorbachev's prestige as a credible political actor. It is not surprising, then, that at a highly secret meeting at a nature reserve in Belarus on December 8, 1991, Yeltsin and the leaders of the Ukraine and Belarus delivered the death blow to the Soviet Union. A "Commonwealth of Independent States" would replace the old USSR (Yeltsin 1994, 11–3; Schmemman 1991). Shortly thereafter, in some legally questionable moves, Yeltsin issued decrees directing the Russian government to seize the Kremlin and take over or replace the functions of the entire Soviet central government with the exception of the ministries of defense and atomic energy. Gorbachev denounced the decrees as illegal but could do nothing to block them. On December 23, 1991, in a meeting in the Kremlin, Gorbachev gave up the last vestige of power when he turned over to Yeltsin the case containing the secret nuclear codes. Yeltsin later justified this final assault by saying that "Gorbachev had exhausted his mental and decision-making resources, making him vulnerable once again to evil forces" (Yeltsin 1994, 112, 115).

REASONS FOR FAILURE

The reasons for the disintegration of the Soviet Union and Gorbachev's fall from grace may be explained along the following lines.

At the most basic level, Gorbachev had attempted the rare feat of bringing about what Zygmunt Bauman calls a "peaceful, systematic revolution" (1994, 15). This endeavor—to carry out nearly simultaneous social, economic, and political transformations—made the leadership task almost impossible. Gorbachev was forced to continuously redirect his attention from one crisis to another, every time realizing how deep the existent problems were (Chernyaev 1993). Comparing his political tasks

to the work of a steeler, he noted on one occasion that "to direct this
stream [of molten steel] into the channels, we have to somehow hold this
stream, so that it doesn't spill over, it doesn't burn and destroy everything." On another occasion, he employed the metaphor of a "reforming
yeast": "In order to start the process [of reforms] we needed a catalyst.
We had to throw it in the fermenting political process." Ultimately, "mis-
calculations took place, the processes went out of control" despite his
attempts to "hold these processes within the boundaries" (Gorbachev
1992, 139, 14–2).

To complicate matters, Gorbachev had no overall strategy for moving from a centralized economy to a free market, from an autocratic system that attempted to control every aspect of life to a democratic and
limited form of government. What he introduced, as Vadim Medvedev has
pointed out, was just a "sum of ideas" (1994, 30). Certainly the "main
virtues of his 'peasant mind' were common sense and the amazing sense
of momentum," wrote the popular Russian analyst Leonid Nikitinsky in
Izvestia on July 16, 1994. Chernyaev (1995, 521), one of Gorbachev's
closest advisers and friends, has suggested that Gorbachev's ideology was
"just simple, human thoughts and desires, simple, 'people's' view on life,
normal 'personal' considerations, and wishes of a simple man; generally
speaking—they were common sense views."

Looking back, Gorbachev remarked, "We simply didn't know much
about our society. We have not been receiving necessary information
about ourselves, about the world around us." His decisions to use tough
measures, he suggests at one point in his writings, were based on his
being deliberately "misinformed" (Gorbachev 1992, 141, 15–1).
Chernyaev made similar observations: "[O]ur scientists did not know
anything about this" (Chernyaev 1993, 280, 127).

In addition to these vulnerabilities, as we have suggested, Gorbachev
had no solid political base for the changes he undertook. Most of those
who remained in the Communist Party after the summer of 1990 were
resistant to fundamental change, as we have seen, and as the Soviet Union
seemed on the verge of disintegration, they became Gorbachev's enemies.
The democratic reformers provided him with no viable alternatives. Most
of them demanded instant change without considering how the change
would be accomplished. Nor did they consider, as Gorbachev had to do,
the possibility of a backlash from those who actually wielded power in the
Soviet Union—the Party, the army, the KGB. As Gorbachev suggests,
"They were romanticists, idealists. They would love to go to bed in the
evening and sleep under the blanket of totalitarian regime in order to

wake up in the morning under the blanket . . . colored by the rainbow's colors. But who should have and who could have conducted those radical changes? Especially at night, when it is hard to see, when it is easy to mess things up" (Gorbachev 1995b, 194). In short, there was no middle ground in the Soviet Union. Compromise was not what the forces on either the conservative right or the new democratic left wanted (Sobchack 1992, 130).

In these circumstances Gorbachev had no good alternatives. If he had deserted the Communist Party earlier, the strongest and most important institution in the Soviet Union would have remained without any check on its actions. If Gorbachev had embraced the economic shock therapy propounded by the "left," he would have had direct responsibility for the anarchy and the disintegration of the Soviet economy that would result. But if he had moved all the way to the "right" and been willing to use force to maintain the Union, a civil war could have resulted. Faced with lose/lose alternatives, Gorbachev procrastinated or attempted to straddle the two sides of an issue. These adaptations made Gorbachev seem either hypocritical or weak, a quality that many Russians scorn. The psychological bases for this procrastination will be suggested in the chapter that follows.

Some suggest that Gorbachev simply might have given up power. But as Chernyaev (1993) has noted, his sense of responsibility and overflowing energy led him to stay on. One could surmise that in the winter of 1991, he was trying to preserve public order and keep the Communist Party from the very kind of coup it later attempted. After the coup, his efforts were to secure, as in his last attempt, some sort of union.

The more deeply ingrained characteristics of the population also contributed to the economic paralysis. Perestroika and glasnost were exciting ideas for many Soviet citizens at first. But as the details and the costs of the economic reforms became evident, resistance to perestroika developed. Communist ideas about equality, too, when combined with economic hardships, reinforced the tendencies of those who had little to envy the new entrepreneurs who had more (Keller 1989b, 1; Doder & Branson 1990, 402). According to Medvedev (1994), Chernyaev (1993), Yakovlev (1992), Shevardnadze (1991), and practically every other major political figure writing about this period, the reaction to the economic reforms was negative throughout the populace.

Indeed, the Soviet political culture was not well suited to the idea that individuals should take initiatives in the economic realm and self-govern in politics. Totalitarian societies promote regressive characteristics in individuals, as Olga Marlin (1990) has noted, creating needs for authority and the tendency to lay problems at the door of external enemies. Dependency is promoted, and people come to need the all-powerful leader who feeds their fantasies and supports their defenses. When a man like Gorbachev comes along and asks people to think for themselves and to take responsibility for their own future (1992, 230), he is upsetting many deep defenses. The publication in 1989 of a National Opinion Research Council poll commissioned by Soviet governmental officials gave explicit evidence of this point of view. Deeply ingrained feelings of dependence on the central government and a strong distaste for economic inequalities were evident in the responses of the people polled (Keller 1989b, 1).

Boris Yeltsin's radical stances, as Glad (1996) has argued in detail elsewhere, contributed to Gorbachev's problems. Blaming Gorbachev for all the problems that the transition was creating, Yeltsin undermined the Soviet leader's authority in democratic circles. At the same time his radical stances increased the resistance of the Communist Party traditionalists to the whole reform movement. His populist assaults on Communist Party privileges, his abrupt departure from the party, his determination to introduce the free market within 500 days, and his lack of concern for the central government—all of these pleased many who were anxious to bury the old regime and/or move more swiftly on the reform track than was Gorbachev. But these stances also fed the fears of the party traditionalists that the whole reform movement would come to no good end, buttressing the commitment of many of them to roll the clock back.

Gorbachev's own contributions to the problems he faced cannot be ignored. He could have strengthened his hand vis-à-vis Yeltsin if he had presented himself to the people in a popular referendum. He might have looked further ahead, initiating the legal changes requisite to the actual functioning of a market economy and the responsible disposition of public properties into private hands. He might have moved strongly toward transferring party assets to the state. In 1990, for example, he gave instructions to begin the transfer of the party's assets, buildings, and communications to the government (for example, to the office of president). The task was supposed to be finished in two months. However, as with previous decisions, he changed his mind and canceled the plan (Chernyaev 1993, 334). Moreover, he could have been clearer in his response to the Shatalin plan. First, he suggested that he would back a commitment to a plan of economic reform that would have moved the Soviet Union radically in the direction of a market economy. But then he refused to endorse the Shatalin-Yavlinsky 500-day program when it was finally ready (Gorbachev 1996, 37–3).

The degree of Gorbachev's political isolation at the end of his regime was also partly his responsibility, as we shall show. If he had shared more responsibility with advisers and other governmental officials who were also committed to reform, he might have secured greater loyalty from them. The psychological bases for this vulnerability will be analyzed in the following chapter.

CONCLUSIONS

In his five years of power, Gorbachev introduced dramatic revisions of Soviet domestic and foreign policies, as we have seen. On the domestic front, by early 1989 relatively democratic national elections to both chambers of the new Soviet congress had been held, and basic decision making had been shifted from the Party to the government. Within the Communist Party, some of the neo-Stalinist element had been swept out of the political leadership cadres, and intraparty competition for office had been introduced. Multi-candidate elections had taken place for the selection of party officials, factory management, schools, universities, and governmental bodies (Taubman 1987a, 1; 1987b, A9; Keller 1987, A10). The party had even been persuaded to surrender its constitutional monopoly on power and had given up on the Politburo as a serious policy-making body. The army was purged of many senior officers who would have been in positions to resist Gorbachev's plans for reducing the size and influence of the military (Bunich 1992, 26–2; Chernyaev 1993, 163). Many ideological "taboos" had been eliminated. With the public denunciation of Stalin and his allies, the very legitimacy of the totalitarian state was undermined. In the new climate of freedom, every fundamental of art and politics was explored. On the international scene, Gorbachev changed the way people thought about the value of nuclear weapons in promoting national security. He ended the Cold War with the West, concluded a treaty limiting intermediate-range nuclear weapons, and began the process that would eventually limit intercontinental nuclear weapons.

In short, Gorbachev ended a totalitarian state without bloodshed. Being exceptionally goal-directed, Gorbachev almost single-handedly moved the rock of totalitarianism. Later he would say that he did not regret anything. "They scream: 'havoc,' 'empty shelves,' 'party is going down,' 'no order.' But how could it be different? . . . Usually such big turns are accompanied with bloodshed. So far, we avoided it. This is a substantial achievement already" (Chernyaev 1993, 51–9, 345). But Gorbachev could not complete the task he undertook. Lacking the backing of a strong party committed to reform and a political culture in which individual initiatives were given a high priority, he obtained no consensus as to the direction reform should go. Nor did he or anyone else in the Soviet Union have a clear idea as to how their country might move ahead in the establishment of fundamentally new economic institutions. That process, as he sensed, would introduce many new problems for Russia and the other successor states.

NOTES

1. Transformational political leadership for the purposes of this study is any leadership that involves undertaking basic changes in the political, economic, or social institutions of a polity. Unlike Burns (1978), who first gave currency to this concept, we do not assume that these changes need result in moral progress. See Bass (1985) for a definition similar to ours. For an overview of the differences between democratic, dictatorial, and despotic leaders, see Schweitzer (1984, 201). For the difficulties of changing habits even in a business organization, see Etzioni (1964, 56–57). Except for the pathbreaking works of Burns (1978) and Wriggens (1969) there have been few empirical studies of transformational leaders in the political realm.

2. For the sources of Gorbachev's "new thinking" and its spread through the Soviet foreign policy see Shevardnadze (1991, 26, 51); Garthoff (1994, 261–65); Checkel (1993, 271–300); and Meyer, (1988, 124–68). For relationships of the "new thinking" to Communist Party doctrine see Thompson (1989, 165–68). For the argument that the "new thinking" involved complex learning on the part of Gorbachev and his allies see Legvold (1991, 684–732).

3. Glasnost is a term that originated from an old Russian word, *glas,* which means "voice." The term glasnost thus can be defined as the voicing of one's opinion openly, in public. Some historians suggest that glasnost was first used as a political term by Konstantin Chernenko in June 1983 in his speech to the Plenum of the Communist Party (Shubin 1997, 161).

4. Yeltsin's speech, published by a local Moscow newspaper, was illegally copied (xeroxing without special permission was unlawful in the Soviet Union), and became known to millions in Russia.

5. "Conservatives" argued that glasnost had undermined authority in the Soviet Union and that the loosening of central controls has been responsible for the economic chaos. In *Pravda* on April 28, 1989, for example, five pages were

covered with such critiques. The Moscow mayor warned that "mindless imitation" of the West was taking place. The party chief of the Vladimir region argued that any program that was as popular abroad as perestroika ought to be regarded with suspicion.

6. In the plan the republics would have been given the right to control their own exports and properties and to adopt additional economic measures as they saw fit. Shortly thereafter, the central government agreed to cede control of the Russian mines and some other industries to the Russian Federal Republic. Approximately a month later the Soviet government announced that 13 republics had agreed on the details of a special work regime in which a ban on strikes would be balanced by wage incentives and the right of enterprises to sell some of their products on the open market (Brumberg 1991, 53–54).

Chapter 2

A Profile of Mikhail Gorbachev: Psychological and Sociological Underpinnings

Betty Glad and Eric Shiraev

INTRODUCTION

What kind of man could climb through a communist political hierarchy, maintain the ability to see the discrepancies between the ideal and the real in the Soviet political system, and once in power, show the commitment to reduce these discrepancies through basic reforms of the whole political system? More generally, how may individuals socialized in a totalitarian regime retain some commitment to humane values as well as intellectual and moral authenticity? The answers to these questions can be explored through an analysis of Gorbachev's character structure and earlier life.

If it was mainly power he wanted, Gorbachev could have done nothing to alter the existing system. As he suggested in 1992, "I could have lived like Leonid Ilyich Brezhnev did: ten years as an emperor." However,

"I haven't regretted a single time that I hadn't used my post of General Secretary in order to just 'be a czar' for several years. I would consider such an action irresponsible and immoral" (Gorbachev 1992, 136, 117).

As general secretary, Gorbachev had other motives. He had long seen the discrepancy between the ideals of communism and its practice in the Soviet Union. When in 1979, Eduard Shevardnadze told him, "You know, everything was rotten," Gorbachev agreed. The night before he was elected to head the Communist Party and, in effect, the state, he confided to his wife, "[W]e cannot live this way"(Gorbachev 1992, 140).

For him the struggle should not touch the system's foundations. In office he made it clear that his goal was to "improve socialism" in the Soviet Union, to make the old social structures work better. The society should be changed, he believed, but no one should touch "worker-peasant" power (Plenum of the Central Committee of the CPSU, January 1987). "More democracy, more socialism" was Gorbachev's formula. He felt that competition is good, but that it should be a competition within the one-party system, a competition among the people, not political parties (Chernyaev 1993, 32, 39, 185).

Not everyone would have undertaken such a difficult task. As George Bernard Shaw noted in the *Quintessence of Ibsenism* (1958), most people deal with discrepancies between their ideals and practices through a somewhat cynical conformity to the prevailing practices. (You cannot beat city hall!) Idealists, who are fewer in number, may attempt to eliminate these discrepancies by getting people to live up to their ideals. They are, however, often surprised by the angry reactions of people who do not want to hear what they are saying. The realist recognizes the discrepancies between the ideal and practice and will stand up for the ideal when it is important to do so. Unlike the idealist, however, the realist understands that many psychological and material interests may be threatened by attempts to realize the ideal. He or she will not be surprised at the resistance these efforts are apt to create.

Only a "realist" of this sort, we suggest, would have had the capacity to rise to the top of the Soviet political system and then seek to reform the whole system from within. Moreover, a person who could carry off such a task would probably possess the ego strength characteristic of innovative leaders more generally. Such individuals, as Bogardus suggests, often show balance and poise and have an awareness of their own weaknesses. Their innovations and skills often become apparent after an awakening move (Bogardus 1934, 89, 166–67, 196). Levinson and Rosenthal (1984, 263, 270–82) come to similar conclusions in their study of several American CEOs. The objects of their study could set goals, relate to peers and followers, reward good work, and punish when they needed to. But they also had such characteristics as the ability to admit self-doubt and other vulnerabilities. Most CEOs, Levinson and Rosenthal also point out, had family members and outside mentors after whom they could model their leadership behavior. A person capable of undertaking these kinds of changes, the literature suggests, must have a relatively strong ego.

Indeed, the ability to act flexibly and function well in the face of stress, as Glad (1969) has suggested, is apt to be a manifestation of a strong ego. To go down routes not well traveled, an individual ordinarily will need a fairly strong sense of competence and self-worth. Open to the world, she or he is aware of the possible gains and many of the possible costs of moving in new directions. Risk-taking behavior, of course, may also be based on repression of doubts and selective processing of data to support the desired action. Yet actions based on repression are apt to be foolhardy and/or stereotyped just because they are based on repression.

Some early observers of Gorbachev suggest he had at least some of the qualities noted above. Irving Janis, for example, argues that Gorbachev had great ability as a vigilant problem solver and that this quality was based on his ability to bear stress. Confronting a wide variety of alternatives, he was able to process information relevant to these various options. In the complexity of his thought, as Philip Tetlock has noted, he ranked among the top 10 percent of all world leaders in his ability to make difficult trade-offs between multiple values through integrated solutions (see "Psyching Out Gorbachev" 1989).

To see if Gorbachev exhibited the kinds of characteristics noted above we shall review in this chapter his earlier life as well as the kinds of leadership skills he exhibited in trying to transform the Soviet Union. In the process we will address the puzzle of how he got through a system that deformed others, retaining a commitment to human values and a capacity for creativity. At the conclusion of our analysis, we will deal with the vulnerabilities that contributed to some of the political mistakes he made near the end of his term in office.

PSYCHOLOGICAL FOUNDATIONS: EARLY EXPERIENCES

The evidence that we have at this time relative to Gorbachev's childhood suggests that he was aware of the darker side of life but that he also developed feelings of competence and an ability to relate well to others at a young age. Mikhail grew up in a time of "inevitable difficulties" (Shiraev & Bastrykin 1988). He was born on March 2, 1931, in Privolnoe, at the time of the widespread resistance to Stalin's collectivization drive in that part of the country. At that time the peasants often slaughtered their herds and withheld grain from the state. In the consequent famine, more than 50,000 people died in the Stavropol district alone (Doder & Branson 1990, 4). In the late 1930s, the village was also heavily hit by the political purges. No one had any guarantee his or her family members would not be arrested for any trumped-up accusation. Then, during World War II the Stavropol district was occupied by the Germans for four and a half months (Gorbachev 1996, 30). Jews were gathered up, deported, and slaughtered (Sheehy 1990a, 119). When the Soviet army reconquered the territory, 80,000 Muslims from the Karachi region were sent to other parts of the Soviet Union for collaborating with the Germans.[1]

In his memoirs Gorbachev indicates that he was touched by these troubles. As a young boy during the period of collectivization, Mikhail was subjected to extreme poverty and back-breaking labor. His first great trauma, however, occurred in 1937–38 when his maternal grandfather Pantelei Yefimovich Gopkalo became a victim of the great purges. He was arrested in the middle of the night, and the Gorbachev family was shunned for several months. Returning home in December 1938, Gop-kalo recounted to family members the torture he had suffered, including being placed in a wet sheepskin coat on a hot stove. He spoke about it only once. Earlier, though this event seemed to be less traumatic for young Mikhail, his paternal grandfather, Andrei Moiseyevich Gorbachev, had been arrested as a saboteur for not seeding his individually worked plot of land. Sent to a forced labor camp in the Irkutsk region, he returned a few months later to Privolnoe with two letters commending him for his work (Gorbachev 1996, 23–27; Brown 1996, 25–26).

A short period of relative peace was followed by the German occupa-tion of Privolnoe. As the Germans swept through the countryside, rumors of mass executions of Jews and communist families, and of machines that poisoned people with gas, spread across the region. On one occasion Ger-man police searched the Gorbachev family home, and the family received information suggesting that a massacre of families such as theirs was sup-posedly planned for January 26, 1943. Five days before this was to happen, the village was liberated by the Soviet troops. Then in the early spring of 1943, when the snow began to thaw, Mikhail and other children came across the remains of Soviet soldiers during one of their explorations of the countryside. They saw "decaying corpses, partly devoured by animals, skulls in rusted helmets, . . . rifles protruding from the sleeves of the rotting jacket." They came home in a state of shock. Finally, in the late summer of 1944, the family received news, false as it shortly thereafter became clear, that Sergei, Gorbachev's father, had died at the front. The family gathered and wept for three days before they received a letter indicating that Sergei was alive and well (Gorbachev 1996, 30, 32–33).

Returning to school in 1944, Mikhail spent his summers doing backbreaking work on a combine harvester. The twenty hours of work and three to four hours of sleep daily still did not bring prosperity to the peasants. As Gorbachev later noted, his generation was "the generation of war time children. It has burned us, leaving its mark both on our characters and on our view of the world" (Gorbachev 1996, 34, 36).

Despite these difficulties, Gorbachev's family provided him with positive role models for adapting to the situation in which they found themselves. His grandfather had been a relatively well-to-do peasant before the collectivization drive, but he joined the movement early and became the chairman of a collective farm in the area. Even after his arrest and torture he set up a pattern of denial that would enable him to function relatively well. Returning to his job as chairman of the *kolkhoz,* he blamed neither Stalin nor the communist regime for his tortures. When Mikhail's paternal grandfather, Andrei Gorbachev, returned to Privolnoe after his arrest, he also adapted to the system. An independent farmer before his arrest, he now joined the *kolkhoz* and was soon managing its pig farm (Gorbachev 1996, 24–26).

Sergei Gorbachev, Mikhail's father, was a patriot who fought in World War II and a hard worker. Most of his working life was spent as a combine harvester driver at one of the machine tractor stations. Moreover, Mikhail's mother, Maria Panteleyevna Gorbacheva, was a strong woman. Neighbors recall that she was "first to raise her voice in village meetings." One neighbor, a former head of the *kolkhoz,* saw her as "very stubborn, willful" (Sheehy 1990a, 116–18; see also Editors of *Time* 1988, 26, 35; Doder & Branson 1990, 5). Mikhail Gorbachev recalled how she faced the German police who came to their house during the occupation; his mother did not "flinch" (Gorbachev 1996, 30).

We have little direct evidence at this time by which we can judge the kind and quality of the parenting young Mikhail received. But Gorbachev's recollections suggest that both his maternal grandfather Pantelei and his father served as moral examples—"their understanding of duty, their life and deeds, their attitude towards their work, their family and their country" made a strong impression (Gorbachev 1996, 39). Moreover his maternal grandparents gave him a great deal of freedom and made him feel as though he were the most important member of the family. In his studies, he recalls, his grandfather simply expected him to do well (Gorbachev 1996, 23, 39).[2]

Gorbachev recalls that his father was a simple country man with intelligence, acumen, and humanity (39). They seem to have become particularly close during Mikhail's adolescence, when the two worked together on the combines they operated on the collective farm. Together for hours at a time, they discussed almost everything. Mikhail suggests that as an adult he was even more fascinated by his father who also set before him a positive model of how to deal with a wife. His father, Mikhail recalls, was always thoughtful toward his mother. Warm to her, he would bring her presents from wherever he went.

The impact of the women in Mikhail's life is somewhat less clear. To some extent they attended to his spiritual needs. One grandmother taught him the words of old Cossack songs (Doder & Branson 1990, 4). His mother took him to church and had him baptized. The available evidence, as noted above, suggests that she was a strong woman who could stand up to authority. Gorbachev told journalist Mainhard Count Mahhauss, that at the emotional level she influenced him the most (Sheehy 1990a, 118, 116).

We do have more direct evidence, however, that his caretakers had an impact on his capacity for duty and hard work. During the German occupation, Mikhail joined his mother and other women in the fields to eke out whatever they could to survive. Later, during the summers, as we have seen, he spent long hours on a tractor on the dusty fields of the collective farms (120–21). For a time during the war, he had little interest in books. But when he returned to school in 1944 he studied zealously. He loved to read and to study, and his grades in school were all excellent except for a "good" in German (Doder & Branson 1990, 7). When he reached the ninth grade, young Gorbachev had to commute 12 miles to the town of Krasnogvardeisk. During at least part of his schooling he stayed in a room in town with several other students from Privolnoe. They were sheltered from the icy winds only by wooden shutters. On weekends they walked back to Privolnoe for food (Gorbachev 1996, 34–35).

The apparent joy and self-confidence young Mikhail showed suggest that he was also well nurtured by at least some of his caretakers. Certainly he had a zest for life. He loved poetry; played *lapta,* a Russian form of baseball; took pleasure in music; and danced, with the girls and by himself. He wore a Cossack-style hat all the time. A member of the school drama club, he played the grand Prince Zvezdich in Mikhail Lermontov's

Masquerade and the czar in Alexander Ostrovsky's *The Snowgirl*. More-over, he was a good-looking young lad and quite popular with the girls. His girlfriend during high school said that Mikhail was "magnetic, fearless" (Sheehy 1990a, 116; Doder & Branson 1990, 7).

This self-confidence was reinforced by early success. At his high school graduation Gorbachev won the silver medal for second place in the class. His work in the fields during the summer of 1949 contributed to the unusually productive harvest of the collective, and as a result he won his "most cherished award," the Order of the Red Banner of Labor (Gorbachev 1996, 38). An honor usually reserved for senior workers after a lifetime of hard and loyal work, this recognition opened for him the doors to Moscow State University. According to his history teacher, he had decided that he wanted to go to university, and it was he who discovered that the award entitled him to such a privilege (Sheehy 1990a, 122). In September 1950, he boarded the train for Moscow.

The evidence, in short, suggests that as a young boy Gorbachev had already developed an awareness of the dark side of life, a commitment to duty and work, and the capacity to enjoy life and relate well to people. He had faith in his own capacities to succeed. Several subsequent experiences, some generational and some specific to him, further developed his self-confidence, feelings of competence, and sense of direction characteristic of the "good Soviet man."

EDUCATION

During his formative years Gorbachev absorbed the communist doctrine and ideology that permeated the educational system, programs, youth organizations, and all other associations. While his father served in the Great Patriotic War, Mikhail worked alongside his mother and other women, living the life of the peasantry, seeking missed kernels of grain. As a member of the Komsomol, which he joined at age 14, he impressed many with his ability to work (Sheehy 1990a, 120–21). At Moscow University, Gorbachev began his political career as a Komsomol organizer for his class. He took his work seriously and was apparently somewhat officious in the performance of his duties.[3] Finally, in October 1952, he joined the Communist Party. In short, Gorbachev was a happy, hardworking, and successful Soviet young man.

At university, however, he had the kinds of experiences that would set him on the road to high political accomplishment. "Without these five years of studies" he writes, "there would be no Gorbachev the politician" (Gorbachev 1996, 55). The university, he notes, provided him with intellectual standards that instilled in him self-confidence and helped him survive when his social element changed drastically.

The system in effect at the time provided him with a more complex socialist perspective than the Communist Party orthodoxy embraced at many other educational institutions. Unlike many of their compatriots at the technical schools, law students at Moscow University were able to study the careers of Marx and Lenin in some detail, as well as their works. Lenin, they discovered, showed a relative humanity in dealing with his Menshevik rival, Julius Martov, as well as pragmatism in making a disadvantageous peace with the Germans at Brest-Litovsk in order to consolidate the revolution at home. Presented as brilliant examples of Lenin's political maneuvers, these stories had an important impact on Gorbachev. As he later noted, the authors who first sowed the seeds of doubt about the ultimate truths were Karl Marx, Friedrich Engels, and Vladimir Lenin (45).

Other courses and lectures introduced Gorbachev to the broader world of ideas. Law students discussed the *Code of Hammurabi;* Machiavelli's *History of Florence;* the works of Thomas Aquinas, Thomas Hobbes, and Jean-Jacques Rousseau; and even the United States Constitution. Gorbachev, according to his friend Zdenek Mlynar, particularly enjoyed the two-year course on the history of political ideas taught by the pre-revolutionary scholar Stepan F. Kechekyan (Editors of *Time* 1988, 53–55; Schmidt-Hauer 1986, 49; Doder & Branson 1990, 157–56).

His exposure to the arts and humanities, moreover, opened up new worlds to him. A friend recalled that during his first year at Moscow University, Gorbachev realized that "he didn't have any culture." But he had enough self-assurance to ask her to help fill in the gaps, and she took him to musicals, taught him the names of the composers, and shepherded him through museums where he learned to appreciate the French Impressionists (Sheehy 1990a, 123).

Gorbachev's choice of a wife further expanded his horizons. A graceful and brilliant but reserved young woman, Raisa Maksimovna Titorenko won the gold medal in philosophy and was first in her class. They were married in early 1954, during their last year at the university. While they were still students they saw plays by Anton Chekhov and Maksim Gorky, as well as other theater classics, and they attended foreign exhibitions such as the abstract expressionism show in 1953 and 1954. Later, back in Stavropol, the young couple were avid theatergoers. Raisa also taught Mikhail philosophy in her course at the agricultural institute and showed him no favors. Responding to his presentation on Immanuel Kant, she told him he was wrong and offered another interpretation. Often, as a fellow student recalled, he persisted in his point of view. "They have the same character," noted one fellow student (180–81).

She also provided him with the emotional security that comes from a loving and committed relationship. Mikhail first met her in a ballroom dancing class and quickly fell madly in love. He was "numb" for weeks until she showed a positive response (124). Their attachment to each other has remained strong throughout the years. As Alexander Nikolaevich Yakovlev, one of Gorbachev's closest political confidants, noted in 1987, "one could only envy them as a family" (Doder & Branson 1990, 19).[4]

During his time at the university Gorbachev was no mere automaton. He sometimes critiqued overly ritualistic teachers. On one occasion he challenged a lecturer who was simply reading to the class Stalin's new work, *Economic Problems of Socialism in the USSR,* published in 1952. Gorbachev sent the lecturer a note saying that they had already read the book and that the mechanical reading was a sign of disrespect. The professor was infuriated and news of incident even reached the Moscow City Committee (Gorbachev 1996, 46). At the height of Stalin's anti-Semitic campaign, during the so-called doctors' plot, Gorbachev seems to have personally avoided the excesses of the time. According to some accounts Gorbachev stood up for a Jewish student named Volodya Liberman in his study group. When another student tried to implicate Liberman as part of a Jewish plot Gorbachev jumped to his feet. "You're a spineless beast," he shouted at Liberman's accuser (Sheehy 1990a, 124).[5] Mlynar supports this perspective on Gorbachev, insisting that he was an open and honest person, and that he had no specific responsibility for the suffering of any individual at the university during this time (Editors of *Time* 1988, 75). Raisa Titorenko, moreover, was one-quarter Jewish, a fact revealed during these attempts to weed out Jews from position of influence. Most of the world, however, would not be aware of this fact until after Gorbachev had become general secretary of the Communist Party (Doder & Branson 1990, 21–22).

Still, throughout his university career, Gorbachev retained his faith in Stalin. For a university examination he had to write a composition named after a popular song, "Stalin our combat glory, Stalin the elation of our youth." His essay was the best among those of his peers and was kept in school for years. And for Gorbachev, as for his wife and most of his friends, the death of Stalin was a shock. As his friend Zdenek Mlynar later noted, "[W]e all deeply believed in Stalin. We deeply believed we were building a

new society for the new Soviet Man" (11). Circumstance and chance, as
they saw it, were responsible for the arbitrariness in the system. So even
after the death of Stalin, Gorbachev retained his faith in the system.

At this phase of his career Gorbachev seems to have been deeply
idealistic. A spiritual core to his communist beliefs was provided through
his studies at Moscow University, as he himself noted (Editors of *Time*
1988, 54). He took his readings and his seminars more seriously than
many other students, always doing his homework and participating in discussions on the works read (Doder & Branson 1990, 11, 14). His faith in
the future was great; Nadezhda Mikhailova, a young woman who
befriended him during his first year at the university, would later recall
that he was "romantic and somewhat naïve—no, the right word is innocent, I think" (Sheehy 1990a, 123).

SEEING DISCREPANCIES

Looking back at these years in the university, Gorbachev does not claim to
have become a free thinker. The first three years of his studies, he recalls,
coincided with the late Stalinist period, when the expression of any independent thought would be completely anachronistic. But he spent his last two
years at the university during the post-Stalin "thaw," a time when people
could express their previously covert doubts and unconventional interpretations of reality and start to reflect seriously on the facts they assimilated.

It was during these last two years that Gorbachev began to slowly
recognize the discrepancies between communist ideals and practices. As
his friend Mlynar recalls, he saw incongruities between official doctrine
and his own experience in Privolnoe, and probed into politically risky
areas. In his dormitory room there were often long discussions late into
the night. Sometimes the students wandered down dangerous paths.
According to one roommate, Rudolf Koitchanov, Gorbachev thought that
the Stalinist collectivization of agriculture had resulted in incredible
injustices, and he said so on these occasions. "We could be sent to jail for
such discussions," Koitchanov would sometimes caution. Mlynar remembers another similar episode. After the two had watched *Cossacks of the
Kuban,* an idealized version of life on the collective farms, Gorbachev
remarked, "It's not like that at all" (Doder & Branson 1990, 13). The
notion that the people on those farms enjoyed abundance was pure propaganda, he told Mlynar. It was "brute force which alone secured working
discipline on the collective farms" (Sheehy 1990a 123–24).

But for Gorbachev, as for many others of his generation, the life-altering events were the revelations at the Twentieth Party Congress in 1956 that Stalin was responsible for the great purges of the late 1930s, that he had mismanaged the war, and that his actions were the cause of the early defeats of the Soviet army. Like many others just beginning their climb up the Communist Party hierarchy, Gorbachev learned of this speech's contents when it was circulated to district and local party committees for discussion. But Gorbachev was in attendance at the Twenty-second Party Congress in October 1961, when Nikita Sergeyevich Khrushchev again attacked the cult of personality and critiqued general prosecutor Andrei Vyshinsky's participation in the purge trails in the late 1930s. Gorbachev, like many others, saw the consequences of these revelations. Stalin's coffin was moved from the mausoleum and buried near the Kremlin wall; thousands of streets, stadiums, libraries and villages were stripped of the dictator's name; and the city of Stalingrad was renamed Volgograd (Editors of *Time* 1988, 84–85, 88–89). In Stavropol, an enormous statue of Stalin was removed from the city center, and Stalin Avenue was renamed Marx Avenue (Gorbachev 1996, 61–63, 69–70).[6]

EARLY POLITICAL ADAPTATIONS

Not every active party member of Gorbachev's generation, of course, responded to revelations at the Twentieth and Twenty-second Party Congresses in the same way. Some, ignoring all contrary evidence, remained true believers. Others, to protect the power and privileges they had secured as party members, cynically went along. But for many of them the speech "was a shattering blow to previously held notions of justice" (Editors of *Time* 1988, 76). From this group of the disillusioned, some dropped out of the system and a few became dissidents. Yet some people learned from these experiences and made a commitment to attempt reform within the existing state and party apparatus. Gorbachev was one of these.

In repressive systems the ways of dissent are difficult. Public disclosures may not be "heard" by a public that is not ready to receive the truth they contain. The truth bearer may pay a price in terms of his or her personal isolation and other punishments. Cynical self-isolation or embitterment may result. Another possibility is that some individuals may be able to find relatively safe arenas where their creative capacities can be expressed and tested with some positive effect. A "second culture" (Havel 1986; Marlin 1990a, b; Shiraev & Bastrykin 1988) can serve to preserve memory and creativity in a nation, even when it is manipulated and divided by totalitarian rule. The adaptation that Gorbachev made was to find an enclave in the post-Khrushchev Soviet system where he could pursue communist ideals and protect his position within the system without feeling false at his base. Committed to the Marxist ideals, he had a base from which he could achieve some positive goals.

FINDING AN ARENA FOR AUTHENTICITY

How did Gorbachev maintain his commitment to communist ideals while climbing up a ladder that created opportunists and cynics out of so many? Key to his adjustment was his ability to maintain a certain amount of authenticity. As a devoted communist, Gorbachev did not have to lead a completely double life. His studies at Moscow University provided him with a spiritual core to his communist beliefs (Editors of *Time* 1988, 54). For him, Marxist theory was not a "collection of axioms to be committed to memory," as one friend recalled, but a guideline for life (Doder & Branson 1990, 11, 14).

Early in his political life he was fortunate to find a relatively open environment in which he could be active, and creative, and implement some reforms. As Communist Party chief in the Stavropol district, he undertook many innovative projects. Work-study programs for children were established that served as models for the entire country (Editors of *Time* 1988, 87). The work brigade system that he established in Stavropol became a model for the region.[7] Teams organized by peasants on the basis of contracts were paid according to the result of the harvest, with some adaptation to their expenses. According to contemporary news accounts, nearly 2,500 such groups were operating in the Stavropol region by the mid-1950s. Harvest yields shot up 50 percent on irrigated lands and on non-irrigated lands some rose 30 to 40 percent. He advanced the construction of an irrigation canal to cope with chronic water shortages and encouraged the introduction of new production techniques in factories. But he could also be a severe boss. For people not inclined to move, he prodded, pushed, and checked up on their implementation of his policies (Doder & Branson 1990, 28–30; Schmidt-Hauer, Christian, & Huber 1986, 59–61).

Stylistically, Gorbachev was able to manifest some of the openness for which he would later become famous. Traveling the length and breadth of his district, he walked through villages and talked to the people. In monthly press briefings he would explain his programs and field questions on a broad range of topics. His reputation was impeccable throughout the region, notes Arkady Shevchenko, the former Soviet UN officer, who visited the region in 1977 (Editors of *Time* 1988, 95–101). He inspired many with his enthusiasm and energy.[8]

His relatively open policies also contributed to Stavropol's development into a cultural oasis in the Soviet Union. The churches were allowed to function in Stavropol. With spas for party leaders and other members of the elite from Moscow, the region also had many more theaters, concerts, and other artistic events than one might expect. Cultured people from Moscow were welcomed by him. Word leaked back to a small group in Moscow that the first secretary in Stavropol was opposed to the repression of the arts then evident in Moscow (Sheehy 1990a, 184).

CONFORMITY

Still, Gorbachev knew he had to play within the rules of the game set by Moscow. He gave the usual accolades when greeting his superiors and followed the strict social ranking system in which Communist Party leaders operated. Directives from the center caused him to reverse some of his programs. In 1977, for example, when Leonid Brezhnev wanted to try out an agricultural reform that directly contradicted his commitment to local control, Gorbachev put his full effort into the experiment. The Ipatov method, as it was called, was a return to the old grandiose, centralized method of production.

He also secured the powerful protectors who would assist him in his local efforts and help him in his climb to national stature. His first mentor, Vsevolod Murakhovsky, guided Gorbachev through several ranks within the local Komsomol organization (Medvedev 1986, 49). Even more influential was the regional boss, Fedor Kulakov, who had earlier served as one of Khrushchev's agriculture experts. In 1962, Kulakov made Gorbachev head of the party organization department (Orgotdel) in the Stavropol Regional Party Committee. Such positions were traditionally among the most powerful in the regional party hierarchy. Eight years later, in 1970, when Kulakov moved to Moscow as the Central Committee secretary for agriculture, he facilitated Gorbachev's appointment as first secretary of the Stavropol district.

Gorbachev also cultivated relations with Yury Andropov, the KGB chief. As local party boss, Gorbachev often met Andropov's train, accompanying him to his government home and then to the nearby spas. To some extent they also became social friends, their two families sometimes taking vacations together. On at least one occasion they cooked *shashlyk* (kebab) and sat around a bonfire. Andropov had a literary side, and he must have appreciated visiting with two such cultured party people as Gorbachev and his wife (Sheehy 1990a, 187). Andropov enjoyed listening to the Russian bards of the 1960s and liked Vladimir Vyssotsky, a controversial singer who often derided the socialist lifestyle (Gorbachev 1996, 95). Eventually, as Medvedev has noted, Gorbachev's honesty, energy, intelligence, and charm led Andropov to become one of his most powerful mentors (Medvedev 1986, 91).

After Kulakov's death, Andropov arranged for Gorbachev to meet Brezhnev when the general secretary's train stopped at Red Rock in the Caucusus in September 1978. As a consequence of that meeting, Brezhnev chose Gorbachev as the replacement for Kulakov as secretary of the Central Committee in Moscow (Boldin 1994, 176; Morrison 1988, 104; Sheehy 1990b, 122–23).[9] Back in Moscow, Gorbachev, at age 47, was now at the center of Soviet political life.

In 1982, when Andropov became general secretary of the Communist Party, Gorbachev emerged as one of the most powerful figures in the country. At the beginning of 1983, Andropov appointed Gorbachev, together with Nikolai Ryzkhov, to lead a think tank group on possible economic reform (Nenashev 1993). Later, in an August 1983 meeting with the Old Bolsheviks, Andropov sent the party a message that he considered Gorbachev his heir. "Comrades, we have to admit," he said, "that each new generation is in some way stronger than the one before. It knows more. It sees further." When Andropov was hospitalized near the end of September 1983, Gorbachev was one of the few who had regular access to the leader and even greater responsibilities (Doder & Branson 1990, 51). Behind the scenes the two men played politics at the highest level. To cut corruption, they purged regional first secretaries and department heads, cracked down on corrupt officials elsewhere, and tried to reform the economy through the greater use of economic incentives (Sheehy 1990a, 188). The arrival of this energetic and bold young man upset the tranquillity of the Politburo. Some powerful members "did not accept the impudent young man from Stavropol" (Boldin 1994, 176).

SELF-RELIANCE

Throughout this whole process of climbing the political ladder of the Communist Party hierarchy, Gorbachev learned to keep his own counsel on a variety of matters. A political system in which rank was based on political maneuver and conformity to a party line was not congenial to the development of real friendships in the workplace. During Stalin's reign of terror this was particularly true. Being a "friend" of the general secretary or his family was dangerous, as Sergei Kirov and Nikolai Bukharin found out. It did not protect them from the violent ends that Stalin employed in the 1930s for every possible rival (Alliluyeva 1967, 31, 140). Stalin's underlings even hesitated to socialize freely with each other. Meetings without Stalin could be seen as possible conspiracies, occasions to plot against the leader or other members of the Politburo.

During the Brezhnev regime political leaders did not fear for their lives. But interpersonal relations at the top remained stilted and difficult. The friendly relations that Gorbachev and his wife had developed with Andropov in the Stavropol district were exceptional. Perhaps the regional boss could be seen as simply the host of those Moscow leaders who came to visit the spas in his district.[10]

But in Moscow, the Gorbachevs discovered that even informal family visits with Andropov were off limits. On one occasion Gorbachev invited Andropov, who lived in the dacha next to him, to attend a hearty dinner in a Stavropol style. Rejecting the invitation, Andropov explained that he wanted to avoid gossip about the event mainly for Gorbachev's sake. Indeed, Andropov never opened up to Gorbachev, and his trust and frankness did not exceed the established framework (Gorbachev 1996, 96).

In Moscow there were formal parties of course. But they were stilted affairs governed by a strict protocol. For the holiday of March 8, 1979, for example, there was a traditional state reception. All the wives gathered in the hall. When Raisa Maksimovna moved to take an open position in the line, Andrei Kirilenko, the secretary of the Party Central Committee, informed her that she was not observing the proper pecking order. "This is your place—at the end!" Generally, in her meetings with other Kremlin wives, Raisa Maksimovna was astonished at the atmosphere of arrogance, suspicion, and sycophancy she found (Gorbacheva 1991, 122).

Going it alone in these circumstances became the means of survival. In this social-political milieu, Mikhail Gorbachev learned to rely on himself, his wife, possibly his friend Mlynar, and a few others—keeping his innermost thoughts and plans to himself. It was a heritage that proved to be a mixed blessing for him as general secretary, as we shall see.

HIDING DISSENT

Along the way Gorbachev managed to hide from his superiors whatever doubts he had about the system. While at Moscow State University, his most probing questions were expressed behind closed doors, as we have seen. Throughout his political career he hid other matters that might make him vulnerable. None of his early biographical materials refers to his life in the Stavropol district during the Nazi occupation. For a long time he hid from the public the fact that his grandfathers had been in the gulag. But he knew he was not the only person who had to make such compromises. At the university he had learned that even Hegel saw the political need to check the full expressions of some of his views, reining in, as it were, "his horses before the Brandenburg Gate" (Editors of *Time* 1988, 56).

Hiding dissent, of course, has its costs. As the Czech playwright and political leader Vaclav Havel (1986, 57–63, 136–94) has noted, the failure to communicate about the nature of truth as one sees it not only impoverishes the public discourse, but it may also cause an individual to lose sight of what is truly authentic within him- or herself. Nonbelievers who remain within a system are particularly prone to this possibility. The cynicism and self-interest likely to result from adaptation to a system that an individual feels is fundamentally immoral is apt to lead to a feeling of falseness at his or her base.

Yet one has also to recognize, as Havel does not, that going public may have its price too. The truths of one's observations may not be heard by a public that has bought into the official lies of the power bearers. The truth bearer, too, is apt to experience personal isolation and other punishments that fence him/her off from life. As the American whistle-blower literature suggests, embitterment is apt to be the consequence of such a choice (see Jos, Tompkins & Hayes 1989, 552–58)

AS GENERAL SECRETARY

At the time of Andropov's death in January 1984, a stalemate between the Andropov and Brezhnev cliques in the Politburo led to the interim selection of the old and frail Konstantin Chernenko as the Soviet leader. During the next few months Gorbachev silently accumulated new posts, won new allies, and generally positioned himself to take over the post of general secretary on its becoming vacant (Schmidt-Hauer 1986, 108–11). Upon Chernenko's death Gorbachev moved quickly, and with the assistance of Andrei Gromyko he secured the position of general secretary. According to some accounts, his main competitor was Grigori Romanov, the Central Committee secretary responsible for the defense industry and administration (Schmidt-Hauer 1986, 111–15).[11]

Finally, Gorbachev had an arena for action that he could use to undertake the basic reforms designed to narrow the discrepancy between the communist ideals and practices. He wanted the democratization of a party that he thought had lost its way. Through a loosening of state controls over speech and the economy he would promote the creativity and productivity he saw as the objectives of a good socialist regime. Moreover, he would tackle the irrelevance in the nuclear age of some of the old ideas about what constitutes national security. The end result would be not only a reduction of tensions between the USSR and the United States, but also a reduction of military expenditures that had become such a drain on the Soviet economy.

Strategically, he saw further than many of his democratic allies. To achieve anything, he had to take the Communist Party along with him. That meant he had to move slowly. To have presented at the beginning of his administration a radical program for splitting up the Communist Party and adopting a free enterprise system, even had he been so inclined, would have led to his overthrow as party secretary.[12] A reform movement led by inexperienced democrats—with no access to the political institutions that governed the Soviet Union and no strong institutions of its own—would surely have been aborted under such circumstances.

Moreover, he was aided in his ability to bring the Communist Party and some leaders of the military along with him, at least initially, by his own commitment to socialist ideals and the well-being of the Soviet Union, as well as his ability to keep his own counsel. Yegor Ligachev, for example, supported his first efforts at glasnost. Marshal Sergei Akhromeyev was one of his main negotiators for the arms limitation talks that led to the INF treaty. These party traditionalists went along with him because they saw him as committed to the well-being of the Soviet regime as they were. But he also won them over because he tried to avoid frightening them at the beginning with any revelation of the full extent to which he would ultimately go in pursuing his reforms.

Gorbachev's extraordinary personal skills also contributed to his early success. In meetings of the Politburo his outlook and logic were impressive. Initially nonauthoritarian in his manner, he often adapted to the general mood in the meeting, according to Anatoly Dobrynin (1995, 616–18). His openness to new ideas enabled him to tap into information resources that previous leaders had ignored and to learn from others (Brown 1996, 38, 59). His clear intelligence was an asset.

Gorbachev also had a unique way of relating to the public. He had a brilliant smile, gave speeches that apparently reflected his own thoughts and feelings, and made himself accessible to crowds. On a sunny May morning in 1985, for example, Eric Shiraev (the coeditor of this volume) happened to be near Gorbachev when he was visiting the city of Leningrad. The crowd around Gorbachev was enormous. People were applauding, and many were screaming, "Way to go, Mikhail Sergeye-vitch! Good health to you! We are with you!" Gorbachev kept smiling and talking. He spoke without notes and without a microphone, just standing in the middle of the crowd. He was young, quick, charming, and persua-sive. Not for several decades had the Soviet people greeted a new leader with such high hopes.

Personally, he was relieved to tear away the mask of hypocrisy that had covered up the lies of the past. He felt that Anatoly Rybakov's *Children of the Arbat* had to be published, and his decision was supported by Ligachev. The novel, as he saw it, would help to conquer the fear that many people still had of the consequences of unmasking totalitarianism. Then he saw to it that Tengiz Abuladze's film *Repentance* was widely dis-tributed. The work, which portrays a despot who looks very much like Stalin, had been produced in Georgia under the personal protection of Eduard Shevardnadze. As Gorbachev notes in his memoirs, he was sad-dened at the time to realize that he could not have been exposed to such works in his student days. "Yes, our generation was spiritually cheated, given meager intellectual rations consisting of ideology alone and deprived of the chance to compare different schools of philosophical thought for ourselves and to make our own choices" (Gorbachev 1996, 207).

On occasion Gorbachev even talked of the personal experiences he had kept secret. As general secretary he publicly noted the importance of the Twentieth Party Congress. In an apparently emotional aside that was edited out of *Pravda,* Gorbachev looked over an audience he was address-ing and noted that most of them were of his generation, political activists who had begun their careers at the time of the Twentieth Party Congress. "We have experienced it all and we know the pluses and the minuses, the gains and the losses," he said. "Let's renew ourselves" (Editors of *Time* 1988, 86). In the fall of 1986, after viewing *Repentance,* Gorbachev con-fided to three Communist Party visitors from Italy that he had to choke back tears during portions of the film. The episode where the secret police knock on the door of an innocent musician to take him away brought back memories of the stories his grandmother had told about the night his grandfather was arrested (Doder & Branson 1990, 3, 183).[13]

At some levels, however, Gorbachev remained a product of the system. Not only was he committed to communist ideals, but as general secretary he also employed some of the techniques he had observed earlier party leaders utilize. Some were productive for him, some were not. These may be summarized as follows.

As had other general secretaries before him, Gorbachev's initial attempt to reform the Communist Party was to replace the traditionalists with his own people. Though many of these new appointees turned out not to be significantly different from their predecessors, a few served him well for some time. The appointment of Shevardnadze is an example of a choice along these lines. The two men first met at the Twelfth Komsomol Congress. Over time they developed a sense of personal trust and an ability to confide in each other their concerns about the system. Once in power, Gorbachev jumped over Dobrynin and other Foreign Ministry professionals to choose Shevardnadze as his foreign minister. Though Shevardnadze had no diplomatic experience, Gorbachev was more concerned with having an intelligent man at his side who was willing to put Gorbachev's new designs into practice (Dobrynin 1995, 575–76). Not only was Shevardnadze free of most of the dogmas of the traditionalists, he was "someone capable of deliberation and persuasion, graced with Eastern affability" (Gorbachev 1996, 180). Over time Shevardnadze and Gorbachev developed a near monopoly over the handling of important foreign-policy issues. The Georgian, as Gorbachev's interpreter Igor Korchilov has noted, became Gorbachev's "most loyal supporter and fellow thinker, and that was an exhausting role" (Korchilov 1997, 60; Ekedahl & Goodman 1997, 229–50, 27, 248).

As had party chiefs before him, Gorbachev also saw political statements as means for influencing men and women to change in the desired direction. His book on perestroika, his speeches, his interviews—all were endeavors along these lines. The emphasis he placed on political messages was also evident in his appointment of Aleksandr Yakovlev to lead the Communist Party on propaganda, culture, and foreign-policy issues. Dismissing the old editors of the Soviet press, Yakovlev sought out "new men who would work to establish a free press and by their examples would demonstrate the new doctrines of glasnost," the new thinking in foreign policy, and perestroika (Matlock 1995, 61–64).

As Gorbachev's difficulties increased, he fell back into the old practice of issuing directives from the center in his attempts to resolve them (Chernyaev 1993, 23). "Problems with cadres? Let's call a plenum. Problems with ethnic minorities? Let's call a meeting. Let's replace the cadres, let's show these bureaucrats their places. Let's fire them!" He waited for "revolutionaries of perestroika" to come and help him. He sincerely wanted to restore "camaraderie, human relationship" within the party, to free it from "'careerism' and 'cultism'" (Tatu 1991, 148). As he wrote later, "Bernstein was right: movement is everything, final goal is nothing, socialism is a constant addition of the new" (Gorbachev 1993, 167). He wrote in his memoirs that "Our world continues to change, as do all its components" (Gorbachev 1995b, 4).

But these techniques did not work as well for Gorbachev as they had for his predecessors. His commitment to the establishment of democratic values and the avoidance of violence inhibited him from systematically employing fear to assure that his new appointees followed his orders. In attempting to dismantle the party and administrative apparatus as it had existed in the past, he also lost control of the institutional mechanisms that had been effective in implementing the policies of the center. As journalist Abraham Brumberg (1991, 60) has noted, "The more *de jure* power he gained, the less power he had *de facto*." And Gorbachev himself later noted, "we push ahead with reform slogans, but everything is quiet just 100 kilometers outside of Moscow" (Gorbachev 1993, 167). Finally he seemed to settle for motion for its own sake.

This straddling between the new and the old gave opponents the opportunity to charge him with being hypocritical and weak. This response is evident in the evaluation of his chief of staff, Valery Boldin. Though Boldin is justifying his own betrayal of Gorbachev in the following statement, he touches on themes that other critics would come to employ:

> Gorbachev advocated democracy and denied Stalinism; yet he ruled the Party and the country practically single-handedly. He talked about 'collegiality', but was silencing his opponents and dissenters. He threatened to dismiss newspaper editors who published material not to his liking. He talked about glasnost, but didn't inform his colleagues of the Security Council or the Supreme Soviet of the results. He fought to protect the independence of the judiciary system, but instructed the prosecutor general on how to pursue certain investigations. He fought against command methods of management, while keeping a tight grip on agencies, ministries, and committees. He talked about transferring power to the regions, but actually concentrated power in his own hands. He called for a modest lifestyle, while keeping for himself the full range of benefits (Boldin 1994, 298–99).

Somewhat more puzzling, in contrast to the charm he exhibited in public, was Gorbachev's insensitivity to persons on his own political team. He sometimes talked at people rather than discussing issues with them. Perhaps more important, he rarely shared credit and seldom thanked those with whom he worked closely. On occasion he reversed the policy commitments of his subordinates without informing them of his choice before acting publicly. Relying on himself, he failed to build a team in which the leaders shared their goals and hung together throughout adverse developments.

These traits can be partly understood as the downside of the extraordinary self-reliance Gorbachev had developed when climbing up the political ladder. While Gorbachev was pushing his early reforms, this ability to think and act on his own was crucial to winning the support of the Communist Party and constraining the more extreme of his democratic allies. Yet it would become apparent that these same qualities contributed to his failure to develop the personal ties of loyalty that would bind other reformers to him over the long haul. Dobrynin (1995, 618) notes that Gorbachev never remained too close for too long with any of his associates. He could easily abandon a former colleague, leaving that colleague bitter and disappointed. Boldin (1994, 106) harps about his "lordly manner," his "contempt for his subordinates," and his inability to defend them when they were in trouble politically.

Dobrynin and Boldin, of course, could have been influenced by their opposition to Gorbachev's policies. But even Gorbachev's close associates developed similar complaints. Nikolai Ryzhkov, chairman of the USSR Council of Ministers from 1985 to 1991, complains that Gorbachev casually discarded him after he suffered a heart attack. Sergei Tarasenko claims that Gorbachev was not easy to get close to because he was egocentric and had little sense of personal loyalty. Aleksandr Yakovlev, one of the most influential of Gorbachev's advisers, says that during the five years he and Gorbachev knew each other, Gorbachev never thanked him for his work (Murray 1995, 26).

The extent to which Gorbachev's insensitivity to Shevardnadze's concerns contributed to the demise of their relationship is dealt with in chapter 3 by Goodman and Ekedahl. Their relationship came to a bitter end on December 20, 1990, when Shevardnadze, without giving Gorbachev any prior notice, resigned his post as foreign minister. Feeling betrayed, Gorbachev stated that "to leave at this time is unforgivable." Six months later, when he was accepting the Nobel Peace Prize, Gorbachev never mentioned Shevardnadze and his contributions. This further exacerbated Shevardnadze's bitterness (Ekedahl & Goodman 1997, 43–48, 240–44).

By the winter of 1990, Gorbachev was politically isolated from his fellow reformers. In addition to the resignation of Shevardnadze, Vadim Bakatin and been dismissed, and Aleksandr Yakovlev had been marginalized. Gorbachev's economic adviser, Nikolai Petrakov, had also resigned.

Shevardnadze would later describe Gorbachev as a "poor judge of people." Certainly, as his former allies deserted him or were fired, his judgments did deteriorate. His new appointees—hard-line party bureaucrats such as Gennady Yanayev, Boris Pugo, and Valentin Pavlov—would all betray him at the end (Murrel 1997, 59). Nor does he seem to even have sensed Boldin's intense dislike of him, as is clearly evident in Boldin's book, *Ten Years that Shook the World*.[14]

By the early summer of 1991, Gorbachev was rejecting any information suggesting that a coup might be in the making. A more alert person might very well have heard the warning bells in the middle of June when Prime Minister Pavlov, KGB Chairman Kryuchkov, Minister of Defense Yazov, and Minister of Internal Affairs Pugo backed a measure granting Pavlov the extraordinary powers that had belonged solely to the president. Shortly thereafter, Gorbachev complacently dismissed a warning from the American ambassador Jack Matlock that a purported coup was in the works and that it could happen at any time. "I have everything well in hand," he said. "You'll see tomorrow." Then he noted that Pavlov had learned from his mistake a few days earlier and was not an experienced politician. Gorbachev even saw Yeltsin as becoming somewhat more conciliatory toward him. The Union treaty would soon be signed, and his visit to London in mid-July for meetings would move the Soviet Union forward into the world economy (Matlock 1995, 543–45).[15]

The next day Gorbachev secured in the Supreme Soviet an overwhelming vote to reject Pavlov's attempt to take over some of his powers. And as he told the Soviet ambassador to the United States, Aleksandr Bessmertnykh, he had given those officials a "good talking to" (Matlock 1995, 544). But he made no effort to remove any of the potential conspirators from their positions. Gorbachev, as Matlock suggests, was "acting like a somnambulist, wandering around oblivious to his surroundings" (Matlock 1995, 544–45).

To understand Gorbachev's vacillations in the fall of 1990, and his failure to confront the possibility of a coup attempt by his own advisers, we can look at several factors. Archie Brown (1996, 276–77) suggests that Gorbachev had become overly self-confident in his own ability to maneuver. Certainly, he was one of the most skilled politicians the Soviet Union had seen, and his earlier successes may well have fortified feelings that as secretary general he was invulnerable.

In addition, there was no clear set of alternatives open to him after the summer of 1990. Yeltsin had occupied whatever base there was for reform on the left. Moreover, any move Gorbachev might have taken to embrace radical economic privatization programs would have created even more serious problems for him in the short run and possibly contribute to the disintegration of the Soviet Union. Should Gorbachev have resigned as general secretary of the Communist Party—at this time completely dominated by the traditionalists—he would no longer be in a position to monitor their activities. But moving to the right presented equally unattractive possibilities. The entire reform process would grind to a halt, and without forward movement the whole nation could become immobilized.

Individuals confronted with such unpleasant choices, Richard Lebow suggests, are apt to resort to the stress-reducing techniques of defensive avoidance—procrastination, shifting of responsibility for the decision to another, or the bolstering of one option. Bolstering, as Lebow notes, "helps a policy-maker forced to settle for a less than satisfactory course of action . . . ," feel as if he is choosing a viable option. But bolstering may also have detrimental effects. It can lull the decision maker "into believing that he had made a good decision when, in fact, he had avoided making a vigilant appraisal of the possible alternatives in order to escape from the conflict this would engender" (Lebow 1981, 110–11).

Gorbachev, it seems, dealt with his difficulties during the last year of his regime along the lines suggested above. At first he procrastinated, making no firm choice on how far to go on economic reforms. When he moved to the right, he buttressed that choice with ukases that gave him no real power. Messages suggesting that he had lost all support within the reform movement without gaining any real ability to control or monitor the right, were simply dismissed. To be open to such information, he would have had to face the near hopelessness of the situation in which he was acting.

FINAL CRISIS: FOROS AND AFTER

Gorbachev's house of cards came tumbling down on Sunday, August 18, 1991, at his vacation home at Foros on the Crimean Peninsula. At 5:00

P.M. a group composed of Chief of Staff Valery Boldin, Central Committee secretary Oleg Baklanov, KGB general Yury Plekhanov, and two other
associates entered the family villa uninvited. After pushing their way to
the second floor of the dacha, they issued Gorbachev an ultimatum: he
must sign the decree they carried declaring a state of emergency.

When Gorbachev refused to either sign the decree or resign, he and
members of his family and a few close aides were placed under house
arrest (Gorbachev 1996, 631–32). A double line of guards was deployed
around the dacha and on the sea, the exits blocked by various vehicles and
guards with machine guns. Their communications cut, Gorbachev, his
family, and the loyal staff around him had no real idea of what was going
on in the outside world for several hours. It was not until Monday morning that they were able, via a small transistor radio they had, to pick up the
World Service of the BBC. (For details given here on coup events, see
Gorbachev 1996, 631–46.)

Fearing for his life, Gorbachev taped audio and video statements so
that if he were killed these tapes would provide testament of his resistance
to the coup. A BBC message picked up on Wednesday afternoon that Gorbachev was "gravely ill" and that a delegation was on the way to see for
themselves, caused Raisa such anguish that one of her arms went numb
and she could not speak. She had suffered a minor stroke from which she
would not fully recover for two years. Gorbachev himself later noted at a
press conference that had the coup been successful, he would have committed suicide.

The immediate crisis ended at 5:45 P.M. that same Wednesday. The
communication lines at Foros were restored and supporters of Gorbachev
were finally able to enter the dacha. Returning to Moscow later that night,
Gorbachev experienced new setbacks. He learned that the leaders of the
Communist Party he had attempted to reform had either participated in
the attempted rebellion or passively responded to it. Moreover, Yeltsin's
heroism in defending the White House marked him as the leader of the
new Russia, while Gorbachev's courage in standing up to the plotters
went relatively unnoticed. The fact that Yeltsin had finally bested Gorbachev in their struggle for power would become evident, as we shall see,
in the meeting of the Russian Soviet the day after Gorbachev's return.

These are the kinds of experiences that could demoralize anyone. As
Harry Stack Sullivan argued in a paper published in 1951, people are apt
to suffer along these lines when "when an elaborate complex of interlock-
ing and mutually supporting and dependent beliefs, convictions, faiths,
and so on, suddenly prove to be built entirely of figments of self decep-

tion." The demoralization may become chronic when "people become convinced that they cannot improve a situation of insecurity or dissatisfaction, or, much more commonly, when they observe that they cannot prevent other people from making their situation worse" (Sullivan 1951, 48–49).[16]

Gorbachev's account of his responses to the above events suggests that his experiences at Foros had not immobilized him. He notes that he was cool and in command—that he retained throughout his "presence of mind and was active" (Gorbachev 1996, 640). Moreover, once communications were restored, he took steps indicating that he was once again in charge of the situation. He talked to George Bush and several republic leaders on the phone; relieved one of the conspirators, General Yazov, of his military command; and ordered a plane to take the family back to Moscow. To some extent, it seems, he had fallen back on a pattern he had seen his grandparents and parents follow during their difficult times. He confronted the threat before him and did what he had to do.

Yet there is other evidence that suggests that Gorbachev did suffer to some extent the kind of demoralization Sullivan sees as typical of any human being in an extreme situation. It was a white-faced and subdued Gorbachev who early on Thursday came down the steps of the plane arriving in Moscow from Foros. His first political instincts upon his return, moreover, were not as sharp as they had once been. Instead of visiting the heroic defenders of democracy in Moscow, he was driven straight to his dacha outside Moscow where he consulted with his aides. At a press conference the following day, he praised Yeltsin and the Soviet people for coming to his aid. But he also spent considerable time delineating the details of his own detention and continued to insist that the Communist Party was a progressive force (Dobbs 1996, 411; Brown 1996, 301).

Gorbachev's handling of his meeting with the Russian legislature on Friday, August 23, gives us further evidence along the same lines. He did compliment Yeltsin on his role in blocking the attempted coup, a statement that led to a standing ovation. But then Gorbachev went on to irritate the delegates, again giving the details of his detention and defending what he saw as the millions of decent people within the ranks of the Communist Party. When Yeltsin, as the presiding officer, engaged in behavior that Gorbachev would later see as "sadistic," Gorbachev floundered. A long line of delegates showered Gorbachev with hostile questions, including some suggesting he had somehow colluded in the coup. At one point in the proceedings Yeltsin insisted that Gorbachev read aloud the minutes of the August 19, 1991, meeting of the USSR Council of Ministers. At first Gorbachev demurred, but when Yeltsin ordered him to "read it now," he complied. (The minutes showed that only two persons opposed the coup.) When Yeltsin signed on the spot an edict suspending the Communist Party of the RSFSR, Gorbachev could only mount a weak protest. Then, despite all the humiliation meted out to him, Gorbachev went off with Yeltsin at the end of the session to discuss other items of business (Gorbachev 1996, 640–45; CNN Broadcast 1991a; Brown 1996, 300–01).

The day after the meeting with the Russian legislature, Gorbachev resigned as general secretary of the CPSU. In the days and weeks that followed the coup attempt, Yeltsin decided not to move forward on the Union agreement, and issued decrees robbing the government of the Soviet Union of all vestiges of its resources and authority. In early November he banned the activities of the CPSU and the Russian Communist Party on the territory of the Russian republic (Brown 1996).

Yet for almost four months Gorbachev continued to fight a rear guard action to preserve something of the Union. Aware of the costs of dismantling the Union, as many of the other reformers were not, he was determined to fight on, against all odds, for some formula that would hold it together. The final death blow was delivered in a highly secret meeting in the Belovezh Forest near Minsk on December 8, 1991, when Yeltsin and the president and prime minister of Ukraine and Belarus declared the USSR dissolved and created the new Commonwealth of Independent States (CIS). On December 25, Gorbachev resigned as president of the Soviet Union in a ten-minute speech broadcast around the world. Less than half an hour later the red flag flying over the Kremlin was taken down for the last time. Two days later—and three days before he had agreed to vacate his office in the Kremlin—Gorbachev was informed that Yeltsin, Ruslan Khasbulatov (the chairman of the Russian Supreme Soviet) and Gennady Burbulis (the first deputy chairman of the Russian government) had taken over his office and were celebrating their triumph by emptying a bottle of whisky (Gorbachev 1996, 665–72; see also Brown 1996, 302–5; Dobbs 1996, 448–49).

In short, the most comprehensive explanation of Gorbachev's maneuvers during his last year in office can be understood in terms of literature dealing with defensive avoidance and demoralization. Faced with alternatives that he could no longer master, he vacillated at first. When he finally embraced one of the two bad alternatives facing him, he bolstered that option by rejecting information suggesting that he had found no real solution to his problems. The attempted coup and its immediate consequences finally cut the ground from under him. Confronted with a triumphant Yeltsin committed to the interests of his own personal power and Russia, Gorbachev could do little. Drained, for a while at least, of the spirit, the energy, and the political ability that had been so characteristic of him in the early phases of reform, he refused to admit defeat. He had never intended that his reforms should lead to the destruction of the Soviet Union, and he committed himself to its survival in some form.

CONCLUSION

Gorbachev was an extraordinary leader—a man who had both the personal integrity and the skills that enabled him to climb up the Communist Party hierarchy in the Soviet Union, while maintaining the commitment to reform it. Gradually, like many others of the so-called Khrushchev generation, he came to see the discrepancies in the communist system between its ideals of equality and ultimate democracy as contrasted to its practices. But he was also a relatively well-educated man who had internalized the ideals of the system and entered onto the track that would eventually give him the power to undertake those reforms. These ideals provided authenticity to some of his efforts while climbing up the party hierarchy, attracting powerful sponsors who assisted him in his ascent. The ideals also provided the moral force that made him remember what his power should be used for. If he had been false—a cynic who simply adapted to the requirements of power—he would have had no motive to even undertake the perilous path he started upon.

Gorbachev's attempts bring the Communist Party along with him on the path of reform was based on his hope that the party could provide for orderly change—as well as his understanding that the disorganized and oftentimes not too politically astute democrats offered no realistic alternatives. He accomplished much—tearing down a totalitarian system without bloodshed and ending a costly and dangerous nuclear arms race. His inability to finish the task he began was in large part due to the difficulties inherent in bringing about, simultaneously, major economic, social, and political reforms in a polity accustomed to rule from the center.

Yet certain personal qualities were contributing factors in his inability to direct, over the long haul, the processes he started. A transitional figure, he carried over from his socialization in the Communist Party some leadership characteristics that contributed to his problems. The use of the appointment process, official statements of doctrine, and the issuance of orders from the center would not suffice in a situation where the force behind these measures was being dismantled. But somewhat ironically, his commitment to democratic values and his pragmatism compounded his problems. In his glasnost policies and his new thinking, he had unleashed new and powerful forces at home and abroad. But lacking any clearly thought-out plan, he was unable to channel those forces into the building, on an evolutionary basis, of the new institutions that would protect the Union, increase economic productivity, and stabilize the forms of democratic participation.

NOTES

1. Mikhail Suslov, as first secretary of the Stavropol region, was responsible for carrying out this program (Tatu 1987, 30).
2. As the organizational literature suggests, transformational leaders who can operate sensibly within the confines of a democratic system often come from families in which parents provide models of leadership behavior and an environment that fosters self-esteem (Levinson & Rosenthal 1984, 263–64).
3. Lev Yudovich, an upperclassman who knew Gorbachev casually, suggests that he had a more officious side, demanding that individuals be expelled from the Komsomol for offenses ranging from telling inappropriate political anecdotes to shrinking from being sent to a *kolkhoz* to work. He also recalls him as having made long ideologically correct speeches (Editors of *Times* 1988, 70, 72).
4. Raisa Gorbacheva's intellectual independence (relative to many of her peers) of party dogmas on various matters clearly has had an impact on him. Her Ph.D. dissertation, published several years later, was entitled "The Emergence of the New Characteristics in the Daily Life of Collective Farm Peasantry," and was an innovative study in that she was one of the first to employ carefully devised questionnaires to see what peasant life was really like (Doder & Branson 1990, 19). Though she noted, in accord with the prevailing party doctrine, that conditions were getting better, she also documented the economic and spiritual impoverishment of the people in the *kolkhoz,* as well as the differential in pay that existed there. Her intellectual independence is evident, moreover, in certain observations about the lot of women in her country, not an au courant concern in the USSR at the time. She noted the differences in pay and work load between men and women, endorsed community kitchens to relieve women of their double burdens, and argued that the stability of this differential could be partly attributed to peasant interpretations of the story of Adam and Eve. Years later the French

Sovietologist Michel Tatu (1987, 30) summarizes his work on this topic as *fortement feministe,* and (somewhat) condescendingly hopes she has out-grown her zeal as she has risen politically and expanded her foreign con-tacts.

5. In his memoirs Gorbachev (l996, 46) recalls the tribulations of his friend Liberman, but he does not present the story that he had stood up for Liber-man.

6. Arendt (1968) sees the beginning of the dismantling of the Soviet totalitar-ian system at the Twentieth Communist Party Congress. Certainly it con-tributed to the ability of a whole new generation of Soviet leaders to later question their system. But Arendt's analysis of totalitarian systems, in which she equates Nazi and communist regimes, does not permit her to explain what would motivate, as it was, what he did. Moreover, her view of a regime in which individuals are reduced to mere automatons, totally controlled by the lies of the leaders, takes on a mythic quality of its own. Certainly, as the experiences of the young Gorbachev indicates, even Stalin at the height of his domination of the Soviet Union could not snuff out normal human emo-tions. Neither was Gorbachev's grandfather rejected by his family when he came back from the gulag, as Arendt suggests is the case for persons in such regimes. Moreover, Gorbachev and his family suffered from war, famine, and the death of loved ones and could wonder about the causes of such evils. For the view that communism is just an extreme development of forces that threaten authenticity see Havel (1986, 136–45). He argues that the arro-gance of scientific rationalism, the use of clichés as a substitute for thought, and the reliance on mindless bureaucracies are much wider problems.

7. Teams of combines would move from farm to farm bringing in the harvest. An extra machine was held in reserve in case of breakdown. The teams were accompanied by repairmen, portable kitchens, and cultural service groups. Gorbachev gave the effort a great deal of hands-on attention, and there was an exceptionally good harvest in the Stavropol region in 1977. On March 1, 1978, Gorbachev received the Order of the October Revolution for his achievements in agriculture (Editors of *Time* 1988, 102; Schmidt-Hauer 1986, 61).

8. Even one of Gorbachev's harshest critics and opponents, Korobeinov, who knew Gorbachev in the 1960s, commends his "obsessive" work style and positive changes in the Stavropol district (Korobeinov 1996, 10).

9. The more orthodox Mikhail Suslov, head of propaganda in the Communist Party's Central Committee, was also a supporter of Gorbachev. It is not clear, however, whether the source of that support was "regional solidarity" or his belief that the young Gorbachev would be able to keep the faith (Tatu 1987, 93; Bunich 1992). Suslov had served at one time as secretary of the Stravopol Regional Party Committee (Doder & Branson 1990, 33; cf Schmidt-Hauer 1986, 45, 63).

10. Gorbachev would later note that he became aware of the kind of distance between individuals in the government elite at the time of Kulakov's death from heart failure in 1978. Neither Brezhnev nor other members of the Politburo interrupted their holidays to attend the funeral. Gorbachev then realized for the first time how incredibly remote people at the top levels of power really are (Gorbachev 1996, 97). The absence of Brezhnev and other leading Politburo members at the funeral also suggests a more malign interpretation. Rumors circulated that Kulakov had run into certain difficulties with the Communist Party, possibly while planning some sort of conspiracy against Brezhnev's leadership or directly opposing his agricultural policies (Editors of *Time* 1988, 104). Loyal to his patron, Gorbachev delivered one of the funeral orations. His face was "waxen," according to a minor official on the spot (Sheehy 1990a, 187).

11. Some witnesses, however, suggest that the decision to choose Chernenko was a result of a simple procedural play, almost an "accident" (Chernyaev 1993, 31).

12. For example, at the end of 1985, Aleksandr Yakovlev wrote Gorbachev a memorandum suggesting that he split the Communist Party. If Gorbachev had followed this advice, he would have been removed from his post of general secretary, as Archie Brown notes. Still, Gorbachev promoted Yakovlev, a tribute to his openness at that time to opposing ideas (Brown 1996, 105–06).

13. *Repentance* is based on complex artistic symbolism and filled with grotesqueries and allegories. This genre, almost forbidden in the Soviet Union before Gorbachev, was radically different from the official "socialist realism" style vigorously promoted and supported by the party officials.

14. Boldin's enmity toward Gorbachev is laced throughout his book. Even when he states something positive about Gorbachev, it is immediately followed by text minimizing the importance of his virtues (See Boldin 1994, 23–24, 78, 80, 152–53, 246.)

15. Matlock's (1995) lack of specificity about the coup may have contributed to Gorbachev's complacent reaction. Matlock did not mention that he received the information from Gavriil Popov, chairman of the Moscow City Council. Nor did he provide details on who the plotters were, though he had a pretty good list, as it turned out.

16. The discovery that one has been mistaken, Sullivan notes, can come about in several different ways. One may learn abruptly from colleagues, or perhaps an enemy, that he or she has been "stupidly and vacantly overconfident." Or it may occur after an "unpleasant discovery that one is not able to affect reality in the way that one always supposed one could." Or it can occur when one discovers that one's faith in the culture complex, "which gives one meaning and value and has fixed one's relations with other people," is "all a mistake" (Sullivan 1951, 52–53).

Chapter 3

Eduard Shevardnadze: Leading the Soviet Union out of the Cold War

Melvin Goodman and Carolyn Ekedahl

Western commentators have tended to underestimate the role played by the Soviet leadership in ending the Cold War because they have focused on the societal problems that precipitated the collapse of the Soviet Union, engaged in protracted debate about the contribution made by Western policies, and miscalculated the importance of Soviet policy changes. The ultimate dissolution of the Soviet empire may have been inevitable and the policies of the West important, but the timing and nature of the collapse and its impact on the international community were determined by the actions of Soviet leaders. Peaceful change was possible only because those who came to power in 1985 were committed to domestic reform, reconciliation with the West, and non-use of force.

Just as the Russian Revolution of October 1917 as defined by Lenin influenced the course of modern history, so the Soviet revolution as defined by Mikhail Gorbachev, Eduard Shevardnadze, and Aleksandr Yakovlev is having a profound impact on contemporary history. The

readiness of these men to halt the arms race, renounce political and military dominance over Eastern Europe, and retreat from the Third World ended the superpower competition that had defined the post-World War II era. Their policies precipitated peaceful anticommunist revolutions in Eastern Europe and redefined the international system. By stabilizing the USSR's external position, Soviet leaders prepared their nation for its nonviolent collapse.

Shevardnadze played a critical role in conceptualizing and implementing the Soviet Union's dramatic volte-face. Considered the moral force for "new political thinking," he was the point man in the struggle to undermine the forces of inertia at home and to end Moscow's isolation abroad. Two American secretaries of state, George Shultz and James Baker, have credited him with convincing them that Moscow was committed to serious negotiations.[1] Each became a proponent of reconciliation in administrations that were intensely anti-Soviet; each concluded that the history of Soviet-American relations and the end of the Cold War would have been far different had it not been for Shevardnadze.

Commitment to the non-use of force became Shevardnadze's most important contribution to the end of communism and the Cold War, permitting the virtually non-violent demise of the Soviet empire and the Soviet Union itself. Shevardnadze was more adamant on this issue than was Gorbachev; he opposed the use of force in Tbilisi, Georgia, in 1989 and in the Baltics in 1990. In his resignation speech in December 1990, he predicted that the use of force would undermine perestroika. The violence in Lithuania three weeks later, condoned by Gorbachev, proved him right.

NEW POLITICAL THINKING

Recognition that the Soviet Union was an exhausted empire was widespread in Moscow long before the new leaders came to power in 1985. The rate of annual growth had been declining since the 1960s, and all important indicators suggested that economic performance would become even worse in the future.[2] The Soviet Union was not keeping pace in the field to which it had devoted the most resources—military technology and production. Its international position was no more promising. Every important relationship was in disarray. Relations with the United States and Western Europe were tense; Eastern Europe was a significant

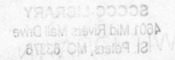

economic burden; and in the Third World its position had been in decline since the 1970s and was draining political and economic resources.

Throughout the 1970s, Soviet commentators debated international trends. They saw an increasingly interdependent international economy and argued that Moscow's vision of separate and opposing capitalist and socialist systems was misguided and counter-productive. Many concluded that exclusion from the world economy was retarding growth in the Soviet Union.[3] The stagnant regime of Leonid Brezhnev had failed to act on these perceptions, but his successor, Yuri Andropov, began the process of reform that was accelerated by the new leaders.

Shevardnadze understood that the Soviet Union's heavy military burden prevented investment in the domestic economy and contributed to stagnation. He recognized that tense relations with the United States, exacerbated by aggressive Soviet actions in the Third World, inhibited progress toward arms control. At the heart of the new thinking was the belief that revitalizing the economy superseded any possible military threat and that security could be served best by improving relations with the West, thereby easing pressure for military spending. The linkage of domestic and foreign policies was critical to new thinking. As they focussed on possible solutions to their problems, the new leaders realized that Moscow's foreign policy would have to change profoundly.

APPOINTMENT OF SHEVARDNADZE

When Shevardnadze was appointed foreign minister in July 1985, it was widely assumed that he would be little more than a mouth-piece for Gorbachev, who would conduct his own foreign policy. In turning to a regional party leader with no foreign-policy background, however, Gorbachev was relying on personal instinct and political acumen. His long association with Shevardnadze was rooted in shared frustration with the inefficiencies and corruption of the communist system, and he believed that his friend had the understanding and political skills necessary to formulate and implement a new foreign policy.

Until 1985, Shevardnadze's career had been entirely within the republic of Georgia, where he had been minister of security before becoming party leader in 1972. The character traits he brought with him from Georgia would serve him well during his years as foreign minister. On the one hand, he was a man of considerable vision, with a strong sense of purpose. On the other, he was a superb politician-opportunistic, flexible, pragmatic, and ruthless. In the words of Victor Israelian, a former Soviet ambassador, he was a "superb actor, as every great politician must be." He was not a diplomat, immersed in the complexities of international discourse; rather, he was a man of action, a problem-solver impatient with obstacles-and a brutal infighter. Perhaps most important, he was not a Russian who distrusted the West.

Shevardnadze used the available instruments of power to advance his career and further his policy objectives in Georgia. He repressed dissidents and removed real and potential opponents. He was an outstanding Soviet apparatchik and acted the role of sycophant to the leaders of the Soviet Union, extolling the virtues of those in a position to help him. At the same time, he took innovative and sometimes risky steps to improve the Georgian economy and to reform its political system. He brought to the Foreign Ministry a commitment to radical change, a willingness to implement reform in an unorthodox manner, and the political skills and strength to accomplish his goals.

As foreign minister, Shevardnadze drew his political legitimacy from his closeness to Gorbachev rather than from the Communist party. His confident assumption that he had the Soviet leader's imprimatur gave him more credibility and authority than any previous foreign minister. He used his political skills to short-circuit normal bureaucratic procedures. Traditionally, Politburo members submitted drafts of speeches to their colleagues for review. However, according to his aide, Sergey Tarasenko, Shevardnadze circulated his drafts immediately before delivering them, leaving any opposition with no time to interfere.[4] And he carefully manipulated his relationship with Gorbachev. During their years of close co-operation (1985-89), the Politburo typically would meet as a whole, then a smaller group would meet, then Gorbachev and Shevardnadze would meet alone. Shevardnadze would not speak in the larger meetings except on matters of foreign policy. He used his one-on-one sessions with Gorbachev, however, to make his points on all issues, and Gorbachev often followed his advice. Shevardnadze also used the process in reverse. He would speak with Gorbachev, encourage him to make a particular point in a speech, and then use that speech to convince others that this was what the general secretary wanted.

Shevardnadze had creative ideas for institutionalizing policy, a rare attribute among leaders in any society, but his ability to impose these ideas outside the Foreign Ministry was limited. It was therefore necessary to co-opt or weaken competing centers of power. He quickly became the

point man for the leadership in a series of challenges to key Soviet institutions, particularly the military and the party. For several years, he and
Gorbachev were extremely successful in undermining opponents and set-
ting the policy agenda. In the end, however, they failed to build legitimate
institutions to pick up the power of those they had weakened.

TAKING ON THE MILITARY

Believing that only deep cutbacks in defense spending could pay for economic reform, the new Soviet leaders moved to end the military monopoly over national security policy. Shevardnadze led the struggle to reduce
defense spending and restructure decision making on national security
issues by challenging the prestige of the military. His commentary constituted both a comprehensive critique of military decision making and a
call for compromise on arms control. He argued that Soviet policy had
contributed to the post-World War II atmosphere of fear and uncertainty
and criticized the military's preoccupation with accumulating weaponry
(*International Affairs* 1988). He called for strategic and conventional
force reductions and accepted intrusive verification and asymmetry as
elements of disarmament pacts.

Gorbachev and Shevardnadze successfully reduced both the influence of the military and the size of the defense budget, entered into extensive arms control agreements with the United States, and staged a major
withdrawal of Soviet forces from regions outside Soviet borders. Shevardnadze registered a series of victories against the general staff, outma-
neuvering the military on intermediate-range nuclear forces, Strategic
Arms Reduction Treaty (START), a chemical weapons ban, conventional
armed forces in Europe, and unilateral withdrawals. Strategic retreats
from Central Europe, the Sino-Soviet border, and the Third World were
accomplished, as was the return of the Soviet fleet to its home waters and
the dismantling of Soviet bases abroad.

REDUCING THE ROLE OF IDEOLOGY AND
THE COMMUNIST PARTY

Shevardnadze understood better than Gorbachev that Moscow's commitment to communist ideology had limited its ability to face reality and
adopt constructive policies. Increasingly, he criticized the emphasis on

ideology over practical experience. In an extraordinary speech to the Foreign Ministry in July 1988, he began his campaign to remove ideology as the basis of foreign policy, asserting that there was no longer any connection between foreign policy and the class struggle (*Pravda,* 1988a). He was the first Soviet official to argue that the struggle between two opposing class systems was no longer relevant.

To gain control over the formulation and implementation of foreign policy, Gorbachev and Shevardnadze had to pre-empt the Communist party institutions involved in national security policy-the Politburo and the Foreign Ministry's main bureaucratic rival, the Central Committee's International Department. Gorbachev transferred some functions to new presidential commissions, and Shevardnadze's aggressive pursuit of the leadership's policies helped render the International Department virtually irrelevant to the policy process.

CENTRALITY OF THE UNITED STATES

The key to success for new thinking was an end to both the Cold War and competition with the United States. From the outset, Shevardnadze focussed on solving the 'American problem' in order to gain a breathing space *(peredyshka)* in which to revive Moscow's failed economy. Complementing his commitment to rapprochement with the United States was his willingness to compromise. In his first two years as foreign minister, he offered concessions on issues important to Washington, particularly disarmament and human rights, making one gesture after another in his efforts to forge a new relationship. His support for deep reductions in the Soviet arsenal led to disarmament agreements that were overwhelmingly favorable to the United States.

The key to progress was Shevardnadze's close personal relationship with his United States counterparts, Shultz and Baker. He used his innate graciousness and sense of humor to insinuate himself into the good graces of both men and to counter the opposition of anti-Soviets in the administrations of Ronald Reagan and George Bush. He developed strong ties to Shultz, who in turn waged a long, intense bureaucratic battle to convince the White House that the Kremlin was genuinely interested in rapprochement. Shultz had major differences with Casper Weinberger, the secretary of defense; William Casey, the director of the Central Intelligence Agency; John Poindexter, the National Security Council advisor; and Kenneth Adelman, the director of the Arms Control and Disarmament Agency, over Soviet-American relations and arms control. Other than the first lady, Nancy Reagan, and Ambassador Jack Matlock at the National Security Council, Shultz had few allies outside the State Department (see Shultz, 1993).

The Bush administration initially ignored radical domestic developments in the USSR and remained convinced that Moscow's gestures were designed solely to seize headlines. The president decided to at least talk with the Soviet leadership in July 1989, when a trip to Eastern Europe made him realize that a meeting with Gorbachev was important to the leaders of Eastern and Western Europe. Baker encouraged Bush, believing that signs of change in Eastern Europe presented the United States with an opportunity that should not be missed.[5]

The turning point in the Baker-Shevardnadze relationship occurred in September 1989, during a visit to Baker's ranch in Jackson Hole, Wyoming, where the two men went fly-fishing and hiked. From then on, according to Baker, they spoke informally at all of their meetings (Baker 1995, 146). The pitch for partnership that Shevardnadze made in Wyoming incorporated more major concessions on arms control. For the first time, a Soviet official declared that Moscow was prepared to sign a START treaty without a separate accord to limit space-based weapons and proposed talks on those aspects of the Strategic Defense Initiative (SDI) that might be compatible with the Anti-Ballistic Missile (ABM) treaty. He promised that the giant phased-array radar at Krasnoyarsk, a violation of the ABM treaty, would be dismantled. True to his word, he told the Supreme Soviet a month later that the radar was a "misguided breach of the ABM treaty" and would be dismantled (Garthoff 1994, 518-19).

Washington used its leverage to gain unilateral concessions from Moscow. This produced satisfying, one-sided agreements, but, in the end, it strengthened Shevardnadze's critics and contributed to his downfall. Soviet ambassador Anatoly Dobrynin, for example, charged that the United States and the West Europeans "outwitted and outflanked" Shevardnadze, who went "further than necessary in concessions . . . on arms control, Eastern Europe, German unification, and the Persian Gulf." Dobrynin particularly blamed Shevardnadze for his "inexplicable rush" to deal with the United States and for "giving away vital geopolitical and military positions" (Dobrynin 1995, 628, 636). Even United States officials believed that Washington got "120 percent of what it wanted in negotiations with the Kremlin."[6] The Reagan and Bush administrations, eager to press their negotiating advantages, made no attempt to be conciliatory.

HUMAN RIGHTS

More than any other Soviet leader, Shevardnadze understood that, in order to change Moscow's international position, it was necessary to change the atmosphere of relations with the United States. Human rights were central to Washington's agenda with the Soviet Union, and the Soviet attitude toward human rights would have to change dramatically if the desired transformation of Soviet-American relations were to occur.

The "human dimension" became one of Shevardnadze's central rhetorical themes when he spoke about international affairs. He was virtually alone among Soviet leaders in understanding that, in large part, the Soviet repression of the individual led to international isolation that reflected its alienation from the Western world. While addressing human rights concerns was not alien to Shevardnadze's own personality and culture, he was not so much a moral idealist as a pragmatist who understood the link between human rights and Soviet-American relations. During the first Shevardnadze-Shultz meeting in September 1985, the latter emphasized that improvement in Soviet-American relations required movement on the human rights issue. A year later, in a meeting with Shultz, Shevardnadze himself stated that human rights-a topic shunned by his predecessors-must be given high priority (Kampleman 1991, 374).

Shevardnadze inherited an enormous problem. Systematic abuse of human rights had produced cynicism and fear at home and undermined Moscow's credibility abroad. For 70 years, Russians had enacted criminal codes that violated international norms and had used psychiatric institutions to house dissenters. The international community condemned but did little to lessen these horrors until 1975, when the signing of the Helsinki Final Act bound the major states of the East and West to abide by enlightened standards of conduct abroad and respect for human rights at home.

Shevardnadze's views at the beginning of his career were no different than those of most of his generation of Soviet officials, and his hands certainly were not clean. He had been brutal to dissidents in Georgia in the 1970s and condoned if not encouraged the use of torture in prisons. There are several explanations for Shevardnadze's volte-face on human rights. One of his enormous strengths as a politician was his ability to adapt to new situations, to change his position to accomplish his purpose. Becoming an advocate of human rights was not difficult for him. His attitudes had been shaped by experiences in the cosmopolitan capital of Tbilisi, historically the crossroads for many nationalities and ethnic groups. When the time to change came, he could do so.

The Helsinki Final Act covered three major areas or "baskets" that included principles of behavior between signatories, economic and technical co-operation, and humanitarian and educational concerns. When he became foreign minister, Shevardnadze argued that, having signed the act, Moscow assumed obligations under international conventions and agreements, including recognizing the right of other signatories to insist that these obligations be met. He insisted that the act must be observed even though it was not a legally binding treaty.

Shevardnadze personally intervened to change Soviet policy on humanitarian issues. When the United States was dissatisfied with the number of refuseniks to be released, Shevardnadze increased the numbers. When Washington wanted the release of so-called troublemakers, Shevardnadze persuaded Gorbachev to make sure the bureaucracy went along. When other ministries dragged their heels, Shevardnadze used the Foreign Ministry and the party's Central Committee to cut through the red tape. When Kremlin opponents wanted to reduce the number of emigrants in order to prevent a brain drain, Shevardnadze pressed for free emigration; by the time he resigned, he had achieved this objective. The role of personal diplomacy often has been exaggerated but, in this case, Shevardnadze's impact on Soviet diplomacy and society was enormous.[7]

EUROPE

Shevardnadze's motives with regard to a retreat from Eastern Europe were clear. The only source for the capital needed to restructure the economy was in the defense budget. Although strategic arms agreements captured the most headlines, the real savings were to be found in conventional arms agreements and unilateral reductions. The obvious focal point was Eastern Europe, particularly the costly Soviet military presence there. The decision to retreat from Eastern Europe, the most dramatic shift in Soviet policy since the end of World War II, had great implications for the East-West rivalry, ending the Soviet threat and undermining the justification for the North Atlantic Treaty Organization (NATO).

More than Gorbachev, Shevardnadze understood that Moscow could not improve its international economic position and implement domestic economic reform until it significantly changed its relations with Western and Eastern Europe. He believed that European economic integration was inevitable and that, without reform, the USSR could never become an integral part of a vigorous Europe and would become even more isolated, backward, and irrelevant. Western Europe was an important source of investment and technology, and Eastern Europe was a drain on Soviet resources.

Shevardnadze understood that increased Soviet tolerance of change in Eastern Europe was one of the keys to improved East-West relations, and he was out in front of the Soviet leadership in believing that reform in Eastern Europe had to be accompanied by radical changes in Moscow's foreign and security policies toward Europe. His calls for global interdependence and a "common European home" required increased political independence for Eastern Europe, and his pursuit of closer economic links with Western Europe required the absence of military confrontation in Central Europe.

In March 1988, Gorbachev formally repudiated the Brezhnev doctrine, which had-proclaimed Moscow's right to intervene to defend communist regimes and had enforced East European submission to Moscow. Shevardnadze emphasized Moscow's commitment to non-use of force and non-intervention, telling James Baker that the use of force to stop reform in Eastern Europe would be the end of perestroika (Oberdorfer 1991, 360). The Soviet Union demonstrated that it would not use force to maintain its empire in 1989 when it accepted the collapse of the Berlin wall, the establishment of non-communist governments in Eastern Europe, and the dissolution of the Warsaw Treaty Organization (Warsaw Pact).

Shevardnadze signaled a major change in approach in a speech to the European Parliament in December 1989 when he acknowledged that the future of Germany had to be discussed and implied acceptance of reunification (Shevardnaze 1989). Certainly he and other Soviet leaders preferred to delay reunification, given their own bitter memories of World War II.[8] Shevardnadze hoped that reunification would at least take place within the framework of European institutions rather than that of military blocs. He wanted the German question to be central to an all-European process that would include the relationship of Eastern Europe to the European Community, the future of NATO and the Warsaw Pact, and military arrangements for the center of Europe(TASS 1989). He wanted to ensure that, when reunification came, Germany would be tied to a geopolitical anchor. But events moved too quickly for the Soviet leaders who had no time to prepare themselves (let alone their constituents) for the political and psychological impact of reunification.

Bowing to the inevitable, Gorbachev and Shevardnadze accepted both reunification and German membership in NATO (TASS 1990a). They still hoped that concessions would be made, such as reductions in the size of the German military, but Shevardnadze argued that Moscow's security could be guaranteed only by cooperation with the West (*Pravda* 1990a). He anticipated that Moscow's concessions on NATO membership would improve Soviet-German relations, and he argued that Bonn's economic support was more important to Soviet security than a continued troop presence in Eastern Germany. He believed that, having accepted the liberation of Eastern Europe, dissolution of the Warsaw pact, and German unification, Moscow would receive Western economic and technical assistance to correct a deepening economic crisis at home. He tried to convince the United States and Western Europe that such aid would stabilize East-West relations and ease the USSR's transition to a market economy (*Pravda* 1990b).

RETREAT FROM THE THIRD WORLD

The decision by Gorbachev and Shevardnadze to abandon confrontation with the United States in the Third World in favor of cooperation contributed to the end of the Cold War and defined the beginning of the post-Cold War era. Two dramatic actions framed this policy reversal: the decision to withdraw from Afghanistan (a policy implemented by Gorbachev and favored by all Soviet leaders) and Shevardnadze's unconditional endorsement of United States policy in the Persian Gulf in 1990 (which faced serious domestic opposition). Both policies reversed standard Soviet practice. Never before had Moscow tolerated the demise of a communist regime on its borders or endorsed the deployment of United States forces close to its borders to engage one of its allies.

The decision to withdraw from Afghanistan was Gorbachev's first major foreign-policy shift, and it pre-dated Shevardnadze's appointment as foreign minister.[9] Soon after becoming general secretary in March 1985, Gorbachev told the Politburo that withdrawal was essential, and the United Nations mediator, Diego Cordovez, observed that Moscow was seeking new ways to move the negotiating process forward as early as May 1985 (Oberdorfer 1991, 238). Once again, Shevardnadze became the chief architect of the policy of retreat; as chair of the Special Commission of the Politburo, his mission was to arrange for withdrawal while maintaining a friendly government in Afghanistan. Ironically, in the case of Afghanistan, it was Shevardnadze who slowed the process of withdrawal by trying to ensure the survival of the regime of Sayid Mohammed Najibullah Kabul. His uncharacteristic stubbornness on this issue reflected his personal commitment to Najibullah, who had been put in place by the Soviet Union because, unlike his predecessor, he was willing to cooperate in the policy of withdrawal.[10]

Shevardnadze and Gorbachev recognized that Washington's cooperation was essential if a withdrawal were to be accomplished with dignity. The "help" they sought was an end to United States support of the Afghan insurgents (Mujahideen) in return for Soviet withdrawal. The United States drove a hard bargain, however, increasing its arms shipments to the Mujahideen and backing away from an implicit commitment to stop such assistance in exchange for Soviet withdrawal. Time and again, Soviet requests for reciprocal action were refused. To a considerable extent, Moscow exacerbated its own dilemma by coupling pleas for a political settlement with intensified efforts to turn the tide of battle militarily in Afghanistan.

The Geneva accords, signed on April 14, 1988, heralded Soviet capitulation to Washington's demands. By February 1989, the Soviet Union had moved its troops out of Afghanistan, even though it had received no assurances that U.S. aid to the Mujahideen would end. Nor did the Soviet withdrawal stop the fighting. The Geneva accords served only to reduce the level of superpower involvement as the Najibullah regime did not crumble immediately and the Mujahideen fought on with support from the outside. Finally, in 1990, the United States and the Soviet Union agreed to cooperate. The Bush administration did not request funding for the Mujahideen in 1991, and Soviet support for Kabul declined. Najibullah's fall in April 1992 was followed by intense fighting among the various insurgent groups. The United States and the Soviet Union were no longer involved in Afghanistan, but the killing continued. The two superpowers had missed an unusual opportunity to shape the postwar environment in that shattered country.

The withdrawal from Afghanistan contributed significantly to Shevardnadze's broader efforts to improve relations with the United States and China, as well as with nations in the Middle East and southwest Asia. The decision to withdraw from a client state with a Marxist government on the Soviet border sent a clear signal to East European and Third World clients, particularly Angola, Cuba, and Vietnam, that there were limits to Moscow's support. When Gorbachev told the United Nations General Assembly in December 1988 that the "bell of regional conflict tolls for all of us," he was giving strong voice to the perception he shared with Shevardnadze that minor confrontations in the Third World adversely affecting the global community should not be tolerated (*Pravda* 1988b).

Shevardnadze was solely responsible for the unprecedented cooperation between the United States and the USSR during the crisis in the Persian Gulf in 1990-91. In pursuing a policy centered on the United States, he had overcome strong domestic opposition and Gorbachev's doubts. Moscow's support for U.S. policy was critical to the success of operations Desert Storm and Desert Shield, and Shevardnadze was the driving force behind that support. Without Moscow's retreat from Central Europe and Shevardnadze's assurances that Moscow's response would be benign, Washington's transfer of most of its forces and armor in Europe to the Gulf would have been far more hazardous—if not impossible. It would have been a "difficult history" without Shevardnadze, according to Brent Scowcroft, the national security advisor at the time, who observed that Gorbachev was "uncomfortable" supporting Washington and could not have managed the policy without Shevardnadze's firm lead.[11]

The personal relationship between Shevardnadze and Baker was the key to the unprecedented cooperation between the United States and the USSR in the Persian Gulf. The two men trusted each other and provided the mutual assurances that enabled U.S. policy to proceed. They met several times during the Gulf crisis, as did Gorbachev and Bush, providing a continuous Soviet-American dialogue to coordinate political and diplomatic actions. This unprecedented coordination was a clear personal victory for the foreign minister in his effort to give Soviet-American relations the highest foreign-policy priority. But his constant battle with internal critics undermined his position in the Kremlin, and his "United States only" approach helped produce his political downfall.

Shevardnadze parleyed Moscow's cooperation in the Gulf into acceptance by the United States of Moscow's inclusion in the Middle East peace process. He called for renewed United Nation's efforts to resolve the Arab-Israeli conflict and, in his speech to the United Nations in late November, he challenged the United States to accept movement toward an international conference on the Arab-Israeli issue and not reject it out of "some occult fear of the word linkage" (TASS 1990b). Bush and Baker initially rejected the idea of linkage, but in January 1991, after Shevardnadze's resignation, Baker agreed. In a joint statement, the two nations included language on the Gulf crisis and on the need to resolve other regional issues, particularly Arab-Israeli tensions; efforts to resolve these issues were to be redoubled after the Gulf crisis ended. Baker's willingness to accept this language reflected his growing concern that Moscow's support for the coalition was weakening.[12]

The policies of Gorbachev and Shevardnadze toward the Third World created opportunities for resolving numerous, previously intractable, conflicts. The decisions to withdraw from Afghanistan and to cooperate with the United States in the Gulf were the two most dramatic examples of new thinking about the Third World but, in the interval between these two decisions, Shevardnadze's Foreign Ministry helped resolve disputes in Africa, southeast Asia, Central America, and the Middle East.

Shevardnadze's emphasis on demilitarization led to a number of proposals for bilateral cutbacks in the Third World, including the withdrawal of U.S. and Soviet forces from the Mediterranean Sea and the Indian Ocean, and the dismantling of both the Soviet naval facility at Cam Ranh Bay in Vietnam and the U.S. naval base at Subic Bay in the Philippines. When Washington failed to respond, he supported unilateral cuts. In 1989, on the eve of the Gorbachev-Bush summit in Malta, for example, Shevardnadze announced a 50 percent cut in the Mediterranean squadron and unilateral withdrawal from Cam Ranh Bay.

Encouraging an active role for the United Nations in conflict resolution, Shevardnadze urged greater use of international military observers and peacekeeping forces. The Soviet Union paid its United Nations arrears as well as overdue assessments for peacekeeping operations which they had previously refused to pay. They cooperated with United Nations observers in Afghanistan, supported peacekeepers in the Persian Gulf and sent observers to Namibia. Shevardnadze favored using the permanent members of the Security Council as guarantors of regional security, and in 1989 for the first time the Soviets cosponsored with the United States a United Nations resolution stressing the importance of Security Council mandates.

Shevardnadze made it clear that Moscow would subordinate the interests of its clients to its national interests. Moscow withdrew its commitment and modified its support to traditional Third World clients, including Cuba, Vietnam, Afghanistan, Ethiopia, Angola, Libya, Mozambique, and Syria. Shevardnadze's message was clear: These states should pursue peaceful resolution of their disputes. In the end, the Angolan government entered talks with the National Union for the Total Independence of Angola (UNITA); Phnom Penh endorsed reconciliation with Prince Sihinouk; the Sandinista regime in Nicaragua negotiated with the Contras; Mengistu Haile Mariam tolerated the secession of Eritrea from Ethiopia; and the Palestinians accepted mediation with Israel.

Shevardnadze helped to alter the political environment throughout Asia. Improved relations with China were achieved by unilateral concessions on the so-called three obstacles: a reduction in the Soviet military presence in Mongolia and on the Sino-Soviet border, Soviet withdrawal from Afghanistan, and Vietnamese withdrawal from Cambodia. Pursuing reduced tensions on the Korean peninsula, Shevardnadze made it clear that Moscow would not permit the policies of a regional client (North Korea) to inhibit its efforts to expand ties to important nations (South Korea). He was out in front on this sensitive policy issue and met with opposition in Moscow, particularly Yevgeny Primakov, who convinced Gorbachev to slow the pace of relations with Seoul. In a meeting with the South Koreans at the United Nations in September 1990, Shevardnadze acted preemptively when he announced that Moscow would establish relations immediately (TASS 1990c).[13]

In the Middle East, the new leaders quickly made it clear that Soviet, not Arab, interests would dictate Moscow's foreign-policy agenda—even in areas where Moscow had previously deferred to its clients. In 1986, Gorbachev lectured Abd al-Salaam Jallud, a visiting Libyan official, about the need for restraint and avoidance of any pretext for imperialist attacks, above all terrorism in all its forms (TASS 1986). In 1987, he urged President Hafez al Assad of Syria to seek a political settlement with Israel and indicated that Moscow would no longer support Syrian efforts to attain military parity with Israel (*Pravda* 1987). In 1988 he encouraged modification in some positions of the Palestine Liberation Organization (PLO), and in 1989 welcomed the opening of a dialogue between the United States and the PLO (*Izvestia* 1989). He expanded ties to Israel and increased Soviet Jewish emigration (from 1,000 in 1986 to 300,000 in 1991).[14] Again demonstrating his commitment to an ally (in this case the PLO), Shevardnadze established consular relations with Israel in 1988, but would not restore formal diplomatic relations until progress was made in the peace process. In January 1991, when the Madrid conference on the Middle East was organized, relations were restored. The Madrid process led to peace agreements first between Israel and the PLO, and then between Israel and Jordan.

The resolution of the Gulf War was the most dramatic manifestation of the impact of new thinking on regional conflict. Following the war, Moscow participated in UN efforts to destroy Iraq's strategic capabilities. United States and Soviet diplomats cooperated to end Ethiopia's civil war and resolve differences in Cambodia and El Salvador; Russian combat forces served with UN and NATO peacekeeping forces in the former

Yugoslavia. Moscow and Washington broke their stalemate over arms shipments to Afghanistan, and the Russians continued to reduce their forces in Cuba and the Northern Territories. Just as the Cuban missile crisis in 1962 convinced the United States and the USSR to put the "nuclear genie back in the bottle," Iraq's invasion of Kuwait revived the notion of collective security and peacekeeping and opened a window of opportunity for the United Nations to engage more actively in conflict resolution.

RESIGNATION

Shevardnadze first threatened to resign in December 1989, following a bitter disagreement with Gorbachev over the use of force in Tbilisi earlier that year.[15] Gorbachev refused to consider his resignation, and Shevardnadze backed down. In December 1990, Shevardnadze had no intention of giving Gorbachev warning. He was extremely angry about Gorbachev's failure to support him on important policy issues. While he had been trying to push the policies of new thinking, he believed that Gorbachev had moved to the right and was trying to slow the process of reform.

In what he described as the "shortest and most difficult speech of my life," Shevardnadze said that he could no longer work with Gorbachev (Keller 1990d). He did not consider the resignation a betrayal of his friend. Rather, he viewed it as a desperate effort to save perestroika by shocking Gorbachev into recognizing the dangers he was facing. Warning that perestroika was headed towards failure and that the nation was threatened by dictatorship, he expressed hope that his radical protest would embolden members of the country's democratic movement to resist the forces of reaction. The resignation drew the curtain on any lingering illusions about the political scene in Moscow. Shevardnadze's chilling statement, with its prophecy of doom, was a shocking defeat for Gorbachev and perestroika and a Pyrrhic victory for the opposition, particularly the military.

By resigning, Shevardnadze distanced himself from a government that was preparing to use force in the Baltic states. Gorbachev gambled that Washington's preoccupation with the Gulf would not permit it to criticize this use of force. That gamble paid off, but he had misjudged the strength of nationalism and forgotten the lessons of Hungary in 1956, Czechoslovakia in 1968, and Afghanistan in 1979—political questions cannot be successfully resolved with tanks and guns.

Moscow's brutal crackdown in the Baltics, its efforts to walk the cat back on arms control with the United States, and its belated steps to stop the ground offensive in Iraq made Shevardnadze look extremely prescient. Unfortunately, his predictions marked the beginning of the end. Several weeks after his speech, the Defense Ministry announced that it was dispatching thousands of paratroopers to several republics where nationalist sentiment was strongest, including the Baltic states and Georgia. Shevardnadze's resignation contributed to the political environment that gave Boris Yeltsin's campaign for the presidency of Russia center stage in an increasingly unpredictable Soviet Union. The abortive coup in August 1991 was an even greater humiliation that led to the collapse of the Soviet Union itself. Unfortunately, Shevardnadze's resignation left the Foreign Ministry without strong leadership during the coup attempt, and his successors caved in to instructions given them by the coup leaders. In spite of his many differences with Yeltsin, Shevardnadze was one of the first to arrive at the Russian White House to support the president and defy the junta's curfew.

POSTSCRIPT

In 1992, Shevardnadze returned to an independent Georgia which was far worse off than when he left it nearly seven years earlier. Civil strife was destroying the country, and the economy was in ruins. As the head of the state, he was forced to pursue a humiliating course, taking Georgia into the Russian-dominated Commonwealth of Independent States and requesting a Russian military presence in western Georgia to counter secessionist forces in Abkhazia. Just as he had been accused of selling out to Western interests when he was Soviet foreign minister, now he was charged with betraying Georgian interests as chairman of his ancestral homeland.

It is one of the great ironies of this period that independence for Georgia brought Shevardnadze, the radical reformer, back to Tbilisi in the familiar role of unelected autocrat. As party leader in Georgia in the 1970s and early 1980s, he had battled corruption and introduced the most liberal political and economic reforms of any Soviet regional leader. In the late 1980s, he pushed strenuously for radical reform of the Soviet Union. When he returned to Georgia, however, he initially ruled by emergency decree, without the legitimacy of law and with the support of corrupt and brutal paramilitary forces. Finally, elected Georgia's second president in 1995, he embarked on another campaign to rid Georgia of corruption, reform the economy, and restore political stability.

The struggle in Georgia will determine whether Shevardnadze can maintain his role as maker of history or whether he will become one of history's pawns, hostage to Russia in the "near abroad." Georgians asked Shevardnadze to return to Tbilisi, because they believed that only he could draw Washington's attention and assistance; they quickly realized, however, that the United States had little time for the Caucasus, despite the energy resources of the Caspian Sea basin. European preoccupation with the Balkans and NATO enlargement allowed Moscow to use force and the threat of force in the Caucasus, invading Chechnya, deploying military forces to Abkhazia and South Ossetia in Georgia, and putting pressure on Azerbaijan. As in the former Yugoslavia, the collapse of communism in the Caucasus unleashed the demons of nationalism that turned long-simmering conflicts into bloody wars. Wars of attrition in South Ossetia and Abkhazia eroded Georgian confidence and euphoria; in its place, apathy, cynicism, and disillusion emerged.

The task facing Shevardnadze is daunting—building a modern state capable of reining in feudal warlords and surviving secessionist movements. He must encourage a market economy and keep it out of the hands of organized criminals. He must carve out an independent niche for Georgia in a violent and tense region, with Georgia's old imperial master, Russia, breathing down its neck, Iran to the south, Chechnya to the north, and Armenia and Azerbaijan next door.

Shevardnadze may be the only Georgian politician crafty and manipulative enough to play the necessary cards in dealing with Moscow. And he may still have his old magic. The Georgian parliament came to life again in late 1995, debating and enacting laws. Inflation, so high in recent years that it could not even be tracked, was under control. The International Monetary Fund made its first loan to Georgia since independence, and prospects for Georgian inclusion in a major pipeline enterprise were promising. Bullet-pocked buildings in Tbilisi were under repair, and Georgians once again were frequenting their favorite cafes at night.

Shevardnadze, a brilliant and ruthless political infighter, is steeped in the twelfth century writings of the Georgian author, Shota Rustaveli, whose epic poem, *The Knight in the Panther's Skin*, extolled the virtues of the free life of a Caucasian mountaineer and his heroic death. Casting himself in the role of a courageous and bold Rustaveli hero, Shevardnadze took on the challenge of bringing stability to his ancient and romantic nation. Success in this venture would enable him to go down in history not only as the statesman who played a major role in ending the

Cold War between the United States and the Soviet Union, but also as the father of the modern Georgian state.

NOTES

1. Interviews with George Shultz, Palo Alto, CA, 24 September 1993; and James Baker, Washington, DC, 14 April 1994.
2. *Allocation of Resources in the Soviet Union and China—1968*, Hearings before the Subcommittee on National Security Economics of the Joint Economic Committee, Congress of the United States, 100th Congress, first session, part 12, 19 March and 3 August 1987, 11.
3. Interview with Ambassador Victor Israelian, State College, PA, 24 March 1993.
4. Interview with Sergey Tarasenko, Providence, RI, 13 April 1993.
5. Interview with James Baker.
6. Interview with Ambassador Jack Matlock, New York, 7 July 1994.
7. Interview with Richard Schifter, former national security adviser to President Bill Clinton, Washington, DC, 15 May 1994.
8. Gorbachev's father had served on the Western front for five years and his village had been occupied; Shevardnadze's oldest brother had been killed in the war; and Yakovlev walked with a limp from a grenade wound. All feared domestic opposition to reunification.
9. Many observers have argued that the introduction of Stinger anti-aircraft missiles into Afghanistan in the late summer and early autumn of 1986 turned the tide against the Soviet Union and forced the decision to withdraw. This position is undermined by the substantial body of evidence which supports the notion that the Soviet Union had already made the decision to withdraw. By 1985, the Soviet leadership overwhelmingly opposed continued occupation; the argument was over how the withdrawal would be accomplished and the nature of the government that would be left.
10. Interviews with Anatoly Chernyayev, former national security advisor to Gorbachev, Princeton, NJ, 27 February 1993; Ambassador Yuly Vorontsov, New York, 6 July 1994; and Pavel Palazchenko, principal interpreter for Gorbachev and Shevardnadze, Moscow, 4 May 1993.
11. Interview with Brent Scowcroft, Washington, DC, 13 December 1993.
12. Interview with Dennis Ross, senior advisor to the secretary of state for the peace process in the Middle East, Washington, DC, 21 May 1993.
13. Tarasenko interview.
14. See *New York Times*, 6 March 1988, p. 3; 30 September 1990, p. 8; 2 and 4 November 1990; *Wiener Zeitung*, 4 February 1990.
15. Interview with Sergey Tarasenko.

Part II

Structural and Contextual Developments

Chapter 4

Yeltsin and the New Political [Dis]Order

Betty Glad

The transformation of the Soviet Union could have been smoother had Gorbachev and Yeltsin been able to work more closely together. The transition in South Africa, for example, was facilitated by the ability of F. Willem De Klerk and Nelson Mandela to negotiate a new set of rules under which the transition would take place in a framework recognizing the concerns of all South Africans. In this endeavor, each man worked to constrain the extremists on his side of the political divide (Glad 1996).[1]

Gorbachev and Yeltsin were never able to come to any such accommodation. For a short time, it is true they served each other's political purposes. At the beginning of the transition Gorbachev needed Yeltsin on his left, so that he, as the more moderate reformer, could bring the Communist Party along with him. During this period Yeltsin also needed Gorbachev. For as long as all the institutions in the Soviet Union—the Communist Party, the bureaucracy, the KGB, and the military—retained their monopoly on power, Gorbachev was needed to keep them from a full right-wing backlash. At first Yeltsin was a simple reformer, winning popular support through populist challenges to the privileges that Gorbachev and other Communist Party leaders enjoyed. But once the communist system had been deligitimated, public expectations raised, and new political structures created in the RSFSR, Yeltsin would be in a position where he could openly challenge the old order in its entirety. Winning a popular election to the presidency of the Russian Republic in 1991, he gained a mandate that Gorbachev had never obtained. But for all the republics, he challenged the most fundamental values of all those committed not only to the old order, but the very idea of a Soviet Union.

Yeltsin's motivations were quite complex. Superficially, he shared certain characteristics with Gorbachev. Both men were born in the same year and started from humble beginnings. Both performed well in school and showed leadership qualities in their early years. Both made their way up the political ladder through the Communist Party and made their reputations as honest and hard-working regional bosses (Yeltsin 1990, 62, 128).[2]

Yet they had very different personalities. While both men were risk takers, Gorbachev sought new routes to achieve the reform of a system in which he believed. The use of irregular legal means toward that end, though on a few occasions he might resort to them, he saw as delegitimating the whole enterprise upon which he had engaged. In short, as Anatoly Sobchack (1992) has pointed out, Gorbachev was a careful statesman, weaving between extremes. Yeltsin, this author suggests, was more oriented toward the accumulation of power for himself. He promised the Russians a free market that he knew little about and changed tactics and goals when it served him well. Above all, he showed that he was tough. Brave enough to voluntarily risk his life by defending the White House during the 1991 coup attempt, he could also employ force against others as he saw political necessity requiring it of him.

The key to Yeltsin's orientation is evident in his own account of his personal history. As he recalls it, his life was emotionally harsh. When he was baptized at the age of one month, a drunken priest dropped Yeltsin in the baptismal fount and left him underwater for several minutes. He described his father as a "rough and quick-tempered" man who did not hesitate to punish young Boris for "whatever happened in our neighborhood" by whipping him with a leather strap. The beatings only stopped when Yeltsin was big enough to physically stand up to his father. At the time of his high school graduation, when his father reached for a strap, Boris grabbed his father's arms and said "That's enough. From now on I'm going to educate myself" (Yeltsin 1990, 22–23, 28).

A good student, Yeltsin was educated in technical matters. At Urals Polytechnic Institute he attained a degree in civil engineering. But he did not have the exposure to the broader world of ideas in his early life that Gorbachev had at Moscow State University. Nor did he have the potentially broadening experience of travel outside the Soviet bloc. He did take off to explore the Soviet Union for a few months after his first year at Urals Polytechnic Institute. But prior to his arrival in Moscow in 1985, he had never visited a capitalist or democratic country (Yeltsin 1990, 31, 33–37).

Adapting to this harsh emotional environment, Yeltsin came to see himself as a powerful risk taker. In *Against the Grain,* he portrays himself as a challenger who often risked his health, life, and career. He recalls that when he was about ten years old he stole a grenade from an army warehouse and accidentally blew off two of his fingers when trying to open it. In ninth grade, Yeltsin led classmates on a long hike into the Ural Mountains. They got lost, drank bad water, and got typhoid fever. As a result, he could not return to school to complete the tenth grade (the final year), but studied at home where he completed his final exams. While attending the Urals Polytechnic Institute, Yeltsin developed a cold that turned into tonsillitis, which led to rheumatic fever. But he continued to play sports and attend school while sick, and as a consequence the rheumatic fever eventually led to rheumatic valvular heart disease (Yeltsin 1990, 29–31, 36–37).

Somehow he always survived his confrontations and self-destructive behaviors. For example, at the graduation ceremony from grammar school, he made a speech before about 600 people concerning the brutal and psychologically damaging treatment given by his homeroom teacher. He was expelled from school and given a citation declaring him ineligible for further education. Taking his case up the education hierarchy, however, he succeeded in having a commission of inquiry set up that reinstated his diploma and dismissed the teacher (27–28).

Even as an adult, Yeltsin continued to gamble with his own health and life. In *The Struggle for Russia* he portrays himself as a Russian type "who needs to constantly prove his physical strength, his ability to overcome something." He goes on to note that the will to win is a quality that has come in handy in his life. He can risk his health, he noted, because he can rely on his "body's resilience." His foolhardiness is evident in a story he tells in which he waved his driver to proceed past a traffic officer who had raised his sign for them to stop. His car crashed into a wooden fence and they were rear-ended by another car (Yeltsin 1994, 29, 117).

Moreover, he portrays himself as a lone wolf who personally faces the forces that would destroy him. In *Against the Grain* (1990, 26–28, 32) there are very few memories of his parents. His younger sister and brother are never named and appear on the scene only once—when Yeltsin was six years old. Most of his childhood memories consist of hard work, fighting with and/or leading neighborhood children, and sports. There are no specific childhood friends mentioned. Nor does he mention the mentors that helped him move up the party apparatus and gain power. In *The Struggle for Russia* (1994) he tells of how he made the decisions all by himself to call for the resignation of Gorbachev in 1991 and to suspend the Russian parliament in the fall of 1993.

His recent memoir also gives us clues to how sensitive he is to slights. He remembers his humiliations, portraying individuals who have made a break with him over policy as somehow dishonest as well as disloyal. Thus he gradually notes features in Gennady Burbulis' character (a close adviser to Yeltsin in 1992 and 1993) that are not particularly attractive. "I think he experiences a special thrill when the escort car raced ahead of his ZIL, its lights blinking and sirens screeching" (Yeltsin 1994, 159). When his vice president (1991–93) Alexander Rutskoi begins commenting on the quality of Yeltsin's shoes, Yeltsin (1994, 32) sees the beginning of the conflict that ended in the standoff at the Russian parliament in the fall of 1993. In short, Yeltsin projects himself as a hardened, impulsive man, a risk taker and power seeker with a short fuse and a long memory for those who have betrayed him.

The deep enmity that developed between Yeltsin and Gorbachev cannot only be understood in terms of their personality differences and a struggle for place. The psychoanalyst Heinz Kohut has suggested that most bitter rivalries between men are based on narcissistic blows they give and receive. Yeltsin began the exchanges with Gorbachev in some subtle digs he made as Moscow party boss in 1986. Traveling around the city on streetcars and buses, he used his own dislike of limousines and marble-walled dachas to contrast himself with Communist Party leaders, including Gorbachev (Felshman, 1992). In his warning in the Politburo meeting of October 27, 1987, of what he saw as the beginning of a cult of personality, he was tacitly comparing Gorbachev to Stalin (Morrison 1991, 60–68; Yeltsin 1990, 128–29). Approximately two weeks later, Yeltsin was the victim of some counterblows. Summoned from the hospital to appear before the Moscow Party Central Committee, Yeltsin had to bear a litany of complaints about his egocentric ways. In February 1988, he was ousted from the Politburo (Morrison 1991, 70–72; Barringer

1988). At a party meeting in July 1988, delegates jeered and heckled him when he attempted to defend his 1987 actions. "I consider that the only error in my speech was that I delivered it at the wrong time." Yeltsin was visibly shaken by the hostility and ended his address with a plea for rehabilitation (Morrison 1991, 81).

When he was removed from his post as a member of the Politburo in early 1987, Yeltsin sank into a depression. Unlike others before him, he was not exiled to Siberia or sent to a minor diplomatic post in one of the far corners of the world, but to the State Committee for Construction, where he held the title of deputy. But he was out of the action, as he realized. Sleeping only three to four hours a night, he felt like a "corpse." While waiting for the telephone to ring, he had time for his wounds to fester, and he finally figured out his relations with Gorbachev. "I have never intended to fight with him personally . . . but why hide it—the motivations for many of my actions were embedded in our conflict" (Yeltsin 1994, 16).[3]

When Yeltsin came into his own, he was able not only to undercut Gorbachev's efforts at reform from the center, but also to further solidify his own political base. Elected speaker of the Russian Supreme Soviet in May 1990, he proceeded to set up a competing government in Russia. Under his leadership the RSFSR Congress of People Deputies on June 12 adopted the Declaration of State Sovereignty proclaiming the supremacy of Russian over Soviet laws. In his walkout at the end of the Twenty-eighth Communist Party Congress in July of 1990, he took a slap at Gorbachev, declaring that "as the highest elected figure in the republic, I can only subordinate myself to the will of the people." That same week, *Newsweek* published an interview with Yeltsin in which he implied that Gorbachev was a weakling (Bogert 1990, 24). "Gorbachev is very fond of power. . . . I think that Raisa Maximovna has a stronger character," he said. "Mikhail Sergeyevich likes it very much when people say good things about him to his face. . . . He likes monologues very much."[4]

In early 1991, after Gorbachev tried to keep him from speaking on television, Yeltsin decided on his own that he would go for broke. "You're afraid of Yeltsin? Well then, you'll get the very Yeltsin you fear" (Yeltsin 1994, 16, 22, 116).

After his election as president of Russia on June 12, 1991, Yeltsin was in a position where he could legitimately claim he was acting as the "voice of the people" as contrasted to Gorbachev, who had never submitted himself to a popular vote.[5] In addition to furthering claims against Soviet resources on Russian territory, Yeltsin met with the leader of

Lithuania on July 29, 1991, and signed a ten-year treaty guaranteeing the civil and economic rights of the Russian people in Lithuania. On July 30, when George Bush was in Moscow for the signing of the Strategic Arms Reduction Treaty, Yeltsin arranged a 50–minute private discussion with the American president in the Kremlin. This was arranged after he had refused Gorbachev's invitation to participate, on a trilateral basis, in some aspects of the conference (Gorbachev 1996, 618–25; Yeltsin 1994).

Other actions undertaken in the summer of 1991 may have convinced the communist reactionaries that they had to act quickly to protect their own positions and to avoid the destruction of the Soviet Union. In a private meeting with Gorbachev in late July, Yeltsin insisted that Marshall Dimitry Yazov, Vladimir Kryuchkov, and other communist reactionaries in the government would have to be replaced after the signing of the Union Treaty. The conversation, which was taped (Gorbachev 1996, 643) by the would-be conspirators, would have alerted them to the necessity of taking action to preserve their own jobs. Then, on August 13, Yeltsin vowed that the Russian government would execute its policy of taking direct control of all the natural resources in Russia as soon as the Union Treaty was signed.

At the time of the attempted coup, the actions of Yeltsin and Gorbachev, though uncoordinated, were in harmony. If Gorbachev had collaborated with the plotters, their claim to be acting in an emergency would have had a patina of legitimacy. Certainly the military would have been more likely to follow the order of the coup leaders under such circumstances. But if Yeltsin had not had the courage to take his stand at the White House, the plotters could have simply moved against Gorbachev and used the media to proclaim that Gorbachev was ill while they silently reestablished their hold over the Soviet Union.

But the shift in the power relationships of the two men, as noted in chapter 2, left Yeltsin in a position where he could treat Gorbachev with an almost complete disdain. The humiliations he imposed on Gorbachev when the latter came to speak to the Russian parliament after the attempted coup in 1991 have been noted earlier. Moreover, Yeltsin never gave Gorbachev even the courtesy of consulting with him prior to the actions he took in December to finally dissolve the Soviet Union and extend Russian power over the Kremlin. Indeed, Gorbachev's office was seized, as we have seen, three days in advance of the agreed-upon turnover.

But the indignities did not stop there. In exchange for a pledge to stay out of politics and to refrain from overt criticism of Yeltsin's government, Yeltsin gave Gorbachev a palatial office building in Moscow to use as headquarters for his new research foundation. When Gorbachev, after months of silence, stated in the early summer of 1992 that the Russian government knows "how to destroy but they have not shown that they can create," his luxurious state-supplied ZIL limousine was replaced by a plain Volga sedan (Bohlen 1992a and b). In early October, after Gorbachev refused to appear before the Constitutional Court to hear the case against the Communist Party, his right to travel overseas was canceled. He was also fined 100 rubles (about 30 U.S. cents). The personal/political feud between the two leaders took a turn for the worse a few days later. When Gorbachev publicly noted that Yeltsin was "clearly not coping with his duties" and should be replaced by a state council, Yeltsin ordered the takeover of Gorbachev's Moscow offices and had him temporarily barred from the premises. The ban on Gorbachev's overseas travel was lifted for one day so that he could go to Willy Brandt's funeral on October 13, 1992. This came only after France, Italy, and Germany protested the way that Gorbachev was being treated (Dahlburg 1992, Bohlen 1992b, Shapiro 1992, Erlanger 1992).

Yeltsin's political battle with Gorbachev served to undercut the Soviet Union. Beginning in 1990, he had proceeded to set up a system of government in Russia that was directly competitive with the Union government. His provocative statements in mid-August 1991, as well as his insistence that the communists then in government be replaced right after the Union Treaty had been signed, certainly set a deadline under which the plotters had to act. In *The Struggle for Russia,* Yeltsin himself noted that the Union might have been preserved. He could have fought for his election as President of the USSR throughout all the republics. Or the Russian parliament could have been declared the legal heir of the dissolved Soviet legislature. Perhaps Gorbachev could have been persuaded to make Yeltsin acting president. But these paths were barred to him. He admits, "Psychologically, I could not take Gorbachev's place. Just as he could not take mine" (Yeltsin 1994, 116).

The irony of these exchanges with Gorbachev is that once Yeltsin was in power he engaged in most of the same practices for which he had earlier criticized Gorbachev. The perks he had condemned, he now sought for himself. In *The Struggle for Russia* (1994, 18) he notes his delight in securing the chairmanship of the Presidium of the Supreme Soviet of Russia. When they first entered the office, an aide said in amazement, "Look, Boris Nikolayevich, what an office we've seized!" Yeltsin describes: "I have seen many an office in my life, but I got a pleasant tingle from the soft modern sheen, all the shininess and comfort. 'Well, what next?' I thought. 'After all, we haven't just seized the office. We've seized an entire Russia'" (Yeltsin 1994, 18).

For each crisis he mentions in that same memoir, he is in a different government dacha. This, he explains, was not because he needed privileges, but because they were necessary for him to do his work. He also had his ZIL limousine. Indeed, at the Novo-Ogaryevo meeting with the leaders of the other republics, he took great pains to make sure that his car was in a place of honor. One evening, when his automobile ended up at the end of the line of government limousines, his security people made a quick U-turn to put him at the front of the line, cutting up the lawn in the process (Yeltsin 1994, 20, 37).

At a more significant level, just as Gorbachev had done before him, Yeltsin as chief executive claimed emergency powers for himself and issued legally questionable decrees on his own authority. In May 1992, he issued a decree that created the Russian army forces and named himself supreme commander of them. In the spring of 1993, when the Congress of People Deputies of Russia voted to limit his powers, he walked out of session and invoked his "emergency powers." His decision on September 21, 1993, to dissolve the Russian parliament led to a most unfortunate confrontation. A majority of the deputies refused to disband and chose Alexander Rutskoi, Yeltsin's deputy, as the provisional president of Russia. At first the Yeltsin government responded by cutting off the electricity and water servicing the White House. But when a group of anti-Yeltsin parliamentary supporters marched toward the television station, the issue was joined. Unlike the leaders of the coup, Yeltsin did not hesitate to use force. The White House, where he had made his brave stand two years earlier, was fired upon, and at least 140 people were killed. Ruslan Khasbulatov, the chairman of the Russian parliament, and Rutskoi escaped unharmed (Hitchings 1993, 702; Schmemann 1993a, b; Bohlen 1993a, b, c).

The increased powers that Yeltsin sought were finally legitimated in the constitution that he and his advisers presented to the Russian public in the fall of 1993. Adopted by a bare majority of the voters in a referendum in December 1993, it gave the president power to name the prime minister and dissolve the Duma (the lower house of the parliament). Moreover, he could call for new elections should that Duma turn down his choice of prime minister in three successive votes.

The principle of regional self-determination, now that it threatened the Russian Republic, also went by the board. The right of secession was explicitly forbidden in the new Russian constitution. When Dzhokhar

Dudayev, a former Soviet air force general and president of the republic of Chechnya, declared Chechnya independent, the gauntlet was laid down. Unlike Gorbachev, Yeltsin was willing to initiate a major military operation to keep the principle of "self-determination" from breaking up the state over which he presided. On December 11, 1994, Russia entered into a conflict that would last 21 months. In the course of that operation the inadequacies of the Russian fighting forces would be revealed, questions would be raised about the morality of the operation, and Yeltsin's favorable poll ratings would fall sharply. After several false statements in public that the war was practically over, he finally found a way out, as we shall see. At last, an agreement was signed ending the conflict. The result, announced on August 31, 1996, was a hedge in which the issue of the Chechen demand for independence would be put aside for five years. On December 29, 1996, Yeltsin ordered the withdrawal of the last two military units remaining in Chechnya (Hitchings 1996, 646).

Yeltsin also differed from his predecessor in his decision to boldly move ahead in privatizing the economy. In December 1991, food prices were officially subjected to the forces of demand and supply, with the hope that the new arrangement would lead to an increase in the food supply. That same month Yeltsin issued a decree ordering the restructuring of state collective farms by the end of 1992. The chronically unprofitable farms would be subject to fundamental restructuring. Other reorganization options were given to the profitable state farms and collectives. The next fall, the privatization of the big state-owned companies was begun. The large companies were to be reorganized as joint stock companies, and vouchers were issued giving citizens access to shares in these new productive enterprises.

The new arrangement, however, did not bring forth the miracles expected. Economic production, which had stalled during Gorbachev's reforms, plunged even further under Yeltsin's shock therapy. Indeed, production fell 19 percent in 1992, and an additional 31 percent in 1993. Overall Gross Domestic Product (GDP) between the 1989 base year and 1995 decreased by 51 percent. At the same time consumer prices increased 82,529 percent between 1990 base year and 1995 (White, Rose, & McAllister 1997, 178). During the first eleven months of 1996, productivity fell another 6 percent from what it had been the previous year. Inequalities in income and living standards became even greater than they had been in the Soviet Union, and the differences in living standards (as shown in chapter 6) became more obvious to those suffering from the changes then underway.

With privatization, corruption increased beyond anything that had touched the Gorbachev regime. Organized crime made its presence felt in almost every new arena of economic activity. Murder became almost a normal part of doing business. Bankers, journalists, and political leaders were killed gangland style. In 1993 ten directors of the country largest commercial banks were killed after refusing underworld demands for "loans." A list of political leaders and journalists assassinated in the next three years includes the following: several members of the Russian parliament (Andrei Aizderdzis, 1994; Valentin Martemyanov, 1994; Sergei Skorochkin, 1995); a Moscow reporter investigating military corruption (Dmitri Kholodov, 1994); the founder of the Russian Agrarian Party (Sergei Kushnaryov, 1995); the General Director of Ostankino, Russia's largest state-owned television and radio network (Vladislav Listyev, 1995); and the finance minister of the Dagestan republic of Russia (Hamid Hamidov, 1996), as he began to set up a commission against crime and corruption (Hitchings 1994, 332, 820; 1995, 94, 175, 270).

The prosecution of the war in Chechnya also went badly. In January 1995, Chechen resistance fighters forced Russian troops back to the edge of Grozny, the capital of the region. Hundreds of Russian soldiers were killed and wounded in the process. The European Commission stopped an interim trade pact with Russia because of the crisis, and Warren Christopher met with Russian foreign minister Andrei Kozyrev in Geneva to discuss the crisis. The Russian Duma, on January 13, 1996, overwhelmingly approved a resolution recommending that the government seek a political solution to the problem. Newspaper accounts indicated that Russian troops in Chechnya had been underfed, ill equipped, and had lacked strategic preparation for their operations. In January 1996, the Russian army and Federal Security Service came under fire for giving false information to the press (Hitchings 1996, 41).

Accompanying these events was a decline Yeltsin's personal popularity. In March 1992 (the peak of his popularity as a president) he had a rating of 4.9 on a 10–point scale. By March 1994 his approval rating had dropped to a low of 3.2 points. By June 1996 his support, in percentage terms, was down to single digits (White, Rose, & McAllister 1997, 169–71).[6]

The elections for the Duma in December 1995 suggested that like Gorbachev, Yeltsin had no solid base in a political party that supported his efforts. The election, held under new electoral rules, consolidated what had been a fragmented political opposition to the Yeltsin government. Only four parties emerged from the elections with the 5 percent vote more necessary for party seats. Finishing at the top of the list were the two political parties that opposed most Yeltsin's policies. Gennady Zyuganov's Communist Party, with 22.3 percent of the votes, finished first, followed by Vladimir Zhirinovsky's nationalist Liberal Democratic Party, with 11.2 percent. Only two reform parties placed—the government's "Our Home is Russia," with 10.1 percent, and Grigory Yavlinsky's Yabloko Party, with 6.9 percent of votes (224). The election, in short, showed that there were three major voting blocs in Russia—the Communists, the next-ranking Liberal Democratic nationalists, and the Yeltsin faction. The Communists had increased their power relative to the Liberal Democrats, and the reformers had lost big. Nine out of ten voters rejected Our Home is Russia, the party most closely allied with President Yeltsin.[7]

The votes also countered the traditional wisdom that Russian voters are apathetic. The voter turnout was approximately 66 percent—much higher than the American congressional elections of 1994, in which 39 percent of the voters went to the polls. Moreover, those at the lower end of the economic ladder—the pensioners, the unemployed, and the communists—voted at a higher rate than the more privileged. The vote was "normal" only in the sense that the voters followed their own interests. Pensioners, the unemployed, the elderly and those yearning for security and order voted for the Communist Party. Persons angered by the loss of Russian international prestige tended to vote for Zhirinovsky's party. Those favoring the free market voted for the reform parties (224–25).

Some observers of the Russian political scene expressed concerns that in these circumstances Yeltsin would postpone the presidential elections scheduled for June 16, 1996. In late April, Boris A. Berezovsky (the senior director of ORT television network, a banker, and a magnate in the automobile and other major industries), along with twelve other leading industrialists, suggested that the elections should be postponed. The idea was subsequently approved by Yeltsin's then chief of security, General Alexander V. Korzhakov (Hitchings 1996, 383). Graham Allison (1996) of Harvard University has suggested that the situation gave Yeltsin three alternatives—hope, steal, or postpone the elections, with the last as the only option assuring that "Yeltsin and his apparatus would stay in power."

But Yeltsin saw himself as the guarantor of the December 1993 constitution, and decided to follow its mandate and proceed with the elections (383). As the subsequent campaign indicated, when it came to his own political survival, he was the ultimate politician. Obtaining campaign funds from the new economic czars his government had aided, he ran a smart media campaign. But perhaps most important was his use of promises to employ the government's purse to aide those hurt by his economic programs. In April 1996, he issued a decree doubling payments to Russia's poorest pensioners, and another guaranteeing the value of private savings that were being wiped out by inflation. At a local park in Astrakhan, when people complained loudly over salary and pension arrears, he handed over some cash on the spot to one of the pensioners. On campaign stops up the Volga River, he said that the debt to the military sector would be completely paid off by the end of the month, and that significant tax breaks would be shortly forthcoming. At a stop in the Arkhangelsk region, he noted, "I came with full pockets. Today a little money will be coming to Arkhangelsk region." Gasping at all these promises, economic minister Yevgeny Yasin said that they were "absolutely unrealistic" and would bankrupt the economy ("The Democrat" 1998; Treismann 1996; for Zyuganov's campaign see Stanley 1996).

To escape responsibility for the negative consequences of his various programs, Yeltsin perfected the tactic he would fall back on throughout his presidency. The blame for the stalled economy and difficulties in pursuing the war in Chechnya was placed at the doors of particular cabinet members or perhaps the entire "government." Those so designated were fired. In the midst of a face-off with the Duma in the summer of 1995, he fired the three ministers who had been most closely associated with the war in Chechnya. In January 1996, First Deputy Prime Minister Anatoly Chubais was replaced by Vladimir V. Kadannikov, director of Russia's Avtovaz automobile plant. Since Kadannikov was an outspoken advocate of the revival of state subsidies and large tariffs to protect Russian production from foreign competition, his appointment was widely seen as an attempt to keep Russian industrial chiefs on Yeltsin's side. Foreign minister Andrei V. Kozyrev was then replaced by Yevgeny Primakov, the head of the Russian foreign intelligence service. These changes were widely interpreted as a move to the center in Yeltsin's bid for reelection in June. Later, agriculture minister Alexander Nazarchuk was sacked. And when the ruble fell a record 845 points, Yeltsin forced Viktor Gerashchenko, the head of the Central Bank, to resign. His prime minister, Victor Chernomyrdin, the man he had chosen to replace Yegor Gaidar in 1992, would survive until the spring of 1998 (Hitchings 1996, 40).

Yeltsin also had the support of one of the most important power centers in the new order—"the oligarchs," as they were called. Privatization had provided major opportunities for many of the old apparatchiks who had headed governmental organizations to funnel state properties to themselves (Bunich 1992, 311). Several of them became very rich. Six of these new magnates—including Boris Beresovsky, the senior director of ORT television network—contributed approximately $3 million to the president's campaign (Hitchings 1996, 831).

An episode on the night of June19 suggests how deeply involved the big-money people were in the Yeltsin campaign. Two Yeltsin associates, Sergei Lisovsky and Arkady Yevstafyev, were stopped by security men as they were taking over $500,000 in cash out of the White House. Lisovsky was a wealthy advertising and entertainment entrepreneur who organized pop and rock concerts for Yeltsin during the campaign and handled some of his advertising. Yevstafyev, a former television news executive, was a close aide to Anatoly Chubais. The next day, the Yeltsin people had conflicting stories of what had happened. Lisovsky claimed that the money had been planted on him by the security agents. Anatoly Chubais denied that the men had been carrying any cash. Prime Minister Chernomyrdin told Russian news agency ITAR-TASS that the aides had had permission to move the cash from the White House. Perhaps most important, the relevant authorities seemed to agree that the episode raised no serious legal questions for the men involved. The new chief of security, Alexander Lebed, told journalists that he had no interest in "the murky case." Chernomyrdin's office ordered the release of the men who had been detained. On June 20, Yeltsin fired the security aides who had made the original detentions. One of these was Alexander Korzhakov, Yeltsin loyal bodyguard since 1987, the man who had stood next to him in 1991 on top of the tank when Yeltsin called upon Russians to oppose the coup ("The Democrat" 1998).

A more complete version of events, published on June 27 in *Obschaya Gazeta,* is indicative of the close ties between the money men and governmental officials. Evidently the deputy finance minister (German Kuznetsov) instructed the deputy head of the National Reserve Bank (Boris Lavrov) to pick up $538,850 from a deputy minister (V. Dmitriev) in the Department of Foreign Credits at the Finance Ministry. Lavrov took the money to the White House, and gave the money to Lisovsky and Yevstafyev, who were then detained as they attempted to leave the building with the cash ("Russia Tackling Crisis . . . ," June 1996).

Still, Yeltsin won only 35.3 percent of the votes in the first round of voting, failing to receive the majority needed to avoid a runoff election. This percentage was far below his 1989 win of 89 percent. The Communist Party candidate, Gennady Zyuganov, followed closely at 32.0 percent, who in turn was followed by Alexander Lebed, with about half Zyuganov's percentage, 14.5. In the ensuing runoff election, Yeltsin won

53 percent of the votes, 13.5 points ahead of Zyuganov (White, Rose & McAllister 1997, 260, 267).[8]

Yeltsin's victory was only possible because he had no skilled challenger who could appeal to a majority of the Russian voters. The one man who was stronger than Yeltsin in the polls, General Alexander Lebed, had failed to qualify for the runoff election and was neutralized when Yeltsin's government brought him in as national security adviser and secretary of the policy-making Security Council. But most important, those who disliked Yeltsin saw him as a better choice than Zyuganov in his approach to the economy. The majority of Russian voters, whatever nostalgia they might have had, did not want to run the risk of turning the clock back. Many of them chose Yeltsin as the lesser of two evils.

After the elections, one difficult problem was resolved. In July, after the Chechen rebels had recaptured Grozny, Yeltsin gave Lebed full authority to settle that conflict. A cease-fire in July and a political agreement for a Russian troop withdrawal in August were signed.

But it was clear that the government had made no progress in dealing with the problem of organized crime. Indeed, in June 1997, Interior Minister Anatoly Kulikov noted that threats and murder had become commonplace under post-Soviet capitalism. There were over 9000 crime groups in Russia, employing around 100,000 people according to his estimates. Moreover, the number of crimes committed by organized groups had increased by 94 percent over the past five years. Indeed the figures had gone up by 6 percent within the last year. Even more ominous for the long run was his suggestion that "organized crime is infiltrating different organs of state power and the forces of law and order, including the police and the judicial system." The problem was due to the weakness of the legal and government systems under which Russia moved toward a market economy (Jones 1997). At the local level, where de facto power had devolved into the hands of local bosses, the corruption was particularly rife (Whitmore 1998).

Moreover, Yeltsin's very obvious health problems raised serious questions about his ability to perform in office.[9] Shortly after his inaugural celebration he left the Kremlin for a sanitarium in Barvikha. Later in the fall he had a multiple bypass heart operation at the Moscow Cardiological Center. In January 1997 he was hospitalized with pneumonia. Responding to these events, several political leaders from the opposition called for Yeltsin to step down in the winter of 1996–97. These included Zyuganov, Gorbachev, and Lebed. In January the Duma approved a 229–63 nonbinding resolution to remove Yeltsin from office.

Yeltsin's increasingly erratic behavior also undermined his authority. Earlier he had amazed observers with antics such as his behavior in Berlin, where he followed up a champagne luncheon by grabbing a baton to lead a nonexistent orchestra, and then took a microphone into which he rendered an out-of-tune song. In 1997, he made so many misstatements that questions began to be raised about his competence to handle the affairs of state. Michael Specter (1997) in the *New York Times* notes the following: once he referred to Japan, a nation with no independent nuclear weapons, as one of the world's nuclear superpowers. Another time he claimed that Russia would disarm unilaterally. He confused Norway with Sweden when talking about a major oil deal that Russia was trying to conclude. Another crowd was informed that Russian troop strength in the Baltic region would be cut by 41 percent. In the Ukraine, he noted that he would remove sales taxes between the Slavic states whose people were friendly with each other, causing his finance minister to go "absolutely nuts."

Russia's difficulties were compounded by Yeltsin's reluctance to accept a possible successor. For a time he hinted that he might run for president again in 2000. Though the constitution limited the president to two terms, his chief constitutional law adviser suggested that the provision did not apply to Yeltsin because his first election had been won under the old constitution of the RSFSR. For a time, Yeltsin got rid of anyone around him who might look like a possible successor. Lebed was fired in a televised statement on October 17, 1996, after publicly feuding with many of Yeltsin's ministers and aides. Lebed's chief crime, however, was that he clearly wanted to succeed Yeltsin as president and that the public placed much more trust in him than they did in Yeltsin. Even the ever-loyal prime minister Victor Chernomyrdin, as we shall see, was let go in the spring of 1998 when he made his ambition for the highest office too obvious (Hitchings 1996, 753).

As if to check any doubts that he might still be the man in charge, Yeltsin continued to play the game of musical chairs with his cabinets. In March 1997, Yeltsin completed another major reshuffling, bringing Anatoly Chubais back into the government as first deputy prime minister with responsibility for overseeing market reforms. But the following November, Chubais was sacked as finance minister, though he remained as first deputy prime minister. During the months in between, Yeltsin fired the defense minister, the justice minister, the privatization minister, and the head of the Federal Bankruptcy Agency over purported misdeeds. In the spring of 1998, Victor Chernomyrdin, who had been prime minister since 1992, was replaced by Sergei Kiriyenko, Russia's young and relatively inexperienced energy minister. The move was widely interpreted as Yeltsin's effort to undercut Chernomyrdin's potential candidacy as his replacement for the presidency.

Five months later, as the *New York Times* reported on October 2 (A10), the worsening financial mess in Russia became a full-blown crisis. In August 1998, Yeltsin devalued the ruble, announced that major Russian banks were in serious trouble, and began printing more money. The International Monetary Fund (IMF), which had already forwarded a $4.8 billion bailout package to Moscow, put on hold another $23 billion that it and other lenders had earmarked for Russia (see also "Taxman in a Tank" 1998).

In this crisis Yeltsin went about creating yet another new government. Responding to the oligarchs' public suggestions that Chernomyrdin might be his successor, Yeltsin first proposed that Chernomyrdin be brought back into the government as prime minister (Hitchings 1998, 589). When the Duma refused to accept this appointment, Yeltsin finally bowed to necessity and recommended Yevgeny Primakov for the position. Acting as foreign minister in the Yeltsin cabinet at the time, Primakov had also been a former Gorbachev foreign-policy adviser and head of foreign intelligence. By late September 1995, Yeltsin had composed a cabinet that reached out beyond the usual circle of Yeltsin associates. Two communists—Yuri D. Maslyukov, the former head of Gosplan, was named first deputy prime minister in charge of economic policy, and Vadim Gustov, governor of the region around St. Petersburg, was named as another top-level aide (Bohlen l998b). The new government also gave more power to regional leaders like Lebed, who at the time was governor of Kranoyarsk. Lebed issued his own crisis decrees that included price controls and a tough tax-collection policy. These new cabinet appointments ended, at least temporarily, the bitter feuding between Yeltsin and the Duma (Hitchings 1998, 589).[10]

As the foregoing suggests, Yeltsin was a man who wanted power; he was very skilled, both in gaining that power and retaining it. His long-term contributions to the Russian polity, however, are mixed. His calls for the self-determination of the Soviet republic contributed to the destruction of a highly integrated economy and threaten the viability of even the RSFSR, as the Chechen revolt indicates. The new regime he played such a central role in creating was rooted in a series of legally questionable acts that contributed to the lawlessness that characterized Russian political and business practices in the 1990s. Privatization, moreover, occurred in a framework in which there was practically no limit to what one could steal from the government, and organized crime has penetrated almost every institution in Russia, seriously impeding the creation of a stable political culture. The governmental economic policies, as we shall see in chapter 6, also contributed to the widespread alienation of both the older generation and the youth.

Certainly the economic crisis of August and September 1998 was the product, in part, of the government's fiscal policies. It is obvious that factors beyond the government's control, such as the failures of several Asian economies and the fall in world oil prices, contributed to Russia's economic plight. But the irresponsible fiscal policies of Yeltsin's own government almost guaranteed a meltdown at some point in time. The failure to collect taxes to cover government expenditures necessitated loans from foreign investors at very high rates of interest. For example, financier George Soros on March 4, 1998, revealed that he had loaned several hundred million dollars to the Russian government the previous year at a "very favorable" interest rate. When approached in December 1997 for another loan, Soros declined (Hitchings 1998, 329).

Some observers of the Russian scene are now suggesting that the problems of the regime run deeper than irresponsible fiscal policies. Converted to capitalism on his first visit to the United States, Boris Yeltsin came to accept the view of many economists in the West that an unfettered free market would somehow work its magic in Russia. But the system did not really work as he thought it would. As Stephen Kotkin (1998), director of the Russian studies program at Princeton University, has noted, Yeltsin's massive privatization and anti-inflationary programs did not bring about investment in Russia as it was supposed to do. Most of the capital staying in Russia went into non-productive short-term treasury notes that paid a substantial interest and other nonproductive enterprises. Moreover, the IMF loans did not substantially help the Russian government, as most of the new dollars coming into the country were shifted abroad and stayed there. Provincial officials formed their own private businesses and awarded them the most lucrative government contracts. Funds from Moscow often disappeared as these same local officials siphoned them off for themselves. In these circumstances the decision to float the ruble compounded a disaster already in the making.[11]

Yeltsin's old nemesis Mikhail Gorbachev (1998) has provided a broader diagnosis of what went wrong during Yeltsin's terms in office.

> Yet it was this decision to break up the Union and subject the economy to shock therapy that predetermined Yeltsin's failure. Yeltsin's

policies abruptly broke the production and market integration that
linked Russia and other Soviet republics much more closely than
even the European Union. As the republics pursued uncoordinated
financial and economic policies, their ability to reform successfully
was undermined. Precipitated decontrol of prices led to a sharp
decline in real incomes and made people's savings, including those
of the large middle class, worthless. Opening up the markets to
imported products at a time when most Russian producers were not
competitive destroyed the chances of many industries to restructure
and "marketize" themselves. As for privatization, it quickly degen-
erated into a gigantic scheme to grab and steal what had been built
during the previous decades.

Since the Primakov appointment, Yeltsin's continuing erratic behavior and health problems have raised the question of who is calling the
shots in Moscow. After announcing the devaluation program in August,
Yeltsin left on a five-week holiday ("Russia's Nightmare" 1998). Early in
October 1998, Yeltsin made a trip to Uzbekistan, his first travel abroad in
six months. At the welcoming ceremony, Yeltsin was described in news
reports as "pale and unwell," and he stumbled and needed assistance. The
ceremony was cut short (CNN 1998; see also Specter 1998).

No longer enamoured with Yeltsin's boldness, the Russian people
began recycling a joke that focuses on his sometimes reckless ways: President Boris Yeltsin addresses the nation. "For years we have stood on the
edge of an abyss," he says. "Now, fellow countrymen, we have taken a
great step forward" (Bohlen, 1998c). Yeltsin himself dropped to an all-
time low in the polls. According to a CNN survey his favorable rating in
October 1998 was at 1 percent.

Where the new government will go is not clear at the present time.
Primakov has suggested that he will try to find a third way in dealing with
the economy—something in between full socialism and the full privatization of all enterprises and unregulated capitalism that has become manifest in what many have come to call the "Wild East." In September,
Maslyukov countered speculation that the government would seek a
revival of state socialism. But he noted that the government must intervene more energetically to salvage the economy that by some estimates
had withered by 50 percent since the collapse of the Soviet Union. And he
has suggested that plants privatized at bargain-basement prices or under
shady circumstances to insiders or criminals would be renationalized.
"We have a crisis instead of a market, as well as a collapse of the financial

system and all the rest," he said ("Russia's Economic Chief Warns of Nationalism" 1998). Both Primakov and Maslyukov were dismissed in May 1999.

Still, there is hope. The new Russian constitution has created a political regime that Yeltsin, as well as the leaders of the other political parties, seem to have accepted as legitimate. Human rights were guaranteed in the document, though much remains to be done on this score. The principles of federalism are gradually being worked out in practice. Yeltsin and the Duma, moreover, were finally able to collaborate in the choice of Sergei Stepashin, as the new prime minister. Russian people may eventually find grounds for collaboration. An economic program somewhere between the publicly owned, centralized, and controlled socialism of the new order, and the anarchic, unregulated capitalism of the early Yeltsin years, may be the foundations for a new beginning.

NOTES

1. Most of the factual material in this chapter is public and has been checked against Facts of File and Russian on Line. Where somewhat controversial material is given, those citations will be given in the text.

2. Boris Yeltsin joined the Communist Party in 1958 and continued to move up through the ranks. In 1969, he was appointed as head of the provincial committee of the party and was responsible for construction in the Sverdlovsk province. In 1976, he was called in for a meeting with Brezhnev and offered the position of first secretary of the Regional Committee of Sverdlovsk province, thus bypassing several others in line before him. He soon started filling the committee for the province with his own people. He served as first secretary from 1976 to 1985 and accomplished several major undertakings, building a 220–mile highway and thousands of apartments for workers who were living in shacks as he had done as a child. On July 1, 1985, Yeltsin was named secretary of the Central Committee of the CPSU. On December 24 of that same year, Yeltsin became head of the Moscow City committee of the Communist Party. Yeltsin was then named as a nonvoting member of the Politburo on February 18, 1986.

3. Gorbachev remained surprisingly pragmatic in his political dealings with Yeltsin for some time. He was the one who let Yeltsin speak at the 1988 Party Conference. In May 1989, Gorbachev blessed political maneuvers in the Congress of People's Deputies that placed Yeltsin in the newly created Soviet of Nationalities of the Soviet Union Supreme Soviet. One winning delegate vacated his spot so it could be given to Yeltsin (Dahlburg 1989). At the Party Congress in the Soviet Union in summer of 1990, Gorbachev also

agreed to an expansion of the Central Committee of the Communist Party to allow room for Yeltsin and several others of the radical reformers. Moreover, in his special speech to the Congress, Gorbachev noted that the Communist Party was willing to cooperate with other mass movements and organizations and that its attitudes toward elected soviets and councils would "drastically change" (Clines 1990c, d; Keller 1990e). Eventually, as Yeltsin threatened the very survival of the Soviet Union, Gorbachev developed a "complex" or obsession of some sort toward Yeltsin. He would talk about his rival for hours, making interpretations of his moves (Chernyaev 1993, 218).

4. In his recent political memoir Yeltsin continues with the disdain. He portrays Gorbachev as a hen-pecked husband who briefs his wife at the end of each day and is influenced by her reactions. Yeltsin, by way of contrast, does not permit politics to be discussed at home (1994, 163–64).

5. Yeltsin won 57 percent of the vote in a popular election against contenders Nikolai Ryzhkov, Vladimir Zhirinovsky, and three other candidates.

6. In the 1993 election Zhirinovsky's Liberal Democratic Party won 24 percent of the votes cast for parties, as contrasted to Russia's Choice, with only 14.5 percent. Thus the communists won 14 percent of the vote.

7. Four other parties—Congress of Russian Communities, Women of Russia, Communists-Working Russia-For Soviet Union, and Workers' Self-Government—followed closely, with percentages slightly below the threshold.

8. Shortly after the election the Russian Communist Party joined several other leftist and nationalistic political parties in the Popular Patriotic Union of Russia. *Sovetskaya Rossiya* on August 8 published a communiqué accepted at the congress pledging respect for political difference and elections as a part of the democratic process for gaining power.

9. In the later half of 1994, Yeltsin had two mild heart attacks and was away from the Kremlin for several weeks.

10. For details on recent cabinet changes see Gordon (1998a, b), "Possible Candidates for New Russian PM" (1998), and "Russia's Nightmare" (1998).

11. For other analyses of the economic crises in Russia, see "Chronology of Russian financial crisis" (1998), Kristov (1998), Liesman (1998), Lind (1998), Sanger (1998), and Suttle (1998). Peter Jennings on *ABC Nightly News* (1988) suggested that one-third of Russians are living below the poverty line. The median cash income is estimated to be $36.00 per month.

Chapter 5

Nation Building and the Russian Federation

Carol Barner-Barry

When Gorbachev took power in the Soviet Union in 1985, he faced a crumbling empire, its people restive and its economic system on the brink of collapse. Ten years later, the Soviet Empire was gone—replaced by a group of motley and struggling new countries. The old Russian Soviet Federated Socialist Republic (RSFSR), had been transformed into a fledgling democracy, the Russian Federation (or, more commonly, Russia). The other 14 union republics of the Soviet Union, having laid claim to absolute sovereignty over their formerly subordinated territories, were emerging on the world stage proclaiming their statehood.

Before these 15 former republics there lies a dual task: the building of viable states and the creation of workable national relationships within those states. Few of these new countries are so ethnically homogeneous that it will be easy for the state-building process to result in a nation-state in the classic European sense. For purposes of this chapter, however, attention will focus on the options that lie before the largest and most influential of these new claimants to statehood, Russia. Although ethnic Russians dominated the ruling institutions of the Soviet Union, by 1991, when the Soviet Union collapsed, the proportion of Russians in the Soviet population was only 51.4 percent. By contrast, in the new Russian Federation, Russians constitute more than 80 percent of the population. If there is significant additional in-migration of Russians from the other former union republics, this figure could increase. When the Russian Republic was created in 1991, it was composed of 55 geographically defined regions, 20 ethnically based republics and 11 national districts. Since then, there have been some changes, but the overall picture remains much the same. While the ethnically defined governmental units occupy 54 percent of the territory of the Russian Federation, non-Russian citizens constitute only 17 percent of the total Russian Federation population (Lynch & Lukic 1996, 15). Finally, according to the latest census, there are 180 distinct nationalities on Russia's soil (Chinyaeva 1996, 33).

When considering these figures, it is natural to wonder whether ethnic nationalism has the potential for divisiveness in the new Russia that it had in the Soviet Union. The recent war and continuing unrest in Chechnya highlight the salience of this question. In order to explore this issue, it is necessary to consider the basic psychological nature of national identity, and then to relate it to the problem lying before Russia as it gropes for a national identity that will bind together this diverse group of people within a unifying state.

NATIONAL IDENTITY

Identity is the product of a process of identification: "A mental operation whereby one attributes to oneself, either consciously or unconsciously, the characteristics of another person or group" (Reber 1995, 355). In the case of national identity, the person would perceive herself as having a primary psychological bond with a collectivity that is based on commonly held characteristics, such as language, culture, religion, a perceived homeland, citizenship or civic values. In the contemporary world, the mediating variable is usually ethnicity.

Esman defines ethnic identity as "the set of meanings that individuals impute to their membership in an ethnic community, including those attributes that bind them to that collectivity and that distinguish it from others in their relevant environment" (Esman 1994, 27). Most persons acquire some sort of ethnic identity at birth in the sense that they are born into preexisting collectivities, such as ancestries, cultures, language communities, religious traditions, and geographical groupings. Even preferences for certain types of food, music and clothing can be used to identify a person (to both himself and others) as belonging to a certain ethnic group. For the individual, ethnic identity brings with it both tangible and intangible rewards. Tangibly, ethnic identity may bring with it automatic membership in a community that "takes care of its own." Intangibly, ethnic identity may bring with it the emotional satisfaction of "belonging" and the psychological security of shared myths about one's ancestral history and place in the world. Politically, ethnic identity is "a useful resource because [it] establishe[s] an 'in group' in the constant struggle for power and domination that comprises politics" (Tellis, Szayna, & Winnefeld 1997, 9).

Strong ethnic identity does not automatically bring with it an imperative toward group political activity. Usually ethnic groups that become significant players in the political arena are referred to as nations. "An ethnic group's transition to a *nation* occurs when political and statist ideas develop within it" (Ganguly & Taras 1998, 10; italics in original). Nations emerge in the political arena as a result of a process of mobilization around political, economic and/or social issues. Generally the precipitating factor is a sense of injustice that results from the existing distribution of power, wealth, or status in a situation where it is difficult for persons of certain ethnic identities to achieve power, wealth and status through channels that are normal for that society. Tellis, Szayna, and Winnefeld (1997) identify five factors that are critical to the mobilization of ethnic groups and their transformation into national political actors.

The first factor is an incipient change in the balance of power in a society. Such "changes may stem either from long-term trends whose cumulative effect is about to be felt or from sudden events that affect (either negatively or positively) a substate group disproportionately."(12) The second is a tipping event that, given the proper conditions, can motivate an ethnic group to become politically active. These are usually "*conspicuous* public events that galvanize group sensibilities, reinforce beliefs in their insular identity, and set off escalating spirals of mutual expectations about collective resistance to the established order. . . ." (12, italics in original). The third critical factor is leadership. Nationalist leaders are people "who, for self-interested reasons (and these may range from material and economic to emotional and personality-related), find it profitable to contribute to creating a group identity and bear the cost of

mobilizing that group for political action." (12) The fourth factor is
financial and organizational resources which can determine the character
of the mobilization effort and the strategic options available to the mobilized group. Finally, the fifth factor is the availability of foreign assistance that can significantly supplement the domestic resources of the
mobilizing group and can also transform domestic power struggles into
international issues.

Ethnicity is not, however, the only basis for national identity. It is
also possible for a group of people to see themselves as members of a
civic nation, an identity "based on common citizenship, a common judicial and administrative system, a central government, and popular sovereignty as the basis of state power" (Ganguly & Taras 1998, 10).
Theoretically, a civic nation grows out of the perception of the occupants
of a given territory that citizenship equates with nationality. (Alter 1989,
14) In the European model of the nation-state, ethnic nationalism comes
first and evolves into civic nationalism. This idea is based on the history
of countries such as England and France.

In the contemporary world, however, most newly emerging states
contain multiple ethnic nations or potential nations. Such multiethnic
states cannot become nation-states on the basis of a preexisting ethnic
community. Rather, their institution-building processes tend to be characterized by significant levels of ethnic mistrust or, even, animosity. If they
are to become nation-states, then, the perception of a common national
identity must be based on something other than ethnic loyalty. Civic loyalty is a possible alternative, but not one that is easy to foster in a situation
of ethnic fragmentation. Also, there are many non-state nations in the
modern world. These are ethnic nations that find themselves in two or
more states. Again, if they are to identify with the state in which they
reside, it must be on the basis of civic commonalities, rather than ethnic
ties.

Because of such factors, the classic European model of a nation-
state growing out of common ethnic bonds may no longer be as useful in
the twenty-first century as it has been in the past. In fact, the idea that a
nation-state must be based on a commonly held ethnic loyalty has
become a source of strife as dominant nations seek to build states in their
own images, and minority nations mobilize against them on the basis of
perceived subordination and deprivations. Indeed, a major source of
intrastate conflict has become the ethnocentrist and even xenophobic attitudes held by nations that find themselves having to deal with each other
under the aegis of a common state, combined with the expectation that

the nation-state model is the most desirable and stable form of macropolitical organization.

In any political competition, the participants must choose how to perceive themselves in relation to the "others" with whom they are in competition. Classically, persons who identify with a certain nationality can experience this relationship in a series of gradations. First, and most benignly, perceptions of the relationship between "us" and "them" can be seen through the prism of patriotism or ethnic loyalty: The "love of one's country and devotion to the best interests of one's people" (Forbes 1985, 63). This is usually associated with the psychological stance of citizens of well-established, traditional nation-states who feel secure in their own national identity and their place in the domestic and world community. The "other" may be seen as less privileged, but is usually not expressly disparaged. Patriotism can be regarded as a form of "good" nationalism. It can be used to mobilize a population to solve a common problem. It can also, however, be used to mobilize the same population to confront a common enemy—real or imagined.

Once the other is defined as the enemy, nationalism can shade over into something less benign than simple patriotism. Ethnocentrism is a psychological stance in which individuals are convinced that their own national group is inherently superior to all others. It is a way of thinking that places one's own group (the ingroup) in a positive light and places other national groups (the outgroups) in a negative light:

> The ethnocentrist either accepts a particular group without reservation or else he rejects it as alien and threatening. The groups he accepts are his ingroups; those he rejects are his outgroups. For the ethnocentric person there are only the two extreme possibilities; there is no such thing as qualified support or moderate criticism. The ethnocentrist cannot be neutral or indifferent; he must reject all outgroups—all groups with which he is not able to identify (Forbes 1985, 23–24).

Ethnocentrism also has its degrees. In its extreme form, xenophobia —everything perceived as foreign or alien—seems threatening and dangerous. And because xenophobics fear the "other" so greatly, they are prone to take measures to eliminate the danger by eliminating or subduing those whom they perceive as a threat to themselves and their way of life. Thus, we have the contemporary phenomenon of "ethnic cleansing." Living peaceably with the "other" is no longer seen as an option.

NATION BUILDING AND STATE BUILDING IN RUSSIA

The processes of nation building and state building are usually conceptualized with reference to the way the classic European nation-state model
arose. In Europe, the coalescence of constructed ethnic nations preceded
and led to the formation of modern nation-states. Thus, the state became
a vehicle for self-rule by the nation occupying a specified territory. In
many places outside of Europe the process was affected by imperialism.
During the process of colonization, the imperial states paid little attention
to tribal and ethnic groupings. They created colonies with boundaries that
were drawn with little or no attention to the loyalties and preferences of
the collectivities that predated colonial rule. Decolonization tended to be
the outgrowth of a common desire among all colonized people to throw
off European rule and to establish political independence from European
imperialists. As the colonial powers retreated, they left behind a group of
states with boundaries that did not reflect the national, ethnic or tribal loyalties of their inhabitants. Once the common enemy—the colonial
power—was eliminated, the citizens of these artificially constructed states
found that their tribal, ethnic and national loyalties were major impedi-
ments to the creation of classic European-style nation-states.

The Soviet Union inherited (with slight modifications) the territory
of the Russian empire (Barner-Barry & Hody 1995, 62–63). Under the
guise of establishing a federal state, it set about the business of creating a
Soviet empire to replace the old Russian one. During this process, the vic-
torious Bolshevik leadership attempted to ward off the state-building
aspirations of various ethnic nations that had seen the fall of the Russian
empire as an opportunity to establish nation-states of their own. In order
to keep control over the territories dominated by these non-Russian
nations, they created an elaborate structure of supposedly ethnically-
based jurisdictions in which the resident nationalities were promised significant self-rule. This promise of self-government was not kept. Despite
its federal structure, the dominance of a unified, hierarchically organized
Communist Party of the Soviet Union (CPSU) made the Soviet Union a
unitary state ruled from Moscow (after a brief, early interlude during
which the rule was centered in St. Petersburg).

The various union republics, autonomous republics, autonomous
regions (*oblasti*) and autonomous areas (*okruga*) were, in many ways, as
artificial as the remnants of colonialism in Africa and Asia. These
"administrative changes in territories . . . reflected political necessities
rather than ethnic or linguistic realities" (Sakwa 1993, 97). From the

point of view of the Bolshevik leadership, however, this was not going to be a problem in the long run. Their ideology told them that ethnic and national loyalties would eventually dissolve into the solidarity of the working class. Also, they began a concerted effort to create a new nation on Soviet soil, a nation based on supposed Soviet commonalities. In this vision, a "new Soviet person" would emerge from and unite all of the various preexisting ethnic nations and groups into one common Soviet nation (*sovietskii narod*). They did not, of course, leave this to chance. Rather they devoted considerable educational and propaganda efforts to achieving this result. They failed.

The suppressed, ethnically based nationalist sentiments did not wither. They lay just below the surface, emerging as a facet of the dissident movement during the Brezhnev years and serving as a focus for many of the independence movements during the Gorbachev years. Emboldened by Gorbachev's policies, particularly glasnost, the newly revitalized nationalities began to make demands for sovereignty or, in some cases, succession from the USSR (a right included in the Soviet constitution, but never intended to be implemented). In this struggle, however, the primary goal was democracy; ethnic nationalism was used by the anti-communists as a tool for mobilization: "In the last years of *perestroika* the rise of [ethnic] nationalism was used as a battering ram against the communist system and, perhaps unavoidably, the old state as well. Democracy and nationalism were ... complementary in the anti-communist revolution; only under conditions of post-communism did a contradiction emerge between the two." (Sakwa 1993, 98) Sakwa adds that "in Russia it was the triumph of the democratic revolution against communism that made possible the rebirth of the [Russian] nation" (98–99). Thus, instead of following the venerable European model for building a nation-state out of a nation, the people of Russia did it backwards. "The Russian state-building endeavor itself became the centre of a new Russian national identity as the government struggled to maintain the unity of the republic." (99)

The fact that a contemporary Russian national identity is emerging from the post-Soviet state-building process stems from the fact that, historically, the ethnic Russians had not had an opportunity to build a firm and lasting Russian national identity. The first Russian state was centered in Kiev, a place that is now the capital of Ukraine. Power shifted to the principality of Moscow as a result of the Mongol invasions. With the final defeat of the Mongol overlords in the fifteenth century the ground was prepared for the development of the czarist empire. The government of this empire was based on autocracy. According to the historian Hugh Seton-Watson, "all Russian subjects owed allegiance to the Tsar, who was responsible only to God. Provided that they loyally obeyed him, they enjoyed his protection regardless of whether they were Russian by speech or religion" (as quoted in Dunlop 1997, 30). Seton-Watson argues that it was not until the end of the nineteenth century that the czarist government began to encourage the development of an exclusive, ethnically based Russian national identity associated with a Russian state. This development was interrupted in its formative stages by the Russian Revolution in 1917 (Sakwa 1993, 103).

Under Soviet rule, the national identity of the Russians was submerged in the development of a Soviet identity. Of all the people in the Soviet Union, it was the Russians who most pervasively accepted the idea of a Soviet national identity. For them, it centered on the status of being associated with a powerful, imperial state. During the Russian period and—to an even greater extent—during the Soviet period the ethnic Russians spread out over Eurasia, establishing strong ties to the places where they settled. For the most part, they saw themselves as the Soviet heirs of the Russian empire: "Russia had never achieved a highly developed sense of itself as a nation state and no distinction between the notions of empire and nation were considered necessary in Russian thought, since Russia's destiny was considered to be an imperial nation" (Sakwa 1993, 104). It was only during the Gorbachev period that the Russians began thinking more exclusively about their ethnically based national role in the Soviet scheme of things.

Unlike the other union republics, the RSFSR had virtually no institutional structure independent of that of the Soviet Union as a whole. For instance, it did not have its own capital. Its capital was Moscow, the capital of the Soviet Union. And a sense of Russia as a union republic—separate and distinct from the Soviet Union—came very late:

> Once Boris Yeltsin had succeeded in achieving election as chairman of the RSFSR Supreme Soviet—in late May 1990—and in declaring the republic's sovereignty, Gorbachev was forced grudgingly to acquiesce to the Russian Republic's gaining the trappings of a "normal" Soviet republic—its own KGB, MVD, and State Committee for Defense and Security; its own television channel and radio station, as well as newspapers officially published by the Russian Republic; and, finally, the activization of a previously dormant and largely symbolic RSFSR Foreign Ministry. These developments suc-

ceeded in bringing Russia into a state of rough ethnic "parity" with
the other union republics (Dunlop 1997, 34).

These developments were the outgrowth of a growing sense among
ethnic Russians that the Russian Republic was not privileged, but was
being sucked dry to meet the needs of the other union republics. Beginning in the late 1980s, Russian nationalists began suggesting that Russia
should secede from the Soviet Union.

The collapse of the Soviet Union caused disorientation among many
of the ethnic Russians living in the non-Russian union republics. By the
beginning of the 1980s, more than 16 percent of the ethnic Russian population resided outside the Russian Republic (Karklins 1986, 232). When
the Soviet Union began its collapse, they increasingly came to be viewed
as "foreigners" in territories they had previously considered subdivisions
of their own country. More significantly, many were unsure as to where
they "belonged," because they considered themselves "Soviet" more than
"Russian."

Thus, the ethnic Russians entered their state-building process in
1991 with a blurred concept of their nationhood. As the leaders of the
Russian Federation struggled to build a new state out of the RSFSR, there
emerged two broad nation-building orientations. Out of the impetus of
the pro-democracy movement during the Gorbachev period, there
emerged a call for an inclusive approach to nationalism. It emphasized
the citizenship and equal rights of all the people residing on Russian soil,
regardless of ethnic origin. The only requirement was the acceptance of
the new Russian state institutions and laws. In other words, this movement called for a state based primarily on civic nationalism. The other
approach emphasized the importance of an ethnically based or exclusive
approach to nationalism. Its advocates wanted ethnic identity to be a cornerstone of the new state. "Therefore nationalism in the anti-communist
revolution had a dual character; both integrative and supportive of democratic state-building; and divisive, when ethnicised or exclusive nationalism was used by old elites or by oppositional patriotic forces to gain
power and to preserve what they saw as threatened national identities"
(Sakwa 1993, 103).

Initially, the first group prevailed. Nowhere is this more evident than
in the name they gave the RSFSR's successor state. In order to see this
clearly, however, it is necessary to appreciate a difference in the Russian
language that is lost in most English translations. Two different terms in
the Russian language are usually translated as "Russian." *Russkii* is the

adjective that is normally selected when the intent is to describe something or someone that is ethnically Russian. *Rossiiskii* is an adjective that is used to describe those who are "of Russia," but not necessarily ethnically Russian (Sakwa 1993, 116). Thus, it becomes significant that the official name of the Russian Federation uses the second variant (*Rossiisksaia Federatsiia*). Thus, the decision makers can be seen as having in mind a kind of civic nation (*rossiiskaia natsiia*), rather than an ethnic nation (*russkaia natsiia)*.

THE EURASIAN MODEL

There are two basic models for building a nation-state in the contemporary world. One, which has already been discussed, is the European model. Here the nation preceded and gave rise to the state. The other is the American model. In this case, the indigenous peoples were defeated and disbursed, their treaty rights little respected and their national identities trivialized. At the same time, in the latter the land was populated by waves of immigrants from many parts of the world. The model was for the immigrants to assimilate into the existing population in a situation where ethnicity was not tied to historical claims to a homeland. Rather, the prevailing perception was that America was a "melting pot" in which former ethnic loyalties were subsumed to a larger civic nationalistic idea of becoming "American." Thus, the state "grew" the nation. Although many Americans still value their ethnic identities, they usually subsume them to their dominant civic identity, becoming Italian Americans, African Americans, Korean Americans and the like. Even the indigenous people are now frequently referred to as Native Americans.

Elena Chinyaeva (1996, 30–35) argues for a third vision to inform Russian state-building—one that falls between the European ethnically based nation-state and the American civic "melting pot." This is a Eurasianist model of a multiethnic state. The idea for such a model has been advanced both in the new Concept on the State Nationalities Policy approved by president Boris Yeltsin in June, 1996 and in the program of the Yabloko Party.

Eurasianism can be traced back to a small group of Russian émigré scholars writing during the early Soviet period. They saw Eurasia as a continent in and of itself, rejecting the idea that the Ural Mountains marked a significant boundary between Europe and Asia. To them, Eurasia was geopolitically discrete from either Europe or Asia, having its own unique history and culture. This Eurasian perspective self-destructed when it was used to buttress the political agenda of its émigré, anti-Bolshevik adherents. Recently, however, it has been resurrected, because it could serve as a model for interethnic relations in the Russian Federation that could claim to be historically based and ideologically supported:

> Superseding the emphasis on territorial and national divisions, it underlines the common value of Eurasian culture for which the contributions of all peoples inhabiting the Eurasian land mass are equally important. The idea of a Eurasian unity does not prescribe the concrete political forms of its realization, which is also an asset in the context of [the] current development of the Russian Federation. Emphasizing the natural rise of the Eurasian union and the advantages of its preservation, the theory provides enough space for the combination of the current ethnically defined federation with the model of national-cultural autonomy. In that way, it escapes both the rigid monoethnicity of a nation-state and the artificial leveling of ethnic differences in a "melting pot" (Chinyaeva 1996, 34–35).

This Eurasian approach would seem to suggest an ethno-federal framework similar to the one that now exists in the Russian Federation.

Lynch and Lukic (1996, 14–17) argue, however, that the ethno-federal principle is a very unstable institutional structure in countries that are emerging from totalitarian rule. The crux of their argument is that "the probability of nationally based politics rather than issue-based politics would seem to be very high in ethno-federal states. . . ." (15). They go on, however, to assert that this will not cause the disintegration of the Russian Federation, as it did the USSR. The reason is that, even though ethnically defined territories represent 54 percent of Russia's area, the titular ethnic populations of those territories are mixed with many other ethnic groups and usually have a heavy Russian presence. In fact, in the republics and autonomous regions, the titular nationalities do not have an absolute majority of the population, "with the sole exception of Chechnya" (Chinyaeva 1996, 33). Also, a large proportion of Russia's population (nine million) is composed of diaspora peoples, such as the Ukrainians, Germans, Kazakhs and Armenians. Finally, many of the ethnic enclaves that do exist are in the center of Russia's territory, having no common borders with third states and no access to the sea.

Moreover, most of the non-Russian nations have for many centuries lived under Moscow's rule. "The memory of lost statehood, so important to the national revivals in the Soviet Union ... is practically absent among the non-Russians of the Russian Federation—who, with the arguable exceptions of Tatarstan and Tuva, have never known independent statehood" (Lynch & Lukic 1996, 16–17). Because of this, they tend to have significant cultural and linguistic ties to the Russians. For example, many of them consider Russian to be their native language.

All of these factors tend to create cross-cutting social and political cleavages that work against sharp national polarizations based on ethnicity. Another factor working against disintegration is the attractiveness of being part of a large state that has the potential for wielding considerable power in the international arena.

None of this, however, should be taken to mean that interethnic relations in the Russian Federation are robust and stable. It is simply that there exists a pattern and a history that can be used as the basis for a more stable nationhood based primarily on interethnic mutual respect, combined with loyalty to a common set of laws and political institutions in which all ethnic groups and individuals are treated equally. Karklins (1994, 14) sees this as being facilitated by democracy and federalism in which "multiple forums with differing balances of power help keep relations in harmony." In addition, she emphasizes the importance of giving nonterritorial ethnic groups collective rights: "Ethnic claims focus on notions of group entitlement in terms of both legitimacy and group worth, and a power-sharing culture accepts this as a positive aspect." Such "ethnic accommodation involves commitment to dialogue and negotiation, as well as legally binding agreements on the basis of free will and reciprocity" (16).

The policies of the Yeltsin regime have, over the years since the demise of the Soviet Union, both encouraged a Eurasian solution and discouraged it. During the first years after independence, the Yeltsin government was willing to allow significant sovereignty to devolve to the subunits of Russia. This led to an asymmetric federalism in which there were two main groups of subunits. One was composed of the republics, which were treated as autonomous states within the Russian Federation. The other was composed of the *oblasti* and other regions, which were treated as administrative subdivisions of a unitary state. This led to considerable unrest and was a factor in the conflict between Yeltsin and the Russian parliament in 1993.

The 1993 Russian constitution "failed to clearly define substantive issues of power-sharing between the center and its federation subjects" (Hughes 1996, 40). It is the power-sharing issue that may prove more divisive in the long run than ethnic separatism. Because a Eurasian model of statehood depends on ethnic equality and civic identity, the wave of bilateral, power-sharing treaties that were signed beginning in 1994 may ultimately prove to have a destabilizing effect. These treaties have meant that all of the Russian Federation's subdivisions do not have equal relationships with the center or equal rights. Even their respective statuses within the federation would seem to vary considerably. Thus, there are many opportunities for local resentments to be mobilized around the key areas of territory, commerce, budgetary matters and foreign ties. For example, there are large disparities in the contribution that the various regions and republics make to the central treasury in Moscow. This means, in effect, that some are subsidizing others. And, in certain cases, the subsidy is substantial. This has been a constant source of tension and is seen by some "as corrupt, irrational, and haphazard" (Treisman 1996, 45). Such factors could easily be used in a process of ethnocentric political mobilization.

For the moment, however, the fact that these power-sharing treaties have taken into a account variations in economic development, strategic importance, culture and ethnicity has been an overall force for stability. It has dampened secessionist imperatives and has permitted Moscow to take into account the particular interests of the various republics and regions. It has also, however, created considerable administrative, legal and budgetary confusion. But the fact that there exist multiple forums with varying balances of power in a context of federalism carries with it at least the potential for successful multiethnic institution-building.

CONCLUSIONS

Identity is a psychological construct. Nation building is a psychological process involving, in effect, the creation of a certain type of political culture within a given space—conceptual or territorial. The basis of the nation built may—and, historically has tended to—be ethnic. Ethnicity is an identity chosen by people in relationship to groups they define as salient, both by reason of birth and by individual choice: By birth, because people are born into situations where they have commonalities with others of culture, religion, language, physical resemblance, music, literature and the like; by individual choice, because people do make choices about the salience of ethnicity in their lives, and in some cases, about the ethnicity they wish to claim.

But, ethnicity, however arrived at, has little political meaning until it is mobilized for political ends and successful mobilization depends on a host of individual and group choices. Each generation (and the individuals within it) must choose the role ethnicity and nationalism will play in the totality of their personal identity. When a state is ethnically-based, it can limit the options of its people to certain ethnic identities and, more importantly, severely restrict or forbid the expression of some identities while encouraging others. If some ethnic identities carry with them certain privileges and others certain disadvantages, ethnic conflict always looms as a threat.

The Russian Federation is not yet a nation-state. Its state-building process is (with all its faults and faltering) is considerably farther along than its nation-building process. In the long run, the building of a Eurasian *(rossiiskaia)* civic and multiethnic nation may lead to greater stability than the attempt to follow European traditions and build a Russian *(ruskiia)* nation based primarily on the ethnic identity of the majority of the population. A Eurasian nation-building process, however, will be an extremely delicate and time-consuming process. Currently existing national identities will have to be reconstructed or deconstructed. A more pervasively Eurasian identity will have to be constructed—or reclaimed.

This process can be regarded as an experiment in the contemporary relationship between state building and nation building. The world today is made up of states with clear (if sometimes disputed) political boundaries. Most of these states contain within them a population that is, to a significant degree, multiethnic and (at least potentially) multinational. For these states, a nation-building process based on either the classic European model or the American melting-pot model is not a clear route to stability. Rather, the twenty-first century is bringing with it the necessity to develop new ways to accommodate ethnic and national diversity within stable state structures. The Russian Federation can be seen as a testing ground for multiethnic state institutions that might eventually be adopted or adapted in other states with multiethnic populations. The problem to be solved is: How do you build a multiethnic national identity in which both ethnic groups and individuals are given a workable combination of rights and duties within a stable complex of state institutions?

Chapter 6

The New Nomenclature and Increasing Income Inequality

Eric Shiraev

Many years ago, Hedrick Smith wrote that in the Soviet Union, the ruling elite was in a very awkward situation: No one could pass on his position and privileges (1976, 49). This statement was relatively accurate, for no one could inherit membership in the Politburo or even a state automobile. However, the Soviet political elite had unlimited and exclusive access to power. What could have been bequeathed from influential parents to their children was the ownership of personal connections, and the access to control over distribution of material resources.

Today, members of the former Soviet nomenclature occupy the top echelons of power in the government and the economy. President Yeltsin and two prime ministers of the 1990s—Chernomyrdin and Primakov—were party and government officials. Most regional leaders worked for the Communist Party organizations in their regions. For example, in the Voronezh region (*oblast*) in the early 1990s, there were only five new people heading local county (*raion*) governments out of a total of 39 officials

(*Izvestia,* 14 July 1994). In the Republic of Tatarstan, 37 out of 52 counties were led by former Communist Party leaders. All top administrators of this republic were former party bosses. In newspapers, stories about young and successful entrepreneurs who "have enormous amounts of contacts" due to their previous work in the party or Komsomol are common (*Nevskoe Vremia,* 7 October 1993).[1] As General Lebed has argued "But it's the same old elite. Nothing changed in this country. And it cannot change" (Lebed, 24 May 1996).[2]

Table 6.1 gives further evidence of this fact.

Though there were no hereditary social classes in the Soviet Union, Communist Party leaders and middle- and high-level bureaucrats developed the skills and wide-ranging social networks that enabled them to take advantage of the opportunities that were opened up in the new regime. The Komsomol, for example, taught its leaders how to organize various projects and how to persuade people to do things they didn't want to do. Many pragmatists who simply wanted to get ahead in the Soviet regime easily found their way up the ladder through this route, adapting to the rules they were given by the regime (*Ogonyok,* #14, April 1998, 11–13).

Like the public officials in the new Russian government, most young entrepreneurs, bankers, and real estate brokers also had a jump-start within the old Soviet social and political establishment. According to one study, 71 percent of them had parents from the middle-class social strata, which guaranteed some status and a particular network of connections. Only 21 percent of Russian entrepreneurs came from the working class (Perepelkin 1995). Many of them had been active in unofficial but widespread trading systems (Simes 1982). These "black market" entrepreneurs were managers of state-owned food and department stores, restaurants, hotels, auto repair shops, and other businesses. Some of them were local officials, people who had access to the distribution of goods and services. A large group of "middlemen" and amateur brokers helped them in the distribution process.[3]

When perestroika was first introduced, some of these people became active in the so-called cooperative movement. With the creation of banks and joint ventures in the late 1980s, many of them were able to transfer government assets into private enterprises.[4] Over time the privatization of governmentally held properties led to a rapid concentration of property and power in the hands of a limited number of business barons. By the mid-1990s, the access to power in Russia, compared to the late 1980s, was extremely limited (Rivera 1995, 65). The oligarchic nature of the

TABLE 6.1

The Komsomol Past of a Select Group of Russian Political and Business Elite

Name	Position in Komsomol	Highest Position by 1998
Gennadi Seleznev	Regional offices (Leningrad)	Chairman, Russian Duma
Sergei Kirienko	Komsomol Secretary (factory, Gorky)	Prime Minister
Boris Pastukhov	First Secretary of Komsomol (Central Committee, Moscow)	First Deputy Minister, Foreign Ministry
Iosif Ordzhonikidze	Secretary of Komsomol (Central Committee, Moscow)	Deputy Premier, Moscow Government
Dmitri Rogozin	Different positions in KMO, a branch of Komsomol (Moscow Headquarters)	Chairman, Congress of Russian Communities
Mikhail Khodorkovski	Deputy Secretary, College (Moscow)	Chairman, Yuksi, Inc. (a major corporation)
Sergei Lisovsky	Regional Office (Moscow)	Director, ORT-Reklama (a major media corporation)
Alexander Degtiarev	Deputy Secretary, Leningrad University (Leningrad)	Chairman, Dalnevostochny Bank

Sources: *Who's Who in Russia* (1996); *Ogonyok*, April 1998, #14:11–13; personal sources.

New Russian elite was noted by both moderates such as Yavlinsky (6 June 1996), and radicals such as Zhirinovsky (22 May 1996).

Privatization also contributed to the new elite's criminalization. The conversion of state properties to private parties created extraordinary opportunities for illegal personal gain. The absence of a legal framework and a shared set of norms about how one should do business facilitated this process. Thus the members of the Russian parliament issued a series of laws that increased their privileges and provided them with immunity against any crime. Officials within the presidential structure maintained close relationships with the companies in which they owned stock. Bureaucrats at all levels (Shlapentokh 1996) offered business elite groups various privileges, such as discounts; tax breaks; low-interest credits; and licenses for export and import protection, including illegal transfer of money abroad. According to some accounts more than 90 percent of properties outside of Russia are either unlawfully obtained or acquired through illegally transferred money *(Argumenty i Facty,* #17, April 1996, 7). Corrupt business elite groups in turn offer politicians funds for their election and relative protection. Many businesses either try to cooperate with criminals by paying them the protection fee, or create their own private security detachments. The richer the business, the bigger its private security army. The coalition of corrupt governmental leaders, bureaucrats, businesses, and criminal organizations threaten to take control of Russia's economy and limit access to it by people who are not in the network (*Segodnia,* 1 August 1995).[5]

Ideologically and psychologically, the entrepreneurs were more prepared to live in a free- market society than the rest of the population.[6] They were more optimistic about Russia's future and more supportive of foreign investments and values (*MMMM,* various polls, 1992–97). Indeed, Russian executives were the least pessimistic group among social groups and the most positive toward assessment of life under the new system. As a group, they were the ones who had most definitely broken away from the norms of the past—from socialism. But many in this group of New Russians, as they were called, were also less educated and less committed to the well-being of their polity than the rest of the population (*Argumenty i Facty* #5, January1996, 13). In the 1990s, their lack of good manners and primitive thinking became a daily source of jokes and anecdotes. Many of these individuals seemed more interested in getting their capital out of Russia than building up new competitive productive enterprises. It is estimated that $400 billion had been taken out of the country by the beginning of 1998 (Borisov 1998). A caricature published in *Argu-*

menty i Facty, illustrated the reality of contemporary Russian life. The picture shows a sign near a reception hall, that says: "Welcome to our VIP special event. Admittance is conducted according to the following order: First Godfathers, Thieves; then proceed New Russians, and finally follow People's deputies" (*Argumenty i Facty,* #5, January 1996, Moscow Edition, 3).

The result of these political and economic changes has been a dramatic increase in economic inequalities. The rich absorb most of the new wealth that has been created in Russia (Abalkin 1995, 23). Moscow and other big cities are full of spectacular mansions and exclusive brick houses. For those who want to display their new status, a newspaper lists the following items as a necessity: an expensive watch ($1,000), expensive shoes ($1,000), a cashmere coat ($1,200), an expensive pen ($30), and a cellular phone ($300) (*Argumenty i Facty,* #14, April 1996). Russian media were filled with advertisements suggesting vacations in the Bahamas, Miami, Mexico, or France. People are daily bombarded with ads for property around the world.

The introduction of the "free market," however, has not brought about a compensatory improvement in the economic circumstances of the average person. Indeed, in some respects living conditions have deteriorated. The GDP per capita in Russia by 1996 was approximately $5,000, which is twice as much as in China, about the same as in Brazil, but four times as low as in most developed countries (*The Economist,* June 1996, 15–21). Indeed, if compared to the stagnant 1970s, today's life expectancy, average income, and educational level are lower. From 1992 to 1995, GDP went down 49 percent while real income went down 29 percent, and inflation was at 650 percent (*Argumenty i Facty,* #27, July 1996). More than half of all Russians report that they do not have any savings kept in a bank (*CISS Index to International Public Opinion,* 1995–96). Those who work for the government or those industries that are still public have joined another class called the "New Poor." They do not receive their salaries for months at a time, and when they do receive something, it is usually only a partial payment.

In major metropolitan areas such as Moscow the newly rich have driven up prices of new housing, public entertainment, and luxury items, to the point where ordinary people find them out of reach. In the mid-1990s in Moscow, for example, the price of one square meter of property was approximately $1,200. This was almost as high as in Helsinki, one of the most expensive European capitals. A small single apartment (Russians call it a one-room flat) in St. Petersburg could easily be sold for $20,000, approximately ten-year's salary of the average Russian adult. For the fine seats at an Elton John concert, many Muscovites paid up to $300, an amount that exceeds an average monthly salary in all Russians regions (*Argumenty i Facty,* #21, May1995). Tigris, a Moscow restaurant listed as "medium-priced," charged $9.80 for a salad, $8.80 for a calamari plate, and $17.80 for a meat filet (*Commersant,* 27 June 1994).

Technological products present in practically every American home are not available for most Russians. For example, in 1996, cable or satellite television was available to approximately 16 percent of the people. Only 40 percent of homes had telephones. Only 22 percent of Russians had VCRs, and only 3 percent had personal computers at home (*The Washington Post,* 13 June 1996). In the United States, the government spends $2,700 per person per year on health care. By the mid-1990s, Russia was spending only $9 per person per year (*Argumenty i Facty,* #8, February 1996, 5). Grigory Yavlinsky, a former boxer who tends to use sharp and precise definitions, called the situation in Russia "the senile dementia of extreme poverty that presses heavily upon every man" (Yavlinsky, 13 June 1996).

Indeed, consumption for the average person has fallen by half since the beginning of the reforms (Zyuganov, 17 May 1996). The official average salary in 1979 was 163 rubles, or about $40 according to the unofficial exchange rate (*Pravda, 21* 1979). Monthly per capita income in 1995 grew up to $62, according to *Izvestia* (22 February 1995). But prices were no longer under state control as they were in 1979. According to our estimations, in the 1970s about 50 percent of an average income were spent on food. In the 1990s the number was close to 90 percent (*Sotsiologicheskie Issledovania,* 1994, 8–9: 9).

The result is that 16 million in the mid-1990s lived below the official poverty level, with a household income of $30 per month. Other sources displayed an even worse picture. Almost 30 percent of Russians belonged to the poverty-level category (*Vesti Statistiki* 1993, 2). Moreover, four out of every ten families with children lived below the poverty level (*Business World,* 23 September, 1994). Between 1991 and 1993, the wide gap between the richest 10 percent and the poorest 10 percent tripled (*Izvestia,* 16 September 1994).

These economic disparities are most evident between the major urban and rural populations. This is suggested in some studies comparing Moscow—the economic, cultural, and political hub of contemporary Russia—and the rest of the country. In Moscow, people spend 2–3 times more per capita than in Russia in general. In 1996, the average employee's salary in Moscow was $145 a month, which is about five times higher than in some other Russian regions. Ford Motor Company suggests that nearly half of all the Russians who can afford to buy its cars live in Moscow. Muscovites, representing just 7 percent of the Russian population, pay twenty percent of the federal budget in taxes (*The Washington Post,* 27 December 1996). According to Romir Gallup Media, Muscovites are twice as likely as urban Russians as a whole to have traveled abroad. Moscow also offers a greater variety and choice of products than the rest of the country. In the mid-1990s, for example, imported and better quality goods comprised almost 70 percent of Moscow's market. As a consequence, people from nearby provinces travel to Moscow to buy better products (*Argumenty i Facty,* #27, July 1996).[7]

Given these circumstances, it is not surprising to find that Muscovites are more supportive of various political and economic changes than are other Russians. They are also more pro-Western (*MMMM,* Various polls 1992–96; Gallup Polls International, 1994–1997). For example, in a 1997 survey by the Mnenie Polling Service, less than 25 percent of Muscovites considered NATO an enemy. Nationwide opinion polls on the same subject showed more negative feelings against NATO in other Russian regions (MacWilliam 1997). Moscow was also more pro-Yeltsin than the rest of the country. Residents of the city provided the president with overwhelming support during the 1996 presidential elections. When Yeltsin underwent his heart bypass operation in the fall of 1996, nearly half of Muscovites said they were worried about his health. Only one in five of all Russians were similarly concerned (*The Washington Post,* 27 December 1996).

Other studies comparing Muscovites to the poor reveal several attitudinal differences. For example, only 40 percent of Muscovites rejected the idea of selling property to foreigners in the capital, but 75 percent of the poor were against it (*MMMM,* March 1992, 6). More than one-third of Russians of all classes supported the idea of "private farmership" (contrary to the "collective farmership"), as compared to only 11 percent of the poor from rural areas (*MMMM,* December 1992). The poorest groups, by way of contrast, had more positive attitudes toward the military than the intelligentsia had (82 percent compared to 52 percent according to *MMMM,* February 1992).

Though many Muscovites are still struggling to find a place for themselves in the new Russia, a relatively high percentage of them are satisfied that they have carved out a place for themselves in Russia. See Table 6.2.

TABLE 6.2

Question: Have You Found a Niche
for Yourself in the New Society?

	Yes	No
MOSCOW	36%	42%
SIBERIA	21%	50%
FAR NORTH	20%	43%

Source: Russian Center for Public Opinion and Market Research. A nationwide poll, October 1996.

Some studies have shown similar contrasts between Russian peasants and urban dwellers. Twenty-five percent of Russians live in small villages and farm the land (Stroev 1996). Most of them are dissatisfied with central government in Moscow and the course of political and economic reforms (*MMMM,* May 1992, 2). Sixty-two percent of peasants opposed the idea of "big private property"—any property with 200 employees or more, when the average opposition to the big private property was at a 40 percent level (*MMMM,* August 1992, 6). Collective ownership for them, at least formally, is over. With exception of land, people now can buy and sell property. But many things have not changed. "[The chances to possess] private property don't change my life," wrote a woman to a central Moscow newspaper (*Izvestia,* #16, 1994).

These class and social differences among Russian regions present a potential for conflict in the future. The New Russians have embraced a post-Soviet social Darwinism that sees the rich and the poor as natural opposites in a world in which the free market is a kind of law of nature. The peasants and the newly poor do not see it that way. Two spokesman for these groups, prominent dissidents of the 1970s, Andrei Siniavski and Maria Rozanova, claim that the growing economic inequality in Russia has little to do with the natural results of competition in a free market-place. But it is making life worse than it was under the communists (*Argumenty i Facty,* # 12, March 1996). It is a discontent upon which Vladimir Zhirinovsky has played during his 1996 presidential campaign when he stated, "Under the Communists, Moscow was well-fed. . . . Everything from sausage onwards came here. Today, all the money is here. Once again, we've overlooked the provinces" (Zhirinovsky, 4 June 1996).

All in all, inequality in Russia today is growing larger while the society rapidly divides into those who have everything and those who have very little. That gap is reinforcing a centuries-old angry feeling of separation between the masses and their masters. But those who predict an inevitable social explosion (Shakhnazarov 1997, 19) will have to wait because in all the wondrous features of the Russian character, there probably has never been a trait so enduring and a quality so exemplary as Russian stoicism.

NOTES

1. There is an ongoing debate in the press about who is able to conduct reforms better, the old, but experienced Soviet-era officials or new, inspired individuals free from communist mentality. The 1996 presidential candidate Sviatoslav Fedorov, for example, suggested that the old bureaucrats are not capable of conducting reforms unless somebody is able to "replace their brains" (*Argumenty i Facty,* #25–26, June 1992). But Boris Nemtsov, then mayor of Nizhny Novgorod, insisted that former party functionaries are more efficient managers than the new "democrats" (*Argumenty I Facty* #28,1992).
2. See *Ogonyok* (April 1998, #14, 11–13) for information on the impact of the Young Communist League (Komsomol) on the contemporary Russian leaders.
3. In some respects the black market during the Soviet regime was simply a patterned deviation from a dominant, official norm. Almost everybody in Soviet Russia was using the "black market" to purchase goods and services, and to solve personal problems. Most of the people involved in illegal trade operations were working full time in other places, raising children at home, and performing basic required citizen's duties. At that time violence wasn't a typical attribute of the Russian "black market."
4. These individuals were more supportive of change than many others. A 1980 study was conducted by the young social psychologist Alexei Khaluta at St. Petersburg University. He compared a wide variety of psychological characteristics of one hundred young "black marketers" with the personal traits of the "average" Russian people, mostly students. The results of this study showed that the young "entrepreneurs" (i.e., "black marketers") had higher IQs, higher achievement motivation, higher levels of optimism, and lower levels of frustration than the "average" people. Khaluta, who has quit his profession and now sells herbal tea to drug stores, was not able to publish the results of his 1980 study. Moreover, some faculty at St. Petersburg University insisted that he himself should have been prosecuted for dealing with "black market thugs," and his paper should be used as evidence to arrest and convict "the criminals."

5. See also opinion polls on anti-legal models of thinking in chapter 10.
6. See available polls published in *MMMM,* June 1992, February 1993, April 1993.
7. The banks in Moscow in 1996 controlled 80 percent of Russian finances. Government employees accounted for 25 percent of Moscow's population. The business barons, criminal bosses, and directors of most influential newspapers and TV networks reside in this city. The majority of local authorities are still accountable before the central offices in the capital (*Argumenty i Facty,* Moscow edition #10, March 1996, 3).

Chapter 7

Old Corruption in the New Russia

Brian Kuns

This chapter concerns the economic and political mores and practices of the Soviet elite, especially vis-à-vis corruption, and how they have survived and changed over the past decade. Studies have shown that more than 60 percent of the Yeltsin-era businessmen in Russia come from the party/state elite of the late Soviet period (Silverman & Yanowitch 1997, 116). Russia's new capitalists, then, are, to a great extent, former Soviet apparatchiki and, notwithstanding the immense political, economic, and legal reforms enacted over the last seven years, these people exert a powerful influence in the new Russian polity. Exploring how these new capitalists were schooled in business goes very far in elucidating the sources of corruption in Russia today. This chapter will argue that the continuing preponderance of the political culture and economic practices of the former Soviet nomenklatura has frustrated the development of a rule-of-law state in the new Russian Federation. It will further be argued that a legalistic conception of corruption obscures a proper understanding of the power struggle currently underway.

FUNCTIONAL CORRUPTION, OR THE WAY THE SOVIET ECONOMY REALLY WORKED

According to Soviet governing doctrine, all economic decisions for every enterprise engaged in some sort of productive or economic activity were made in Moscow, in the government organs of Gosplan (the Central Planning Agency) and Gossnab (The State Committee for Material Supply). Production targets—output—were determined for each enterprise, as were the inputs necessary to produce this output. Individual directors and others responsible for economic output, such as local or regional party bosses, were under tremendous pressure and were offered great incentives to fulfill these targets. Although "in theory, the targets were knowable and coherent, . . . an ongoing renegotiation process made them obscure and contingent. The enterprise manager bargained with the *glavk* (Soviet economic administration for particular products) that administered his operation; the *glavk* represented him in the ministry, which in turn dealt with Gosplan" (Stephen 1991, 36). To some extent, then, production quotas were changeable, though technically the plan carried the force of law. In any case, directors and other notables in the economic sphere knew that they had some leeway when it came to the central planners in Moscow.

Nevertheless, the pressure from the center to produce was unrelenting, and when the economy began to stagnate in the 1960s, the pressure only increased. Enterprise directors, within the context of growing shortages, increasingly began to resort to novel and/or otherwise illegal methods in order to produce. Enterprises hoarded inputs and final products and secured other vital supplies through the black market. The use of *tolkachi* (pushers), unofficial intermediaries who traded hoarded products on the black market, became commonplace. It was not uncommon for officials, directors, or *tolkachi* to resort to threats, bribery, or, on some occasions, violence to secure their necessities. Thus was born a massive informal economy whose participants included official enterprises and ministries, black marketeers, and outright criminals. Such practices, of course, violated many elements of the Soviet criminal code, which outlawed speculation, hoarding, bribery, report padding, etc.

These illegal tactics required falsification of production data, or *ochkovtiratel'stvo* (eyewash). Sometimes, officials engaged in *ochkovtiratel'stvo* for truly criminal purposes, which is perhaps best illustrated by the famous Uzbekistan Cotton Scandal. During the late 1970s and early 1980s, up to half of Uzbekistan's officially reported cotton crop was fictitious (Stephen 1991, 44). The "successful" managers and bureaucrats in the various enterprises, farms, and state and party organizations involved enjoyed great bonuses and, at great profit to themselves, were able to direct vast resources, officially designated for cotton production, to the informal economy. This was a massive conspiracy involving elements from the political and economic elite of Uzbekistan as well as major figures in the Soviet central government.

However, often enough, *ochkovtiratel'stvo* and other more mundane deceptive tactics were employed merely to shield the enterprise from the ire of the central government for not fulfilling the plan. Typically, this deception involved such practices as concealing the redirection of funds that had been earmarked by the central planners for special purposes (such as housing for workers or capital maintenance), and forsaking quality for quantity—to the extent that often necessary parts of a manufactured item would be missing when the item in question was shipped to the shops.[1] Accounting books for enterprises engaging in these tactics were doctored, of course, to reflect a more normal state of affairs. Such deception was in part fostered by the intense secrecy that surrounded all official economic activity. Accurate economic data was "compartmentalized" between departments and enterprises, and was transmitted up the hierarchy only reluctantly (Stephen 1991, 36).[2]

The ubiquity of official mendacity in the Soviet system inspired the frustration of the highest circles of leadership, even while the norms of Soviet economic practice encouraged it. Nikita Khrushchev (1958–64), who in general tried and failed to make the Soviet system work according to its stated norms, declared *ochkovtiratel'stvo* and other such crimes to be a major threat to the economy: "An important task of the central agencies . . . is to block deception, account padding, local interest tendencies, bribery, the squandering and theft of state property, etc. Instances of this kind are unfortunately widespread" (Pomorski 1978, 301).

However, the behavior of the courts with respect to these crimes reveals how the regime, notwithstanding the objections of some elements within the political leadership, viewed this illegal behavior. William Clark (1993) reports that in 1971, 87.7 percent of the officials convicted of report padding did not lose their jobs. Similarly, between 1965 and 1990, only 11 percent of the officials convicted of abuse of authority, exceeding authority, or neglect of duty, received prison sentences, while 31 percent of these officials received only fines and reprimands.[3] (The remainder lost their jobs.) Hoarding, the use of *tolkachi,* and other economic crimes were punished less frequently. In fact, Clark's data (95), though incomplete, show only three dozen convictions for these offenses from 1965 to

1990. Receiving or offering a bribe, however, was punished more vigorously by the regime (83). Thus, as Clark concludes, these so-called functional crimes became a sort of informal business regime, the participants of which included officials at all levels from the ministers to the plant managers. Officials generally were not punished for crimes committed in the interests of their particular enterprise or organization because such crime helped to keep the Soviet economy working. Officials were usually only punished for violations of the criminal code if the offense (such as bribery or speculation) was particularly egregious and the goal was personal aggrandizement.

THE IMPORTANCE OF PERSONNEL

Notwithstanding the exhortations of communist ideologues to remain loyal to communism, an earnest, career-minded functionary's loyalty was intensely and personally focused on his immediate superiors. Such loyalty was crucial because (1) job mobility was decreasing in the 1970s owing to stagnation in economic growth; (2) the Soviet bureaucracy was strictly hierarchical with officials having great power over their subordinates; (3) "the decisive criteria for promotion [were] not 'neutral' rule-bound achievement norms but the evaluation of superiors"; and (4) "promotion within the bureaucratic hierarchies [was] the only path to political power" (Klugman 1989, 98; Rigby 1970, 177; Gyula 1983, 167). Through such intense loyalties, Soviet officials—despite the party dictum to "carry out unswervingly the party line in the selection of personnel according to their political and work qualifications"—were able to develop and exploit loyal patronage networks that followed them up the career ladder (Hough 1979, 321).

However, the ties that bound Soviet officials were not only vertical. In order to deflect the harsh scrutiny from the center and effect a degree of material security in their lives, officials would create or participate in "family circles," fashioned out of the previously mentioned patronage networks and other horizontal ties. Merle Fainsod (1958, 85) describes in detail several family circles that ruled Smolensk in the 1920s and 1930s:

> The so-called family circles [strive] to build an ever-widening entourage that embraces the key points of power in the area and seeks to suppress or regulate the type of criticism on which effective control depends. Under the cover of such arrangements for mutual

protection, it was apparently possible for all kinds of local abuses to flourish for months and even years, simply because the *guberniya* or *oblast* leadership had put together an effective machine which at least temporarily maintained its own discipline.

In a sense, these machines constituted informal political and economic regimes within the state apparatus. These informal regimes were crucial in fostering the development of the functional corruption described earlier. They provided the protection, or *krisha* (roof), that officials needed in order to conduct their semi-legal, illegal but regime-sanctioned, or blatantly illegal business. Family circles thrived under Leonid Brezhnev's administration (1964–82), which is not surprising given the fact that Brezhnev's entourage was one of the biggest and most corrupt political machines in the Soviet Union (Farmer 1992, 239).

A study (DiFranseisco & Gitelman 1984, 611) conducted in 1984 of Soviet émigrés found that 64 percent of the respondents listed *sviazi* or *blat* (connections), as their first or second response to the question "What is the main condition for success in life in the USSR?" Given the increasing scarcity of goods and services, the use of *sviazi* became quite ubiquitous, as very often one would have to call in a favor in order to receive even the most elementary service or material good, such as plumbing repair or spare automotive parts. As Hedrick Smith (1976) writes:

> Almost any transaction can work *po blatu,* by connections . . . from hockey tickets that [one may pass] on to [a] food store director as a favor, to a general's getting a professor to give his son a good grade on a university entrance exam and the professor getting the general to arrange a draft deferment for his son (an actual case).

Thus personal ties, be they defined by patronage, *blat,* or family circles, served to significantly dilute the effectiveness of the Soviet bureaucracy. Public office was used illegally for the protection of one's career, for the safeguarding of others', or for private gain, because, to a great extent, trading the privileges that one's office conferred was the only means possible to secure basic, but scarce, necessities. By the 1980s, everyone from the highest official to the common citizen was complicit in this system.

The successful Soviet enterprise, in short, was run contrary to the norms of the law, and this behavior was known, tolerated, and, to some extent, tacitly encouraged by the Soviet regime (Clark 1993, 40). Given this toleration, enterprise directors "learned . . . that their protection came not from the force of law, but from their political connections and their ability to bring pressure on their trading partners" (Katherine Hendley 1996). Thus, contrary to the stated goals of the Soviet leadership, the exigencies of the command economy bred a respect for force or power, and not the law.

As the Soviet state continued to crumble, Soviet managers assumed de facto ownership rights over their enterprises. First, many directors brazenly consumed resources that belonged to the enterprise, and second, varying amounts of their product were either sold on the black market or, by the late 1980s, shipped abroad for their own personal profit (McFaul 1995, 222–23; Sergeyev 1997). Also, according to the 1988 Law on Socialist Enterprise, all property of a Soviet firm was placed under the complete control of the firm management, thereby significantly decreasing the accountability of Soviet managers to the state. Thus, by the end of the Soviet Union, directors and managers throughout the Soviet economy came to amass great wealth and power, especially vis-à-vis the central government. They had a strong vested interest in ensuring that the privatization of state property—promised by the fledgling Russian Republic—would not erode their profitable and powerful position in society.

CONTINUITY AND CHANGE

Although the structure of the economy and polity have gone through great changes, former members of the Soviet nomenklature have managed to accommodate their business ethic and practices within the new structures. This accommodation has, in effect, perverted the course of Russian economic and legal reform. On the surface, the economic reorganization that has taken place seems astounding. As of 1996, 77.7 percent of the economy was in private hands. However, the majority of shares of these newly privatized enterprises, as alluded to earlier, were cornered by their Soviet-era directors, and, it should further be noted, the state maintains a significant share in many of these "privatized" companies (Kolko 1997, 25; Blasi et al. 1997, 202).[4] This is not to challenge the premise that significant economic and political reforms have fundamentally altered the Russian political landscape. Rather, the juxtaposition of the mores of the Soviet nomenklatura and the new political and economic realities has resulted in a mix of continuity and change.

Taxation constitutes one area where Soviet-era business practices, under a new guise, work to weaken economic reforms and the development of a rule-of-law state. For the past several years, tax collection has been at 50 to 60 percent of planned revenues, and has declined even further in the fall of 1998 (Shlykov 1997, 7; Humphreys 1998). Several factors contribute to poor tax collection. First, the government's poorly organized tax policies encourage non-compliance. There are more than four thousand decrees, government orders, ministerial instructions, legislative acts, and sub-legislative acts that regulate taxes, the number of which reached two hundred by the end of 1997 (Shlykov 1997, 7; "Broken Code," 1997). Plus, these rules change so fast that it is impossible to keep track of them. Finally, the tax load is so enormous, some enterprises estimate that compliance with all taxes would completely eradicate profit (Witt 1996).

Second, large enterprises, corporations, and banks, such as Gazprom, Lukoil, and Uneximbank, view the taxes levied on their operations as subject to negotiation. Gazprom and other large utilities make deals with the government according to which they continue to supply energy to non-paying customers (various cash-strapped localities and regions throughout Russia) and the government grants them huge tax breaks ("Taxman in a Tank" 1998, 72.) The banks also agreed finance enough of the government's operations to keep them going in return for political favors, such as bargain prices for potentially profitable state enterprises.[5] Also, companies go to great lengths to hide their income. One study (Shama 1997) found that 90 percent of all private production goes unreported; and an astounding 80 percent of the population thinks that it is OK to cheat on their taxes (Caryl 1998).

Thus, in many ways the relations between the Russian tax collector and private business approximate the relationship between the Soviet central planner and the state-run economy. The state sets blindingly complex, unrealistic tax goals, just as the Soviet five-year plans were unfulfillable. Russian businessmen engage in all sorts of deals with the government to avoid and/or delay paying taxes, just as Soviet directors sought to influence and/or change their production quotas. The same secrecy surrounds the actual income of a Russian firm as surrounded the actual output of a Soviet enterprise. Finally, Russian citizens feel no compulsion to pay their income taxes, just as the theft of state property was a pervasive fact of Soviet life.

Technically, tax evasion, though illegal, should not fall under the category of official corruption, as it is performed by private firms. However, the extensive ownership of shares on the part of the state in private industry, and the close relationship between many of these firms and officials in the state, would seem to put the source of the problem of tax collection closer to the state bureaucracy. For example, the former prime minister Viktor Chernomyrdin (1992–98) was previously the head of Gazprom, which, as mentioned earlier, has very successfully avoided paying taxes. In addition, in June 1998, the head of the Russian national statistical agency, Goskomstat, was accused of altering his statistics to help large companies avoid taxes. Police found close to $1 million at his apartment (Hoffman 1998, Philips 1998). Finally, the tax police themselves have been accused of corruption ("Russia Tackling Crisis . . . ," 1998).

Efforts of state enterprises to evade taxes serve to highlight the close relationship between the state and privatized enterprises. These relationships in many cases are products of the old Soviet family circles. In contemporary Russian political parlance, family circles are referred to as "clans." Their membership is more fluid today than in the past, but then, the present political situation is significantly more volatile than the stagnant, but relatively peaceful Brezhnev years. Also, the clashes between the different clans is much more open, brazen, and deadly than in the past, as the political and economic stakes have greatly increased.

Generally, clans are composed of alliances between directors or managers of a particular industry and state officials in the appropriate federal or regional ministry. Due to the vast sums of money to be made from the market and from the government, there may be several clans within one industry, representing different firms. Each has its share of corrupt state bureaucrats to provide *krisha,* or protection. The clans fight for rents from the government (subsidies, tax privileges, price supports, tariffs, import quotas or licenses), market share, and profit (Shlapentokh 1997, 61; Galuszka & Brady 1996). The major banks in Russia, which either own the major profit-making private firms or are owned by them, have engaged in particularly ferocious competition, as they attempt to purchase as many profitable former state enterprises as possible. One battle, between Boris Berezovsky, one of the richest men in Russia, and Vladimir Gusinsky, head of the Most bank, led to a fire-fight between troops from the Presidential Security Service under Alexander Korzhakov (a close confidant of the president up to 1996), and policemen supplied by Moscow mayor Yuri Luzhkov (Korzhakov 1997, 282–92; Shlapentokh 1996, 78). Vladimir Shlapentokh (1997) considers these clans to be the real arbiters of power in Russia. The degree of power and influence that these clans possess, then, constitutes a significant change from the previous era, as the Communist Party in the Soviet Union, until the very end, was always able to maintain some discipline among its officials.

The opening of the Russian economy to the global economy is perhaps the most significant factor leading to the increased levels of corrupt behavior present in contemporary Russia. It is now legal to have hard currency and to spend that currency wherever and on whatever the heart desires, without fear of punishment. Bureaucrats are important in this situation because "they control access to the privilege of becoming rich" (Glinka 1998, 21). A bureaucrat's signature or a state license is still needed to conduct much economic and trading activity. Thus, given the depressed economic conditions and the meager salaries many bureaucrats receive, the boost in corruption is not surprising. The manifold possibilities for corruption are too numerous to list here, for they touch on all spheres of society and the economy from banking, law enforcement, export and imports, foreign aid, and the procurement of raw materials to the sale of ambassadorships, privatization, and the dispensation of state credits.

However, some acts are more ubiquitous than others. For example, placing state funds in banks and reaping the returns off high interest rates was a popular way of abusing one's official position for profit (Sergeyev 1997, 119). Or, as is common in developing countries, customs control and export registration is rife with corruption. Indeed, it has become a widespread practice for officers in the Russian Customs Service to accept bribes for underreporting the value of goods crossing the border so that the payer of the bribe can avoid export taxes, or for officials in the Ministry of Foreign Economic Relations to take a bribe in order to influence the distribution of export rights (Tikhomirov 1997, 596–99). The possibility of acquiring real wealth, combined with the declining power of the state to punish transgressions of its laws, has made bribery much more extensive and lucrative than in the past. Russian businessmen devote between 30 to 50 percent of their profit to maintaining relationships with the bureaucracy and organized crime figures (Glinka 1998, 20). Moreover, it is estimated that 70 percent of all bureaucrats take bribes, which in 1993 and 1994 amounted to around $100 million in bribes or other forms of illegal income (21; Waller and Yasmann 1995). Whereas in the Soviet era, public office was used to gain elementary services and other favors, now, as money—especially dollars—has become a real medium of exchange, public office is a source of monetary wealth.

Some official agencies directly engage in economic or criminal activity. The military and security services are the most egregious offenders in this regard. In the early 1990s, a report prepared by a joint government committee—corroborated by press accounts—found widespread corruption in the military (Yasmann 1993, 16; Mathers 1995, 167–68). Army officers in Eastern Europe, the report alleged, set up commercial ventures to buy food and liquor, which were then sold on the free market in Poland or Russia. The report also stated that military officers were selling supplies from their military stocks to German criminals. Evidence has also been presented concerning the illegal commercial activities of the security services. Former KGB operatives allege that KGB agents engage in money laundering and drug trafficking. A 1991–92 Parliamentary commission found similar evidence, but was unable to substantiate it due to the stonewalling of then foreign intelligence service director Evgenny Primakov (Waller & Yasmann 1995).

By all accounts, then, it would appear that corruption has immobilized the Russian state. This stands in contrast to the Soviet era, when corruption to some extent facilitated the maintenance of the Soviet economic system. In other words, whereas some corruption in the Soviet era was viewed as functional and kept under control, in the Yeltsin era, corruption appears to be not only uncontrollable, but extremely dysfunctional to the regime. Nevertheless, the roots of corruption in the Russian Federation are to be found in the inadequacy of the Soviet command economy. The debilitating nature of the present-day corruption supports the views of Western businessmen, journalists, and diplomats (and many Russian commentators as well), who paint corruption in simplistic black-and-white legal terms and blame it for the precipitous economic decline of the last seven years. However, in order to understand the role that corruption plays in the contemporary Russian political system, it is necessary to move beyond both its undoubtedly tragic economic effects and the moral condemnation of it.

RUSSIAN POLITICS AND CORRUPTION: A RECONCEPTUALIZATION

Seeking a more nuanced conception of corruption, James C. Scott (1972, 21–24) holds that corruption is the un-institutionalized influence of wealth in a political system. Conceiving of corruption as influence permits Scott to draw a distinction between influence on the input side of policy (lobbying) and influence on the output side of policy (what we typically refer to as corruption). He argues that such post hoc influence on policy should be considered as an "alternate means of interest articulation." He offers two instances in which powerful or wealthy personages may seek to effect policy output, rather than policy input: (1) "where the narrowness of loyalties or the scarcity of organizational skills inhibits the formation of political interest groups"; and (2) "where the administration of law is so loose and erratic that existing law bears little relationship to administrative behavior—it may be more efficient to make demands known at the enforcement stage than at the legislative stage."

The second of these circumstances certainly applies to Russia. One would expect that wealth seekers, who in general are not proficient in the ways of democratic lobbying—after all, their country has only been "democratic" for a few short years—may prefer the efficacy of bribing a state official in order to seek a desired policy outcome. Russians have traditionally held their government in low esteem, the administration of law in Russia is indeed very erratic, and, in any case, Russian businessmen are not very confident of or proficient in the "proper" ways to effect the new political institutions. Scott's formulation thus suggests that Russia should simplify its tax code and export procedures in order to legitimize, with respect to the law, some of the current activities of Russian businessmen. The Russian authorities could then focus their resources on other cases of corruption, such as those involving the banking industry.

Joel Migdal's elaboration (1988) on the dilemmas facing the authorities of developing countries with shaky state institutions and unstable political circumstances fits present-day Russia very well. He writes that the exigencies of political survival in such situations necessitate that rulers "make eunuchs of their underlings" (209) so as to prevent the establishment of potential rivals, or "power centers" (211) that could challenge their authority. According to Migdal, there are several ways to accomplish this. First, they can create a huge array of overlapping and competing state organizations to prevent any one agency from gaining prominence. Second, rulers can permit and may even encourage corruption so as "to wed potential rivals to the regime" (22). Third, they can conduct the "big shuffle"—the regular rotation of officials so they do not establish too much comfort and power in their positions.

Yeltsin has employed each of these techniques. First, the Russian bureaucracy has grown tremendously in the past few years. In 1995, the government bureaucracy of the Russian Federation was 1.7 times the size of the Soviet government bureaucracy (Walter & Yasmann 1995). As a result of this growth, there has been a widespread duplication of compe-tencies, especially between presidential administration departments *(upravleniie)* and cabinet ministries, creating much institutional conflict and confusion. The once-mighty KGB, for example, has been divided into several different agencies. Second, Yeltsin winks at corruption in the mil-itary and in the successors to the KGB, because this weakens them as potential rivals or coup-plotters. For example, Yeltsin retained the corrupt Pavel Grachev as defense minister for four years, even though he was by far one of the least popular cabinet ministers. However, once the 1996 election made it clear that Yeltsin would not need the army to maintain his rule, he unceremoniously fired Grachev (Parish 1996, 9). Finally, Yeltsins' March 1998 mass dismissal of his entire cabinet—months before the financial crisis necessitated some fast backpedaling on his part—attests to his willingness to shuffle his personnel so that no one person (or clan) becomes predominant.

Migdal also explicates the pressures facing local bureaucrats. With the center distant and engrossed in its own Byzantine game of survival, local and other lower-level bureaucrats are left to fend for themselves. It is in their interest, then, to seek an accommodation with local, powerful personages or "strongmen," as they cannot expect any support from their superiors. He writes "no career-minded bureaucrat wants to be identified as a zealot for a state policy . . . if there is a strong chance that he or she will be left out on the limb long after its creators and the agency chiefs have turned to other endeavors" (241). Thus policemen, judges, and other local representatives of the Russian state are unwill-ing to vigorously pursue their duties because they know that the state cannot even safeguard their lives, much less their livelihoods. It is for this reason that a mutually profitable modus vivendi has been estab-lished in Russia's regions between locally powerful personages—be they mafiosi, bankers, businessmen, or a combination of the three—and local representatives of the state apparatus, such as the police and courts. Many such officials are no doubt disgusted with this state of affairs, but they cannot do anything about it. The result of this accom-modation, according to Migdal, is increasing social fragmentation and a further erosion of state control.

These circumstances do not bode well for the near-term prospects of the rule of law or even a reassertion of state authority in Russia because, as Samuel Huntington writes, weak states "lack the ability to curb the excesses of personal and parochial desires." In such a situation, "politics is a Hobbesian world of unrelenting competition among social forces—

between man and man, family and family, clan and clan, region and region, class and class—a competition unmediated by more comprehensive political organizations" (1965, 411). Yet all hope is not lost. There are members of the political elite who are honest, and earnestly support the development of the rule of law. Yuri Boldyrev, the former deputy chairman of the Federal Audit Chamber (similar to the American General Accounting Office) and a rising St. Petersburg politician, is one such example (Whitmore 1998a, b). Boris Fyodorov, the recently fired head of the Russian Tax Service, who for the past year has sought to improve tax collection, is perhaps another example. Even the youthful Sergei Kirienko, prime minister for a few short months in 1998, provides another example of a relatively honest politician. A characteristic shared by these three men is their relative youth compared to other members of the political establishment. Their youth suggests that, just as a generational shift in leadership contributed to the Gorbachev revolution in Russian politics, it will probably take yet another generational shift to complete the transition to a rule-of-law state.

NOTES

1. Soviet production targets were in gross quantitative units, which did not take into account quality. For example, a shoe factory would produce many shoes of just one size in order to fulfill the plan, which called for a certain number of shoes. It was more efficient to produce one size than to recalibrate the machines in order to make other sizes. Examples of this sort of deception would require a separate book to list completely.
2. It is important to note that such practices occurred on an individual level as well, as workers and farmers deceptively shirked their duties in order to wait in long lines at the stores or work on their private plots of land, or simply stole from their employers. As Stanislaw Pomorski asserts, such behavior on the part of the Soviet elite and general citizenry constituted a "political culture of lies" (Pomorski 1978, 310) that became characteristic of Soviet life in the 1970s and 1980s.
3. One should not forget the courts in this period were not independent, and often were under the influence of the local political bosses.
4. Gabriel Kolko writes that the state retains "an interest of up to 49% in most of [the privatized companies], establishing a crucial government link that has also provided many new proprietors with enormous, continuous government subsidies." However, according to Joseph Blasi, Maya Kroumova, and Douglas Kruse (1997), the state owned an average of 32 percent of the shares in privatized companies.

5. According to *The Economist* (8 April 1995, 19–20), "in other countries rich in gas or oil, ranging from Indonesia to Norway, the energy-producing sector generates tax revenues equal to 5 to 8 percent of GDP. Russia's oil and gas sector pays taxes equal to less than 2% of GDP."

Part III

Popular Adaptations

Chapter 8

The Psychological Dimension of Transition: A Stage Model

Gordon B. Smith

The profound political, economic, and social changes that have transformed the former USSR have had a significant psychological impact on Russian citizens. As Berger and Luckmann noted three decades ago, "Radical changes in the social structure . . . may result in concomitant changes in psychological reality" (1966, 200). One need only look to the statements of political analysts in both the East and West to see these revolutionary changes depicted in terms of a national psyche. The Russian public is routinely described as feeling "empowered," "euphoric," "paranoid," "insecure," "angry," "betrayed," or "anomic" (Remnick 1993).[1] Russian leaders also tend to view the transition process as incorporating important psychological elements. Shortly after coming to office in 1985, Mikhail Gorbachev, addressing a plenum of the Communist Party (CPSU) Central Committee, noted, "Little can be changed in the economy, management, and education without changing [our] mentality and developing a desire and ability to think and work in new ways" (Gorbachev 1985).

Two years later one of his major policy initiatives would carry the appellation "new thinking" *(novoe myshlenie)*. Even more telling are the numerous observations by Russians that the most important place for perestroika is in the mind. People are urged to "restructure themselves" *(perestroitsia)*—a reflexive verb based on the root perestroika. The Moldovan reform advocate Oazug Nantoy echoes the sentiment: "The worst legacy we have from the Stalin era is the way we think. And we cannot obtain new thinking on credit" (Martin 1990).

This chapter begins by developing a stage or phased model for understanding the transition process, that incorporates political, economic, social, and psychological dimensions. We explore the psychological impact at each stage in the transition process by pointing to public opinion, demographic statistics, and observational data to support the generalizations. It should be noted at the outset that this chapter is a preliminary exploration of a phenomenon that will require much more thorough and systematic inquiry in the future.

The effect of fundamental social, political, and economic change on the values, beliefs, and emotions of Russian citizens is conceived here as complex and interactive. In other words, it is hypothesized that each phase of the transition process brings about attitudinal and emotional changes in Russian citizens. These changes, in turn, affect citizen support or resistance to the transition process, in a feedback loop. These reactions then influence subsequent phases of the transition.

Transition, as discussed here, is a complex variable encompassing fundamental political, social, and economic changes. As noted in this chapter, at some points in the transition process political change predominates, at other points economic or social change predominates. Furthermore, the rate of change (and the rate of each of these three components of transition) may fluctuate across time.

The second variable, psychological change, as discussed later, consists of citizens' attitudes, emotions, and feelings. These are distinguished from public opinion, in that public opinion is generally conceived as being relatively well formed and discrete, and having a specific referent (see, for example, Rose 1994, 1995, 1996; Miller, Reisinger, & Hesli 1990–91; Gibson 1995; Hahn 1993). The attitudes, feelings, and emotions that are examined here are less specific and well defined, and the object to which they are addressed may be quite general.

The changed psychological state of Russians under conditions of rapid social, political, and economic change can be either supportive of or resistant to the transition process. The incidence of regime-supportive and regime-resistant psychological states are, to some extent, predictable in time and across the population (see, for example, Grilli di Cortona 1991; Ekiert 1991; Davis & Speer 1991; Tobacyk 1992; Gibson 1995; Miller, Reisinger, & Hesli 1990–91). Furthermore, for a significant portion of the population the changed psychological states manifest themselves in pathological, self-destructive behaviors, including suicide, alcoholism, drug addiction, and crime. These will be explored in some detail with particular reference to the latter stages of transition.

PSYCHOLOGY AND TRANSITION

In recent years an extensive literature has developed concerning transitional societies. Studies of transition have been especially appealing given their occurrence across divergent cultures—Latin America, Southern Europe, and Central Europe—and because of the rapidity and magnitude of change in central Europe and the former USSR (for good examples of this literature, see Linz & Stepan 1996; Przeworski 1991). Several notable articles on transition, especially relevant to transitions in post-communist societies, have noted certain identifiable stages in the process of transition. For each stage, authors have identified common political, economic, and social dimensions (see Bova 1993, Remington 1993, Arato 1985). Below I develop a stage model of transition. For each stage of the transition process I suggest potential psychological manifestations deriving from these political, economic, and social changes.

Stages or phased models have long been recognized as a useful way to conceptualize social change and democratization. Dankwart Rustow's 1970 pioneering *Comparative Politics* article "Transitions to Democracy" conceptualized the process of democratization as a sequence of tasks requiring certain "ingredients," each driven by "its own logic." Richard Joseph (1991) adapted Rustow's model to analyze democratization in Africa, identifying eight phases of transition: decay, mobilization, decision, formulation, electoral contestation, hand over, legitimation, and consolidation.

I identify here six stages of the transition process. As in most developmental processes, these stages do not have clear and distinct starting and ending points, nor are they of uniform duration. Furthermore, the stages are not mutually exclusive; rather there may be significant periods of overlap.

Stage analysis does assume a sequence and directionality to the transition, but it does not presume a specific outcome (such as democracy). In this sense, I do not consider the model to be deterministic. The model presented below builds on the empirical case of transition in Russia (with some consideration given to other cases of transition in other former communist countries). Stage 6 is, at this point, a hypothesized stage for Russian transition. Other outcomes are possible in stage 6, but I have developed here what I consider to be the most likely next stage in the Russian transition.

For each stage discussed, I briefly characterize the nature of the political, economic, and social policy changes. Then I attempt to link these to observable psychological changes in the Russian populace. Where possible, I attempt to differentiate the impact of transition policies on different segments of the population. One final caveat: The model presented in table 8.1 incorporates ethnic and regional factors that are beyond the scope of this chapter and that will be developed further in other research.

TABLE 8.1
Stages in the Transition to Democracy in Former Communist States

Stage 1: Delegitimation of the Old Regime

Political System:	corruption, stagnation, mounting policy failures
Economic System:	state ownership, declining economic performance, black markets
Social System:	status and privileges dependent upon personal connections, social protection by the state, inefficient state controls
Psychological Level:	delegitimation, decline of ideology, youth counterculture
Ethnic/Regional Level:	increasing demands and frustrations against center

Stage 2: Mobilization

Political System:	grass-roots movements, parties, reduced risks of coercion
Economic System:	spontaneous privatization, black markets legalized

Social System:	social/culture sphere opens (glasnost); cultural relativity and diversity
Psychological Level:	euphoria, rapidly rising expectations
Ethnic/Regional Level:	national fronts form, calls for independence

Stage 3: Deinstitutionalization—Purge or Pact?

Political System:	destroy former institutions, purge elites (or form pact with them), gain legitimacy by rejecting the past
Economic System:	destroy former institutions, barter, engage in small-scale entrepreneurship; end of state planning
Social System:	abolish state controls and state protection, abandon commitment to social equality
Psychological Level:	polarization
Ethnic/Regional Level:	nationalism, secessionist movements

Stage 4: Romantic Reforms—Institution Building

Political System:	elections, creation of new institutions (parliaments, presidencies), proliferation of parties
Economic System:	shock therapy, rapid privatization, income differentiation; prices freed
Social System:	new class formations, deterioration of social infrastructure, freedom from social controls
Psychological Level:	euphoria, unrealistic expectations
Ethnic/Regional Level:	independence movements become mainstream

Stage 5: Institutional Failure—Reaction and Retrenchment

Political System:	gridlock, political conflicts, old guard regrouping to defend traditional values
Economic System:	slowed privatization, widely differentiated incomes, insider advantages, hyperinflation, unemployment, bankruptcy; trade and budget deficits
Social System:	crime; collapse of social institutions and social policy

TABLE 8.1 *Continued*

Psychological Level:	anomie, disillusionment, naglost'
Ethnic/Regional Level:	nationalism, chauvinism

Stage 6: Consolidation—Redefinition of the Course and Pace of Reform

Political System:	coalition governments, moderation of extremes, new constitutions, new elections, desire for strong leader
Economic System:	rejection of shock therapy, privatization, return to social protection
Social System:	return to selective state protection (capitalism with a human face)
Psychological Level:	unifying appeal of nationalism, exhaustion
Ethnic/Regional Level:	devolution and reintegration

STAGE 1: DELEGITIMATION OF THE OLD REGIME

The process of transition in communist societies generally begins, not with grassroots revolutions or mass civil disobedience, but with the delegitimation and erosion of support for the communist system. The Brezhnev years (1964–82) are referred to today in Russia as "the period of stagnation" *(zastoi)*. The transition process began in the USSR when an exhausted communist regime began to lose the support and legitimacy it needed to continue to operate. On a political level, such a phenomenon manifested itself in pervasive corruption, leadership stagnation, mounting policy failures, rising ethnic demands, and an inability to recruit people into communist youth organizations and the party. During the Brezhnev years the average age of the ruling Politburo increased from 58 in 1960 to 72 in 1982 at the time of Brezhnev's death. By the mid-1970s, Komsomol activity was declining, especially among older youth (Unger 1981). Between 1985 and 1988, Komsomol membership dropped almost 10 percent (Eklov 1989, 46). Evidence of the persistence of these problems in the USSR are ample. The Soviet political system, as well as the economy, functioned on the basis of *blat* (connections). Throughout the Brezhnev period identifiable networked groups that were organized around regional party organizations or individual ministries promoted people and looked after one another's best interests (see, for example, Skilling & Griffiths 1971; Hough & Fainsod 1979; Moses 1976; Clark 1989).

On the economic level, the delegitimation phase was associated with stagnant or declining economic performance, pervasive economic crime and corruption, and thriving black and gray markets that diverted personnel and resources from the realm of the official, state-controlled economy. The Soviet GNP growth rate declined steadily through the Brezhnev years from 4.7 percent per year in the 1961–65 plan period to only 2.0 percent in the 1981–85 plan period. Declining growth rates were paralleled by declines in industrial production, agricultural output, labor productivity, capital formation, investment, and per-capita income (Hewett 1988, 52).

Results of the surveys of Jewish émigrés conducted in the 1970s tend to support a view of regime legitimacy based primarily on the provision of social welfare benefits. However, by the early 1980s the ability of the regime to meet the social welfare needs of the citizens was seriously eroded; and the cronyism of the top leadership jeopardized its ability to provide people with any real avenues for participation.

At the level of social relations, the communist system under the Brezhnev leadership was associated with the provision of social protections by the state, inefficient state controls, and an ideologically dictated policy of income/social leveling and equality. At the same time, there was an unofficial policy of providing perks, status, and privileges based upon *blat*.

The psychological states associated with this stage in the transition process include declining feelings of legitimacy and support for the communist system, its ideology, its policies, and its goals. Documenting this decline is difficult, since the communist regime under the aging leadership of Leonid Brezhnev sought to suppress any information that would substantiate the phenomenon of declining systemic legitimacy. Yet evidence can be pieced together that shows declining legitimacy and regime support. For example, people manifested cynical, disengaged behaviors, and there were marked differences between public and private modes of behaving. The black market flourished. Private agricultural plots, which constituted only a tiny fraction of arable land and investment, nevertheless accounted for approximately 25 percent of the total production (Raig 1984). Theft of state property became so prevalent and accepted that some engineers and technicians left their posts in research and design bureaus to work in restaurants where they had the opportunity to steal food. Public disaffection can also be seen in declining labor productivity. On any given day as much as 20 percent of the labor force showed up at work drunk or failed to show up at all (Turovskii 1984, 197). There was a thriving counterculture, especially among the young, and corruption and cronyism were widespread and generally tolerated by officials and the citizenry.

STAGE 2: MOBILIZATION

The very conditions of stagnation that characterized stage 1 and resulted in declining support for the communist regime and its strict control of access to and participation in decision making began to break down in stage 2. In the case of the USSR, the catalyst for change came from the leadership in the person of Mikhail Gorbachev. Entering office with a mandate for reform, Gorbachev sought to unleash public opinion to apply pressure on conservative bureaucrats. Under his policies of glasnost Gorbachev encouraged the airing of citizens' grievances, and criticism of public policies and the performances of officials. Views that would have resulted in criminal prosecution and long periods of incarceration just three years earlier were not only tolerated but encouraged by the leadership. With the reduced risks of coercion, Soviet citizens not only began to voice their demands and grievances, they began to organize into grassroots movements and proto-parties.

In the economy, Gorbachev's policies of perestroika brought the once-underground economy above ground. Private co-ops sprang up, many former black-market activities became legal, and some small-scale enterprises became privatized despite the absence of laws governing privatization of state property.

In the social sphere under the influence of glasnost, cultural and social interaction rapidly expanded. Distinctions between public and private behavior patterns began to diminish. The rapid increase of black and gray-market activities, the legalization of cooperatives, and the spontaneous proliferation of citizens' grass-roots organizations expanded the realm of private citizen activity. Greater emphasis was placed on diversity and cultural relativity, rather than on the previously dictated party line. One of the fundamental contributions of glasnost was providing multiple avenues for the expression of divergent ideas. Implicit in glasnost was the notion that there was no longer a uniform party line or an official history that dictated what constitutes "truth."

The rapid mobilization of the public in support of Gorbachev's political, economic, and social agenda resulted in popular euphoria, a growing sense of empowerment, and rapidly rising expectations. Two surveys conducted in 1988 captured the optimism of the time. A CBS/New York Times (CBS/NYT) survey found that 74 percent of respondents strongly endorsed Gorbachev's reforms and 23 percent supported the reforms with some reservations. A similar survey conducted by Marttila and Kiley and Market Opinion Research (MK/MOR) found 70 percent strongly supporting the reforms and 23 percent supporting them with reservations (Willerton & Sigelman 1991). Finifter and Mickiewicz's 1989 survey indicated widespread support for the goals of democratic reforms at this stage in the transition process. Some 95 percent of the respondents supported competitive elections, and 58 percent preferred free speech to social order (Finifter & Mickiewicz 1992, 859).

The relatively fresh memories of the stagnation under Brezhnev were catalytic agents in public responses to Gorbachev's reforms. Animosity toward the old regime was a powerful force in mobilizing support for Gorbachev's reforms. The CBS/NYT survey found that 48 percent of the respondents evaluated Brezhnev as negative or very negative, while the MK/MOR survey recorded similar views among 64 percent of the respondents (Willerton & Sigelman 1991). Unrealistically optimistic responses were also noted in the 1988 surveys, with 53 percent of the respondents expecting perestroika to improve their personal financial situation during the next five years, while only 24 percent feared that their personal financial situation would worsen.

STAGE 3: DEINSTITUTIONALIZATION—PURGE OR PACT?

The combined forces of a mobilized citizenry demanding reform from below and the political elite applying pressure from above presented a real threat to entrenched interests favoring the status quo—the CPSU, state bureaucracies, state enterprises, the military, and institutions of law enforcement. For the reform process to succeed, resistance from such powerful bureaucracies had to be overcome.

Unlike a truly revolutionary transition, in which the revolution removes the preexisting political, economic, and social institutions, the transition process in the former USSR necessitated the replacement of functioning institutions and the dismissal of people in positions of power. In most communist systems this stage of the transition process was accomplished by purge rather than pact. "Purge" is used broadly here to refer to replacement of elites—by dismissal, election, or (as in the case of Romania) violence. In Poland this stage of transition was accomplished by forming a pact between Solidarity reformers and the Jaruzelski government representing the party and the military, thus co-opting the potential opponents of the reforms.

At the Nineteenth Party Conference in mid-1988, Gorbachev first proposed contested elections for local and regional party secretaries, as well as state officials at all levels. The first semi-democratic elections to a newly created national parliament, the Congress of People's Deputies, were held in March 1989. The following year elections were held to regional and local soviets. The importance of these exercises in democracy was multifaceted. On the one hand, citizens were being entrusted to make decisions. This encouraged and gave substance to the feelings of empowerment that derived from glasnost. The elections also removed from office scores of conservative, Brezhnev-era party functionaries who had actively opposed Gorbachev's reforms. Pro-reform liberal deputies constituted a majority of newly elected councils in Moscow, Leningrad, and many other cities. One voter noted that it was easy to decide who to vote for: "I simply crossed out any name that I had heard of before and voted for the 'unknown' candidates on the assumption that the candidates I had heard of were former members of the Communist apparat" (Interview with anonymous voter, 13 June 1991, Leningrad).

Article 6 of the constitution of the USSR, guaranteeing a monopoly of power to the Communist Party, was amended in March 1990. Almost overnight nascent political parties sprang up. Within six months some 250 parties had registered in Moscow; the relatively small republic of Georgia registered more than 160 parties. Such parties were narrowly defined, poorly organized, and locally based. The term "couch parties" was coined to describe a party whose entire membership could sit on a single couch.

Reforms also necessitated the breakdown of former institutions, including the central planning apparatus, and state control of virtually all production decisions, production quotas, and delivery schedules. In the absence of strict central controls, small-scale entrepreneurship flourished. Even within state enterprises, the most profitable activities were hived off into private operations, usually to the great financial benefit of the managers. The breakdown of the state-controlled economy resulted in real hardships for Russian citizens. By early 1990 nearly three-quarters of all respondents in a public opinion survey conducted by *Ogonek* (1990) reported that they had experienced shortages of necessary food items "quite often" or "constantly."

At the level of the social system, the deinstitutionalization phase was characterized by the erosion of state controls and protections. State control in the hands of the party, the KGB, and the police had long been resented by Russians, and it is not surprising that these were the targets of public wrath. In the aftermath of the abortive coup of August 1991 thousands of people streamed to Dzerzhinsky Square in front of KGB headquarters, and toppled a mammoth statue of Felix Dzerzhinsky, the founder of the Chekha (a forerunner of the modern KGB).

In a similar vein, citizens rejected Marxist-Leninist ideology that tried to equalize the social and economic status of citizens, especially workers and peasants. The breakdown of communist social controls ushered in a new rhetoric of individualism, self-reliance, and physical and social mobility. In the winter of 1990 more than two hundred thousand people boldly ignored Gorbachev's ban on public gatherings and marched to the Kremlin to voice concern for the future of reform. Peter Juvelier observed that "millions of Soviet citizens [had] unlearned fear and experienced a sense of numbers and empowerment" (Julevier 1991, in Ahdieh 1997, 101).

The combined effects of the deinstitutionalization stage were manifested in a marked polarization of public attitudes in Russia (Willerton & Sigelman 1992). A large segment of the population, perhaps a majority, strongly supported the destruction of the communist system. However, a significant minority, especially among the elderly, rural, and least-educated segments of the population, feared the loss of centralized control and order and resented what they saw as the denigration of the values of the Soviet system to which they had devoted their lives. A *Moscow News* (21–28 January 1990, 9) survey found that attitudes toward the term "capitalism" were almost evenly divided, with 34 percent positive and 38 percent negative responses.[2] A survey conducted in the winter of 1989–90 by the All-Union Center for the Study of Public Opinion (*New Outlook* 1990, 22) found that 42 percent of the respondents felt that they had lived better in the past, while 32.6 percent disagreed and 25.4 percent had no opinion. These figures suggest that public dissatisfaction with the communist regime and the Brezhnev legacy was waning. Such a polarization of attitudes was also apparent among deputies to the second, third, and fourth sessions of the congress, from December 1990 to May 1991, who were arrayed in a classic bimodal distribution between liberal reformers and conservative defenders of the communist regime (Remington et al. 1994).

The polarization of public attitudes was manifested in the rise of hate groups such as Pamyat, an increasing intolerance for diversity, and nostalgia for the Brezhnev and Stalin eras among a certain segment of the population (Gibson & Duch 1993). By 1989, Pamyat was claiming twenty thousand members in Moscow and thousands more supporters around the country (Dunlap 1989). Anti-reform demonstrations were mounted in Moscow and many other cities on May Day 1990, attracting thousands of pro-communist marchers. Hundreds, if not thousands, of conservative national front organizations were established, mobilizing frustrated members of the working class. Many of these national front groups began to espouse extreme Russian nationalistic positions.

The clash of pro-reform and anti-reform public attitudes was most starkly seen in the events surrounding the August 1991 attempted coup d'état. Almost immediately following the public announcement of the formation of the eight-man State Committee for the State of Emergency in the USSR some 50,000 Muscovites began streaming to the White House, the seat of the Russian Soviet Federation of Socialist Republics' (RSFSR) parliament and presidency. On August 20 another 200,000 people demonstrated outside the Moscow City Soviet, while 200,000 rallied in Leningrad's Palace Square. When the coup collapsed on August 21, some 150,000 Muscovites celebrated in front of the Russian White House. Gibson's analysis (1993) revealed that 56.4 percent of citizens surveyed nationwide took some form of action against the coup, while only 11.6 percent took some action in support of the coup. Resistance was more common among those who supported the collective good of democratic governance, expected resistance to be effective, and approved in general of protest activity. Citizen activism against the coup also benefited from the newly found empowerment; citizens who participated in anti-coup activities were more likely to have some experience at unconventional participation than those who remained inactive, and were generally recruited to political activity by family, coworkers, or friends.

STAGE 4: ROMANTIC REFORMS—INSTITUTION BUILDING

The August 1991 failed coup d'état accelerated the pace of political change and fragmentation in the USSR, resulting ultimately in the breakup of the USSR. With the destruction of the political, economic, and social institutions came the necessity of constructing new institutions to take their place; thus there was a substantial natural overlap between the deinstitutionalization process and institution-building process. One leads naturally to the other.

The breakup of the USSR left the surviving institutions of the RSFSR largely intact. The Russian presidency was occupied by Boris Yeltsin, who had been elected in June 1991 in a landslide popular vote with 57.3 percent of the vote against five challengers.[3] The Russian parliament—the Congress of People's Deputies—had been elected in March 1990. Although the majority of deputies to the congress had been members of the Communist Party, they were generally considered to be more reform-minded than the members of the defunct Congress of People's Deputies of the USSR.

The period of romantic reforms was associated with the economic policies of shock therapy, rapid privatization, price reforms, and widespread entrepreneurship. While Gorbachev waffled on the full and rapid implementation of radical economic reforms, the Yeltsin administration in 1992 aggressively began to implement Yegor Gaidar's policies of shock therapy. Price controls on most goods were lifted, and Anatoly Chubais, deputy prime minister for privatization and chair of the State Committee for the Administration of State Property, began to develop a plan for selling off state property.

The freedoms and social dislocations caused by changes in the USSR created the potential for new class formations and afforded citizens greater freedom from social controls. The term "New Russians" began to be used in referring to people who had managed to accumulate some wealth in the private economy. However, these social and economic changes also resulted in a deterioration of the social infrastructure and a decline in the standard of living for many Russians, especially pensioners (Zaslavsky 1995).

The word "romantic" in reference to this stage of the transition process reflects the widespread euphoria and unrealistic expectations with which many Russian citizens greeted changes in the political, economic, and social realms following the August 1991 coup and the breakup of the USSR later that year. The success of popular resistance to the coup helped to create a sense of empowerment and optimism in Russians that appears to have lasted into 1992. In fact, Gibson (1996) argues that support for democracy did not wane appreciably from 1990 to 1992, despite the chaos resulting from the breakup of the USSR and the destruction of the command economy.

Yeltsin, whose popularity would never be higher than after the defeat of the coup, was granted special powers by the Fifth Congress of People's Deputies. These measures substantially increased his powers vis-à-vis the parliament and set up a cycle of events that would eventually result in the shoot-out at the White House in October 1993. Throughout 1992 and 1993, Yeltsin sought to expand presidential powers, arguing for a presidential republic since a parliamentary republic under current crisis conditions would amount to "suicide" (Remington et al. 1994). Despite the opposition of many deputies, he favored at the same time the creation of a new parliament, which would have necessitated a new round of elections.

Throughout Russia, newly elected politicians, convinced of their democratic mandate, sought to intimidate holdovers from the former system. Energetic young managers sought to privatize profitable segments of state-owned enterprises, despite the fact that legislation on privatization had yet to be passed.[4] The phrase "the Wild East" (Dikii Vostok) was coined to depict the wide-open, unruly society in which fortitude and ambition were unfettered and potential material gains were unbounded.

STAGE 5: INSTITUTIONAL FAILURE—REACTION AND RETRENCHMENT

Perhaps the most prolonged phase of the Russian transition (and the one that some observers would argue is continuing today) has been characterized by the failure (or inadequate performance) of newly created political, economic, and social institutions. The new political institutions, established in the period between 1989 and 1993, began to encounter resistance almost immediately. Inept leadership of novice politicians, institutional gridlock between executive and legislative bodies, unclear or nonexistent legal guidelines, and the absence of popular legitimacy resulted in faltering institutional performance.

In the economic sphere, the effects of shock therapy were sudden and severe. Inflation soared to 3,000 percent in 1992 and another 900 percent in 1993, and GDP fell by more than 40 percent in the period between 1991 and 1993, while industrial production dropped 43 percent. The privatization program became bogged down in bureaucracy, and the public was uninformed about how to invest their savings and privatization vouchers. Meanwhile, well-placed figures in government and industry, recognizing an opportunity, used their insider positions to obtain large blocks of stocks in the most promising industries. Hyperinflation especially hit people on fixed incomes. By 1993 some 31 percent of the Russian population was existing below the poverty line. During the 1991–96 period the GDP fell some 52 percent and industrial production was down 60 percent—twice the impact of the Great Depression in the United States.

The failure of newly created institutions resulted in an institutional vacuum that gave rise to lawlessness and invited organized crime. Economic collapse resulted in the inability of the government to sustain social policies. Government support for education, culture and the arts, science, pensions, the military, housing, and health care dwindled. People were forced for the first time to fend for themselves. Truancy rates skyrocketed; there was little incentive for children to attend school when the "big money" was being made in street trade. An estimated 1.5 million school-age children were not attending school regularly (*RFE/RL Newsline*, 10 March 1997). Public-sector workers went months without paychecks, precipitating a brain drain of talent from research institutes, universities, and laboratories.[5]

It is during this Institutional Failure phase that the most damaging psychological effects of transition have been felt. Widespread cynicism and disillusionment prevail. Among much of the Russian public this has translated into dwindling support for the goals of reform. A survey conducted in October 1992 by the Media and Opinion Research Department of Radio Free Europe/Radio Liberty Research Institute (Rhodes 1993, 42) found that 78 percent of all respondents were dissatisfied with the current political situation; of these, 43 percent expressed complete dissatisfaction. The New Russian Barometer III (Rose & Haerpfer 1994, 29) public opinion survey taken in spring 1994 found that 23 percent of the respondents agreed with the statement, "It would be better to restore the former communist system." Responses to the same question over the next two years rose to 32 percent in 1995 and 39 percent in 1996 (Rose 1995, 51; 1996, 57).[6] Public anger was evidenced in the 1995 parliamentary election when right-wing and communist parties combined won some 55 percent of the vote. Meanwhile, the liberal reform parties, which had amassed some 35 percent of the vote in the 1993 parliamentary election, dropped off to 11.1 percent. Support for all democratic institutions declined, while support for the church and the army increased (1996).

Other manifestations of the Institutional Failure phase can be expressed in a newly coined Russian word, *naglost'*. *Naglost'* is difficult to translate into English, but a close approximation would be "sullen insolence." Traffic officials in Moscow reported widespread disregard for traffic rules, stop lights, and other restrictions. Vandalism exploded in between 1993 and 1995.

For some, the psychological stress of transition—the economic uncertainty, absence of a social welfare net, and general state of lawlessness—has manifested itself in alarming increases in suicide, alcoholism, drug addiction, domestic violence, crime, and other anomic behaviors. Suicide rates have been rising, making a 9 percent jump from 1994 to 1995. Since 1993 suicide has been a major cause of the decrease in life expectancy for men in their fifties. In fact, for this segment of the population suicide is the second leading cause of death behind heart attack. Today only 54 percent of men over 16 are likely to live to the age of 60, whereas at the end of the nineteenth century 56 percent of men over 16 lived to the age of 60. The increase in suicides has been especially troubling in the military. In 1991, 15 out of every 100,000 soldiers committed suicide. By 1996 the suicide rate had more than doubled, to 36 out of 100,000 (*RFE/RL Newsline,* 9 June 1997). Defense Minister Rodionov reported that more than 500 Russian military officers committed suicide in 1996 alone (7 February 1997).

Alcohol consumption per capita rose by more than 68 percent from 1987 to 1996, from 10.7 liters per person to 18 liters (10 March 1995). During the same time period deaths attributed to alcohol poisoning increased 124 percent and accounted for 262,000 fatalities per year. The examples of anomic behavior are often manifested quite differentially across the population, and alcoholism is no exception. Men are four time more likely to become alcoholics than women; however, the number of women treated for alcoholism is steadily rising. In 1995 more than 2.5 million people received medical treatment for alcoholism, and experts estimate than another 10 million citizens should have received treatment but did not seek help.

Drug addiction, while still substantially lower than in the West, has risen dramatically in recent years. Drug-related crimes in Moscow rose by 53.3 percent, from 3,000 in 1995 to 4,600 in 1996 (3 January 1997).

Crime steadily rose from 1991 through 1995. Murders increased in 1993 by 27 percent, on top of a 22 percent increase the previous year (*Izvestiia,* 2 October 1992, 8; *New York Times,* 30 January 1994, 6). Rapes increased by 15 percent in 1993 (*Izvestiia,* 7 December 1993, 6; 12 August 1993, 8). In the past few years there has been an explosion of property crimes, especially theft and robbery. These categories of crime increased 75 percent from 1991 to 1992 (2 October 1992, 8). Crimes involving weapons rose by 250 percent in 1993, while crimes resulting in serious bodily injury jumped by 24 percent (*New York Times,* 30 January 1994, 6). In recent years, crime by teenagers has been rising faster than adult crime, accounting for 68 percent of all recorded crime in Moscow oblast (*RFE/RL Newsline,* 10 March 1997). One-half of all juvenile delinquents neither work nor attend school.

The single largest cause for the surge in crime in recent years has been the rise of mafia-on-mafia violence. Violent acts by organized crime groups motivated by either revenge or economic greed are outside the realm of behaviors discussed in this chapter. Behaviors more expressive of the public's psychological state might include vandalism, hate crimes, rape, domestic violence, and theft.

STAGE 6: CONSOLIDATION—REDEFINITION OF THE COURSE AND PACE OF REFORM

The traumatic effects of the transition experienced in the protracted stage 5, Institutional Failure, eventually begin to become attenuated. Fledgling political institutions that initially struggled to meet rising demands from citizens begin to improve their performance. Overcoming the combined effects of the transition may require the moderation of extremist views, the formation of coalition governments, or the introduction of a strong presidency. New elections and enactment of a new constitution can be important events in the consolidation process.

In the case of Russia, the 1993 constitution formalized extensive presidential powers. With the Duma dominated by conservative forces of the "red-brown" coalition, Yeltsin has chosen to rule by decree, making extensive use of his constitutional authority to issue binding unilateral decrees. Yeltsin's authority was further enhanced by his reelection in July 1996.

On the economic front, it appeared until recently that Russia had moved beyond the crisis of economic collapse experienced in stage 5. Official statistics place GDP growth for 1997 between 0.4 and 1.2 percent. However, actual GDP growth was probably somewhat higher, as a substantial amount of economic activity goes unreported. According to some estimates that take the underground economy into account, production has been increasing by 5 to 8 percent since 1994 (*Wall Street Journal,* 24 December 1997, A10). Also, inflation slowed to 11 percent for 1997, well within International Monetary Fund (IMF) target levels. Finally, the percentage of people existing below the poverty line dropped to 22 percent in 1996, down from 26 percent the previous year and 31 percent in 1993. This progress, however, was overwhelmed in mid-1998 by the

Asian financial crisis that resulted in the massive exodus of investment capital out of "emerging markets," including Russia.

The consolidation stage may entail the moderation of many of the economic policies that were central to the transition at earlier stages. For example, the consolidation stage may result in the rejection of shock therapy, retardation of the pace of privatization (or even sporadic de-privatizations where assets were privatized illegally), and a return to social protections to buffer the effects of the transition. All of these adjustments are being advocated not only by Yeltsin's opponents, but by members of his cabinet as well. The communists, who represent the largest bloc of votes in the Duma and have strong support in the countryside, have nevertheless indicated their willingness to live within the confines of the 1993 constitution, and support competitive elections and civil liberties. However, they are arguing for a reassertion of the state's interest in maintaining a minimum quality of life for all citizens.

Ironically, at this point in the transition process in Poland, the public, angered by several years of economic collapse and political chaos, voted overwhelmingly for a return of the communists. In Russia, too, there appears to be a perceptual lag between economic improvement and public awareness of the improvement. Half of all Russian families now own their own homes or apartments, usually acquired from the state at a marginal sum; 36 percent own a dacha, and 9 percent own a second or third apartment ("Russia Survey," 12 July 1997). Some 62 percent own land.

The psychological impact of the transition has been differentiated by age cohorts. The Russian Market Research Company finds that 73 percent of those aged 16 to 24 and 60 percent of those aged 25 to 34 think life got better in 1996, whereas 67 percent of Russians over 65 feel it got worse, much worse, or unbearable (12 July 1997).

The adaptive behaviors that have helped some communist countries through the traumas of transition may not be available to the Russians. For the Poles, as for the Latvians, Estonians, Lithuanians, Czechs, Hungarians, and others, the reassertion of sovereignty and national independence may prove to be a powerful palliative that helps to maintain national unity and cohesion through the transition process. In contrast, Russia cannot claim renewed national sovereignty; rather it must face the ignominy of the loss of its empire and status as a global superpower. Nationalism and patriotism are, however, potential unifying forces in Russia and help to explain the appeal of leaders such as Alexander Lebed, especially among those hardest hit by the reforms.

Many Russians also report feelings of "emotional exhaustion" at all the changes they have endured in recent years. Such feelings of exhaustion may be adaptive in lowering the levels of political, economic, and social conflict and minimizing the chances of citizens becoming mobilized in support of anti-democratic "quick fixes." The relative calmness that the Russian public has so far (through October 1998) exhibited with respect to the recent government financial meltdown is further indicative of their emotional exhaustion. Skepticism and cynicism toward all politicians and public figures may be emotionally healthy responses that make it less likely that Russians will fall prey to an extremist demagogue.

CONCLUSION

The preceding analysis has attempted to suggest that there has been an important psychological dimension to the transitions taking place in Russia and other former communist countries. Inexplicably, the psychological dimension has been neglected in much of the rapidly expanding body of literature on transition. As I have suggested, the manner, intensity, and scope of impact of the transition on citizens' psychological state and well-being vary considerably at different stages of the process. Furthermore, psychological manifestations, whether in the form of eroding trust in democratic institutions or a surge in suicides and alcoholism, inevitably will have an impact on the course of the reforms and the likelihood of their success. Unfortunately, a systematic and comprehensive assessment of the psychological dimensions of transition in Russia is hampered by a lack of standardized survey and observation data covering the past two decades. Finally, while the model delineated above is grounded on the Russian experience, hopefully it affords some generalizations about the transition process and its psychological dimensions that will inform future broadly comparative studies of transition.

NOTES

1. *The Economist*'s "Russia Survey" (1997) recently described the popular mood of Russians using words such as "despair," "bitter," "outraged," and "weary."
2. Twenty-eight percent were undecided or neutral.
3. Yeltsin had been selected president of the congress in May 1990 from among its members, but the June 1991 election marked his mandate as a popularly elected president.

4. For example, Alexander Fedotov, procurator of Nizhnyi Novgorod, confirmed the widespread practice of "spontaneous privatizations" (Consultation with author, Nizhnyi Novgorod, 7 April 1993).

5. In July 1997 it was estimated that total unpaid wages to public-sector workers in Russia amounted to 11 trillion rubles ($1.9 billion) (*RFE/RL Newsline,* 9 July 1997).

6. Note that the question in New Russian Barometer (NRB) III allowed for a "difficult to answer" response, while the later surveys did not.

Chapter 9

Attitudinal Changes during the Transition

Eric Shiraev

Bringing representative government to a people accustomed to auto-cratic rule requires more than lifting the yoke of repression under which they have suffered. A society must also build the institutions for linking the people to the government and develop the attitudes and practices that maintain a respect for the rules that support that republic and make the compromise of differences possible. When this task is compounded by the need to move from a command to a market economy, the transformational process is bound to be fraught with difficulties (see Miller, Hesli, & Reisinger 1994). In this chapter we will delineate the major adaptations that the Russian people as a whole have made during this transformational process and note the implications of their adaptations for the continuation of a representative government in the future.

When Gorbachev first introduced glasnost and perestroika in the Soviet Union, he had enthusiastic supporters at practically every level of Soviet society (Smith 1990, 6). But with the breakup of the Soviet Union

TABLE 9.1

Overall Russian Satisfaction with the Transition in Russia (1994–96)

Question	1994	1995	1996
Do you personally feel that the creation of a market economy is wrong for our country's future? ("Yes" answers)	53%	67%	65%
On the whole, are you satisfied with the way democracy is developing in our country? ("No" answers)	71%	83%	86%
How much respect is there for individual human rights in our country? ("No respect" answers)	75%	83%	85%

Sources: *Index to International Public Opinion* 1995–96, 1994–95, and 1993–94.

and the political and economic turmoil related to the transition, a profound disillusionment set in among the people. Over time, as difficulties mounted, the free market and new democratic institutions increasingly disappointed the majority of Russia's people. See table 9.1.

Satisfaction with one's life was also low. By summer of 1995, the ratio between the number of people in Russia satisfied with their life, compared to those who were not satisfied was 1:8 (*Segodnia,* 2 August, 1995). Compared to other European nations, this was a significantly lower level of satisfaction. The Eurobarometer surveys between 1993 and 1995 indicate that Russian respondents repeatedly scored the lowest (with the exception of the 1995 Ukrainian sample) in satisfaction with current events (see table 9.2; see also Wyman 1997, 21–23).

Moreover, most Russians did not have much hope for the future. Surveys conducted between 1994 and 1996 show that only one in ten people was convinced that strikes and other industrial disputes would decrease in the near future (CISS, 1995–96; 1994–95; 1993–94). Only 13 percent of these people were looking to the future more or less optimistically (Shlapentokh 1996). In 1996, 87 percent of Russians were dissatis-

TABLE 9.2

Question: In General, do You feel that Things are going in the Right or Wrong Direction?

Answer	1993	1994	1995
Right Direction	31%	16%	19%
Wrong Direction	47%	68%	67%
Don't Know	22%	16%	14%

Sources: *Index to International Public Opinion* 1995–96, 567–85; 1994–95, 545–63; 1993–94, 612–23.

fied with the direction of the country's movement (Ferguson 1996, 44). In a 1995 survey only 26 percent of urban residents assessed optimistically the perspectives for dealing with the economic crisis in Russia, while 17 percent suggested that they were hopeless (CISS, 1995–96, 50).

Popular disillusionment with the way things were in the country was accompanied by increasingly negative attitudes toward the Yeltsin government. By 1994 opinion polls showed that only 4 percent of Russians fully supported the actions of the Yeltsin government, and 31 percent believed that he should resign. (*Ekonomicheskie I Sotsialnye Peremeny: Monitoring Obshchestvennogo Mneniya* # 6 1994, 63). In 1995, 60 percent of the respondents favored a change of the country's leaders based on the opinion that they had exhausted their potential (Poll conducted in July by Boris Grushin's Vox Populi service; *Izvestia,* 13 October 1995, 6). Some even came to look at the past with a different eye. On July 1995, 80 percent of those surveyed in a Vox Populi poll thought that their rights were less protected under Yeltsin than they had been under Brezhnev (*Izvestia,* 13 October 1995, 6). Sixty-five percent of the respondents said that the attitude of Russians toward the existing government is worse than it was in the former USSR (Grunt et al. 1996; Wyman 1997, 63–73,125–27).

The distrust extended to other major Russian institutions. In 1995, the church and army were approved by only 33 and 32 percent of the surveyed people respectively. Political parties and social movements received a 7 percent approval rating, while the heads of banks had only 6 percent of the people's support. Even judgments about individual Russians were colored by this lack of faith. According to sociologist Yuri Levada, interpersonal trust was significantly down between 1989 and 1991, as compared to studies conducted in early 1980s (Levada 1993). By

1994, only 30 percent of Russian respondents interviewed in a poll agreed with the statement, "People should be trusted." By way of contrast, up to 90 percent of those in Western countries agreed with the assertion (*British Journal of Political Science* #24, 1994, 208).

In a survey conducted in Moscow and Perm in 1995, 60 percent of those interviewed agreed that there had been a negative change in the way Russians behave (Grunt et. al. 1996). Vladimir Pankov (1991), deputy editor of *Rodina* magazine, noted that Russians have lived apart from one another for a long time and nothing can unify them. Russian collectivism is not brotherhood or selfless service to the good, but rather "a dictatorship of indifference, a revelry of dependence, cowardice of consciousness."

Pessimism of this sort, under some conditions, could lead to political protest and other acts of greater political involvement. In Russia, however, it has been accompanied by a decline in political interest and participation. Most people react with indifference to public issues (Shlapentokh 1996). As the popular weekly *Ogonyok* noted, most Russians do not care at all about the control over the government (#12, March 1998, 6). Indeed, only 10 to 12 percent of the Russian population participate directly in political decision making. Nuzgar Betaneli, director of the Institute of Sociology of Parliamentarism, expressed his opinion about the nature of contemporary Russian public opinion and voting behavior, suggesting that in the end, everything is decided not by a majority, but by a small and politically active part of the population.[1] As Boris Kagarlitsky (1997, 53), a former Soviet dissident and now politician, suggested at a Gorbachev Foundation meeting, political struggles in the former Soviet Union are among the elites, not between the people and the system.

This apathy[2] is perhaps a function of a widespread feeling among many Russian people that there is little they can do to influence the course of political events.[3] In a comparative *Times-Mirror* survey in 1991, only 47 percent of Russians expressed their agreement that voting gives them a chance to express their opinion on how the government runs things.[4] In a study in 1996, 56 percent of the respondents said that officials in Moscow are unable to make improvements in ordinary people's lives. More than 60 percent said that politicians are only interested in helping themselves (Ferguson 1996, 44). Expressing this feeling of hopelessness, General Lebed noted on one occasion that "The state is beyond our reach. It is beyond us. It can do with us what it wants" (Lebed 14 May 1996).

The fact that the government is beyond the control of the public is in part the result of real inadequacies in the institutions that link the government to the populace. The large number of political parties makes it difficult for people to know which political party to join or what to stand for. Before the state Duma elections in 1995, for example, there were as many as two hundred political parties competing on the ballot. In April 1995, 49 percent of respondents said (in a survey organized by the Obshestvennoe Mnenie Foundation) that they don't understand the division of parties as left, right, or center. Thirty-one percent said that they could not explain their voting and political preference. The electoral system compounds the problem. The four parties that were able to pass the required 5 percent barrier in voting for the Duma elections in 1995 collected only 50.5 percent of the total ballots cast. That means that almost half of Russia's votes in 1995 were "wasted" on the small parties that were unable to collect the required minimum of votes (Ferguson 1996, 44).

Yeltsin's ability to remain in power is a reflection of these institutional failures. The opposition to his government was ineffective, in part, because it consisted of uncoordinated groups of unsatisfied people identified with a variety of factions (Abalkin 1995, 30, 40). The support he did receive was based, to a great extent, on the fear of many Russians that the alternative to him could be worse. In the election of 1996 many voted for Yeltsin because of the anxiety that the communists would come back to power and take away their newly acquired perks (Kara-Murza, 5 May 1996). As the VTSIOM poll suggests, a majority of Russians either think a return of the communists to power could be worse for the country, or remain uncertain about its consequences.

TABLE 9.3

VTsIOM Poll Question: Will the Situation in the Country change if a Politician of a Communist Orientation becomes President of Russia?

1998	Agree	Disagree
Will Improve	30%	32%
Will be the same	19%	20%
Will worsen	27%	25%
Don't know	24%	23%

Source: *Ogonyok*, #10, March 1998, 8.

The long-term consequences of these feelings of pessimism and powerlessness, however, are hard to gauge.[5] Individuals who are uncertain about the future and disappointed with the present are apt to search for external limitations as the guarantor of stability and order (Mikulski 1995). Certainly many Russians today long for greater stability, and many are willing to pay a price in terms of the sacrifice of certain liberties. One-third of those surveyed in 1992 favored maintaining public order above all, even if it meant limiting freedom of speech. More than a half said that the state should forbid the publication of "dangerous ideas" because of their destructiveness (*USIA Research Memorandum,* 16 March 1992). Compared to Americans, almost twice as many Russians thought that freedom of speech should not be guaranteed to the least-liked social groups. Moreover, people were generally in favor of the idea of "liquidating" murderers (72 percent), homosexuals (34 percent), drug addicts (28 percent), and prostitutes (28 percent) (Wyman 1997, 136).

The Russian people have been inclined historically to seek out a strong man to give them the order they need. Their experience under a totalitarian regime compounded these problems (Gozman & Etkind 1992). Indeed, as Betty Glad has suggested in this book, Yeltsin's victory over Gorbachev was the result not only of his commitments to "democracy" and self-determination, but also the fact that he seemed tougher than Gorbachev. The Russian ambassador to the Ukraine, Leonid Smolyakov (1997) has noted the culturally inherited nostalgia for a strong and wise czar (Grunt et. al 1996). In a poll conducted in St. Petersburg in 1998, 72 percent of those respondents who were unsatisfied with Yeltsin's government named the former head of Riga's Special Militia Department (OMON), Cheslav Mlynnik, as a person who could rebuilt Russia as a state in the shortest period of time (*Ogonyok,* #11, March1998, 8). By the end of 1992, according to Moscow-based polling firm ROMIR, 51 percent of the population began to support the idea of a strong leader, a 22–point gain over the course of one year (*The National Journal,* 13 March 1993, 654).

Moreover, several political leaders in post-communist Russia have toyed with the possibility of offering themselves in the role of authoritarian leader. On a televised interview, democrat Grigory Yavlinsky suggested that he wouldn't mind becoming a dictator if the goal is to defend democracy (June 8 1996). Anatoly Chubais, one of the long-lasting top Yeltsin aides, expressed his disappointment about the low level of discipline in the country by calling for a dictatorship of power (*The Washington Post,* 22 October 1996). Vladimir Zhirinovsky justified autocracy by implying that without it, few in Russia would obey the law (21 May 1996).[6]

Nationalism and the notion of a "Russian destiny" are ideas that remain attractive to many. In both the 1993 and 1995 Russian Duma elections, popular support for Zhirinovsky and his party was much stronger than anticipated (Ferguson 1996, 44). The national-patriotic path, which emphasizes the greatness of Russia's past, cultural accomplishments, and pride for the past victories, has also been taken by General Lebed: "If this is nationalism, then I'm nationalistic" (Lebed, 13 June 1996). Communists also embrace the national-patriotic idea. As Zyuganov stated in 1996, "Russia prospered when the idea of statehood and patriotism was inspired by the idea of national culture, language, and tradition [supported by] all people who inhabited our country" (Zyuganov, 9 April 1996).

The potential for nationalistic appeal extends beyond political parties. Many Russians regret the disintegration of the Union and think it could have been prevented. Back in 1991, more than 70 percent of Russians voted for the preservation of the USSR in the all-Union referendum. (Openkin, 1996b). In a survey conducted in July 1995, more than 70 percent of Russians expressed regrets about the collapse of the Soviet Union (*Izvestia,* 13 October 1995, 6). In a March 1998 survey, 66 percent of those polled regretted the collapse of the USSR. In addition, 58 percent suggested that the collapse could have been prevented (*Ogonyok,* #12, March 1998, 6. Poll conducted by VTSIOM, February-March 1998).

Russians are also clearly divided over the virtues of the free market and the "inevitability" of the growing inequalities in income noted in chapter 6. The New Russians have adopted a kind of social Darwinism that provides a justification for the unfettered operation of the market system as it has developed in Russia. However, socialist ideas continue to attract strong pluralities among many Russians. A survey organized by the Obshestvennoe Mnenie Foundation in April 1995 revealed that 43 percent of the respondents wanted their children to live "under socialism." Only 20 percent of the surveyed preferred "capitalism." Others were uncertain: Twenty-one percent could not find an appropriate answer, and about 16 percent reported that the political system didn't matter to them at all. Another poll suggested that a majority of Russians are opposed to the unregulated operations of the free market. Only 15 to 20 percent supported free market prices as an alternative to state-controlled rates (Openkin 1996). In addition, 55 percent of Russians support state subsidies to families (*Argumenty i Facty,* #6, February1996).

Some Russian politicians argue that these differences between the old and new Russians are emblematic of a political and cultural divide deeply rooted in Russian history and culture. General Lebed sees the ideological and psychological divisions apparent in Russia in the 1990s as dating back to the civil war of l9l7. "We have forgiven the Germans," said he in 1996, "we defeated them and we have no claims to them today. But the Reds and the Whites cannot forgive each other. Divided in Reds and Whites, they are now called communists and reformers, or communists and democrats" (Lebed, 13 May 1996). Gennady Zyuganov even predicted that the ideological differences evident in the mid-1990s would grow deeper (Zyuganov, 3 February and 25 June,1996).

Even social scientists warn of a coming clash between various groups in Russia. Moscow sociologist Boris Grushin, for example, anticipated that in the 1990s tensions within Russian society would grow. According to him, there would be opposition between the executive and legislative powers, the elite and the working people. The hired personnel would clash with the owners of private business; the proponents of opponents of change would also fight against each other, as would the regions and the center, Russians and non-Russians (Grushin, 8 October 1994). In 1996, famous playwright Viktor Rozov saw riots on the horizon (Rozov 1997, 59). At exactly the same time, Georgi Shakhnazarov, a top ideologist in the Gorbachev government, predicted that without substantial changes in the next three months "an explosion would be unavoidable" (Shakhnazarov 1997, 19).

Yuri Shlapentokh (1996) has suggested that Russian politicians are no less disjointed and egotistical than feudal lords. Boris Grushin (December 1994) claims that one of the most remarkable characteristics of Russian conflicts is that they all appear to be deadly. He blamed lack of traditions, know-how, and skills for the inability of Russians to resolve any controversial problems. Certainly the communist regime was not one in which individuals were prepared to deal with conflicts through "mutual recognition of interests of others as equals" and a desire for accommodation though some sort of compromise (Grunt et al. 1996, 61).

Extremist proclivities, moreover, were evident in some of the parliamentary debates of the late 1980s and early 1990s. With the eclipse of the old order, new positions of power were opened up and verbal attacks and counterattacks became a part of the maneuvering for those positions (Abalkin 1995, 43). As Gozman and Edkind (1992, 69) wrote about the Russian character, "enemies change but the struggle against them is unvarying."

The dictatorship itself, from a psychoanalytic perspective, contributed to this hostility. At first the dictator eats his subjects (63), and toward the end they eat the dictator. In other words, when leaders are presented as godlike figures, they will be scorned when they make mistakes or falter in any way. Thus, Russians ridiculed Leonid Brezhnev in the 1980s. Gorbachev was admired at the beginning of his tenure in office and then quickly dethroned after his fourth year in power (Chernyaev 1993). Yeltsin's approval ratings were high for several years. But as the economy faltered and the new political institutions compounded problems, his popular standing steadily dropped to single digits in 1996 and 1998 (VTsIOM, RIISNP, ROMIR, an online archive www.cs.indiana.edu /hyplan/Dmiguse/Russian/polls.html).

But the future is not entirely bleak. For the public as a whole, conflicts over ideological and ethnic identity are no longer ideologically "charged." Most Russians are rather neutral and indifferent about political issues (Kliamkin & Lapkin 1996). Indeed, few of them even identify with any single political party.[7] Only 5 to 10 percent of Russians consider themselves members of any political association, or sympathizers of any specific politician in the government or in the opposition (Shlapentokh 1996). Except for their anti-communist feeling, even the supporters of reforms lacked ideological reasoning. Opinion polls confirm this assumption. People identify specific issues, such as corruption, alcoholism, speculation, theft, technical backwardness, and bureaucracy, as the major causes of the Soviet Union's problems in 1988–89. Political or ideological reasons were on the bottom of their lists (Levada 1991).[8] The relative prevalence of new, pragmatic attitudes in the Russian people was demonstrated in another study (Gorianinov 1996). Respondents were asked to rank a list of values according to personal importance. The results showed that among the most important values were private ideals of family, human rights, spirituality, humanism, love of work, professionalism, security, personal dignity, and societal order.

Russians also relish some of the new freedoms they have achieved and recognize the need for a multiparty system. According to the USIA Research Memorandum (16 March 1992), a majority of those surveyed supported citizens' rights to live wherever they want, free of government regulation. More than a half of those surveyed felt that people should be free to say whatever they want, even if it increases tensions in society. Half the public regarded strikes and political demonstrations as acceptable forms of political conduct. Most Russians (69 percent) agree that political parties are necessary for democracy. Only 15 percent said that parties aren't necessary. In addition, a 42 percent plurality felt that, ideally, there should be several political parties rather than one (17 percent) or many (10 percent). Despite the low level of political efficacy, a majority of Russians (58 percent) indicated that political parties were relevant to the concerns of the electorate (Ferguson 1996).[9]

Indeed, the very passivity of the masses seems to reflect their determination to avoid the kind of bloodletting they have experienced in the past. Egor Stroev (1996) has noted most Russians don't want to solve their social and political problems on the barricades. Most people are unhappy but nobody wants to do anything about it.[10] Everyone prefers to dig his or her own trench to hide in. Boris Grushin suggested that despite the growing contradictions in modern Russian society one cannot find any forces that wanted to enter into a fight on a national level (Grushin December 1994). Zhirinovsky has also admitted that the Russian people are "laid-back" by nature. "First they wait for war to break out and only then take up arms" (Zhirinovsky, 29 May 1996).[11]

What they want at this point in the Russian transition is a job with wages paid twice a month; decent housing; medical care for themselves, their parents, and their children; the freedom to say what they want; ability to walk safely on the streets and breathe air that is not dangerously polluted; and a government in Moscow that acts on their behalf.

NOTES

1. Even warnings from public officials about the expansion of NATO to its border did not excite most Russians. In January 1997, in a nationwide poll carried out by the Russian Center for Public Opinion and Market Research, only 41 percent of Russians indicated that they would regard the entry of former Warsaw Pact countries into NATO as negative. But 44 percent either were unsure of its consequences or said it would not matter. In a similar poll, 73 percent of Muscovites thought that the NATO expansion would make no difference in their lives (MacWilliam 1997).

2. Political efficacy, one's belief that one can effectively participate in politics and in this way have some control over the action of political decision makers, has been relatively low since the beginning of the 1990s. As experts suggest and polls confirm, after the collapse of the Soviet Union ordinary people realized that the real power was far away from ordinary people, as it was 20 or 30 years ago.

3. As it had been 10 or 20 years ago. In 1982, when ailing Leonid Brezhnev was still in power, Konstantin Simis wrote about the Russian people's mood

of "complete alienation" from the state, and "indifference and even hostility" toward the government (Simis 1982, 254).

4. According to the survey, 83 percent of Americans said the same (Wyman 1997, 130).

5. Boris Berezovsky, a Russian financial tycoon and the gray cardinal of Russian politics of the late 1990s, once said that dictatorship, from his standpoint, is a system of external limitations. Democracy is a system of internal ones (*Argumenty I Facty*, #19, May 1996, 3).

6. Autocracy assumes that someone else should impose behavioral standards and instill them into individuals. However, totalitarian violence on the vertical level, imposed by the Communist Party, has been already replaced by a new blend of economic insecurity, social pessimism, and fear of violence on the horizontal level. In this situation, a strong hand is expectedly seen as a solution.

7. Traditional Western textbook divisions of the spectrum of political attitudes on liberal, moderate, and conservative scales make little sense in Russian politics today. Russian conservative groups support bigger government involvement in business, including nationalization of private industries. They stand for more substantial government support for the needy, higher capital gain taxes, and the urgent restoration of Russian military power (Barsukov 1996). Many communists, on the other hand, identify themselves as social democrats. Anticommunists consider communists to be national socialists. National socialists call themselves patriots. Pro-socialist attitudes are more often identified by the Russian media as conservatism.

8. Later polls conducted by the Russian Center for Public Opinion Research showed no substantial changes in public mood in favor of democracy (*Ekonomicheskie i sotsialnye peremeny: Monitoring obshchestvennogo mneniya*, #4, 1993, 45) The same trend was confirmed by Wyman (1997, 131–39).

9. Half of the Russians said that their country needs a real multiparty system, whereas only a fifth disagreed.

10. Most Russians don't participate in these heated debates that take place within the elite circle.

11. Despite many problems, Russians have managed to maintain a predominantly positive individual self-assessment. Since the late 1980s, people's assessments of their happiness or unhappiness have been relatively stable. According to VTsIOM and Vox Populi data, approximately 15 percent of the population felt either very happy or extremely unhappy, with the vast majority of people expressing only relative satisfaction or dissatisfaction with their lives.

Chapter 10

Generational Adaptations
to the Transition

Eric Shiraev and Betty Glad

A totalitarian culture in a process of transition is likely to present difficult psychological problems for its populace. Those who have been socialized and spent most of their adult lives adapting to such a regime are apt to carry some of the values and habits it has inculcated in them. Certainly the dependency that the system engenders has consequences for their attitudes toward personal initiative and authority. People in such situations need their authoritarian leaders to provide checks on their behavior (Gozman & Edkind 1992). If asked to act on their own, individuals tend to become frustrated. Many Russians, as Gorbachev found out, wanted him to tell them how to use their new freedoms (Chernyaev 1993). People in their middle years, many of whom made somewhat cynical adaptations to the Soviet regime and still have their lives ahead of them, may simply employ the skills developed in the old system to adapt to the new order. The young, socialized as they are during the transition, are apt to have problems if they are given no solid framework of values.

Freedom for them, those who are mostly unaccustomed to self-restraint, may result simply in a hungry embrace of what had been forbidden in the past. In this chapter we delineate the adaptation that three Russian generations have made along the foregoing lines.

THE SENIOR GENERATION

The Soviet regime had positive values for those Russians who had been socialized under Stalin and spent most of their adult lives living under Brezhnev. The power and the claims for justice of the old order enabled many men and women to feel that they belonged to a great, strong, and righteous nation. Indeed, the leaders of the regime suggested that the path the Soviet Union took represented the future, that the country was traveling down the main route of civilization, and that its justice was superior to that of capitalist countries. The simplicity of this state dogma provided individuals with an understanding of issues around them and offered them symbolic control over these issues (Gozman & Etkind 1992, 40–43). Even the acceptance of subordination to a powerful state and to the party—which could not be criticized publicly—contributed to a sense of common purpose and security.

When Gorbachev and other new authorities lifted the curtain on the crimes of Stalin and his henchmen, the very foundation of the regime to which these people had committed themselves was undermined. Stalin was not a hero but a murderer, they were told. The Communist Party in the show trials of the late 1930s had collaborated in Stalin's undertakings. To prosper economically, the new regime would have to adopt the values of the former capitalist enemy—with its emphasis on individual initiative, private property, and free enterprise. To adapt to this new order Russians would have to admit that their "old" values were outdated, that people had followed false gods, and that their lives did not have the meaning that they had believed they had.

These revelations were profoundly disturbing to those who had identified with the Soviet system. In the short run, many of them reacted with anger, carrying, for example, anti-Gorbachev signs in May Day demonstrations. In the long run, several special adaptations were made. Some insisted on reclaiming the good from their past. As Boris Pasternak wrote in 1947, "Amid this sea of lies, there were honest dreams." Indeed, the idealism, romantic ideas, and impressive visions of life under the old regime had a certain excitement (Vail & Genis 1989, 55, 57). Innovations and experiments conducted by the government had been a part of their lives, and many still insisted that they were proud of their commitments and sacrifice for the promotion of those dreams. As a veteran wrote in the *Izvestia* daily newspaper on July 15, 1994: "I was a good communist, I am very proud of it. Indeed, if you are a member of the Party, so you have to be a believer, you have to give all your strength and energy to the work that everybody did. . . . How could [my commitment] be different if during all my childhood I was surrounded by book shelves with math and education textbooks on them, and with most important books in the red cover with Lenin profiles on them?"

Others would cling to many of the values associated with the communist regime. They were less satisfied with the course of development of democracy in Russia, less favorable toward complete independence of Russia. They were also reluctant to accept free exit from the country and firearms in private possession, and more inclined to accept "the communist political cause" than younger age groups (*MMMM,* November 1991, June 1992; October 1992; USIA Research Memorandum, 6 March, 1992). Opinion polls also show that most senior citizen's groups tended to support more authoritarian views on politics than other age groups (*MMMM,* June 1991). Cognitively, many people of this generation tend to minimize the evil of the old regime. As a whole, Russians realized that Soviet Russia was a police state in which millions of innocent people were terrorized (Riasanovsky 1984). But some members of the older generation argued that during Stalin's reign most people outside the central and local elites were not targets of arrests. Some even refused to change their favorable views of the dictator. For them, Stalin was not just a person but a great leader and a symbol of stability and order. As one veteran wrote in the *Ogonyok* weekly: "Here you think about Stalin; we have to use his tough methods in order to bring everything to order, and not only in Russia" (*Ogonyok,* #12, March 1998, 4). Indeed, in the early 1990s almost two-thirds of those 60 or older still believed in Stalin's great leadership (see different opinion polls conducted by the Grushin's center published in *MMMM* in 1991–92).[1]

The problems in addressing the past are compounded for these older Russians because the future looks particularly bleak to them. When 50–year-olds were asked in 1991 about their future, many gave very pessimistic answers, as contrasted to the younger persons polled (*MMMM,* February 1991). In a series of surveys conducted by Institute of Applied Politics (1992–93), there was a stable ratio (approximately 2:1) between the opinions of the oldest and the youngest groups of respondents on issues such as support of private property (57 percent to 32 percent), the condemnation of the economic gap between rich and poor (82 percent to 45 percent), and the criticism of democracy (28 percent to 14 percent) (Wyman 1997, 207, 217–19). The senior generation cannot wait for another 30 years before the horn of plenty will be accessible to everyone, including them.

What is surprising, given the kind of alienation one would expect from these people, is that they were more likely to vote than many in the younger generations. More than one-half of senior citizens expressed a strong desire to vote in the 1995 Duma elections, 15 percent more than younger adults (Kara-Murza et al. 1995). Generally, people over 55 years old are almost twice as likely to vote compared to those under 25 years old (*Izvestia,* 11 November 1995; survey by the International Foundation for Election Systems, July 1995).

This willingness to vote may be attributed to the activities of the Communist Party as an outlet for the expression of their frustration. In 1990, 34 percent of the senior respondents saw the Communist Party as able to lead the country in the next decade, as contrasted to 20 percent of support of the entire sample (Vox Populi, July 1990). More recent figures indicated than 45 percent of persons 60 and older voted for Zuganov in the second round of 1996 presidential elections while only 35 percent of adults between the ages 45 and 59 showed the same support (Mitofsky-CESSI 1996). The Communist Party of Russia draws 55 percent of its support from pensioners (Ferguson 1996, 44).

Despite their many frustrations, one factor from the past enables these people to continue on. They have lived through so many drastic changes that many find the strength to deal with the present difficulties as just another stage of their lives. As Carroll Bogert writes, "All Russian history has been scarred by enormous suffering, and the present is no exception" (*Newsweek,* 21 June 1993, 45). For many the troubles experienced during the transition could be placed in a broader context of Russian suffering. "*Nichego*" (that's okay), say Russians, who, like their ancestors, try to outlast and survive the next unexpected turn on their path. General Lebed (1996) said, "This is the way we were brought up: keep your head down below the pain threshold and somehow scrape by."

THE BREZHNEV GENERATION

The "in-between generation"—those people who were reared and commenced their careers during the Brezhnev era—seem to have identified with the Soviet regime to a lesser extent that their parents.[2] It is true that as young people they were socialized in an ideologically consistent educational system coupled with reinforcing propaganda in the media (Vail & Genis 1989, 94). But early in their lives they experienced the relative openness of the Soviet system as a result of Khrushchev's thaw. Many came to both realize and internalize contradictions in their lives. What this generation was taught and what it really saw have often been completely opposite. "Nobody believes that wind doesn't exist, even if the wind was forbidden," wrote Andrei Makarevich, a popular rock singer in the 1970s.[3] Their adaptation was to live a two-dimensional life. On the one hand, they had a relatively "normal" emotional life with their families, in the company of their friends, and often at work. Only what went on in society at large depressed them (Gozman & Etkind 1992, 71).

At the time of the Russian transformation some of these people were Communist Party mid-level officials, Youth Communist League influentials, university professors who taught Marxism, or mid-level managers of the state-owned factories appointed to their posts by local Communist Party authorities. It is very likely that had the Soviet Union not been eliminated as a political entity, they would have continued their careers under the communist regime, adapting to circumstances as they saw necessary. With the change in regime, these leaders would transfer their skills to the new government or begin to build their fortunes in other fields.

For most of the members of this generation Gorbachev offered hope for an integrated life and more freedom. In the late 1980s many embraced the radical social changes that they thought would reform their world for the better. As late as 1991, many of them saluted the collapse of the Soviet Union. Young Russian adults under 40 years old were about twice as favorable toward complete independence of Russia as people over 60. These younger Russians were about twice as satisfied with the political changes of 1991 as those over 60 years old (30 percent). The younger and the better educated also favored decentralization of the economy (*USIA Research Memorandum,* 6 March 1992).

Their hopes were dashed, however, as it became clear that reform would not come overnight (Openkin 1996a, b). In 1991, only 40 percent of Russians believed that most of the contemporary entrepreneurs were "driven and ambitious individuals." A common belief was that the success in the new economy was based on personal connections and the ability to manipulate the system (*MMMM,* December 1991). People soon found that a new elite simply replaced the old one. Many members of this group, the Communist Party leader Gennady Zuganov charged, had believed in the "sirens who told them lies about so-called democracy, in which power was usurped by the Mafia rather than transferred to the citizens of the country, and today they are paying for this" (Zuganov 1996).

Politically this group provides the backbone for Grigory Yavlinsky and his Yabloko Party, one of the most democratically oriented political parties in Russia (*Izvestia,* 11 November 1995).[4] Voters under the age of 40 made up 57 percent of his supporters. Almost a third of the adults in this generation group also voted for Yeltsin in the 1996 presidential elections.

But there was also a surprisingly high degree of political apathy in this group. Younger adults in this generation, in particular, express a very low level of interest in political life. Only 35 percent of men and 24 percent of women in 1993 indicated that they were either strongly or very strongly interested in politics (Wyman 1997, 215).

Even though the members of the in-between generation were more inclined to embrace the new order than their elders, many of them were still influenced by their earlier leanings. This is evident in the reluctance of a sizable minority to adopt and accept all the new values. Only a third thought that Russia should accept a "Western" system of beliefs, values, and norms, as contrasted to half of the younger people (*MMMM,* polls taken in 1993). Only four out of ten of these adults believed that reinstating private property is a way to solve the crisis in Russia (*MMMM,* August 1992). By 1993, according to the Institute of Applied Politics, support for private property was expressed by only 45 percent of adults between 30 and 44 years of age (Wyman 1997, 218). Some of them were also part of the 20 percent of those below the age of 44 who cast his or her ballot in 1996 for the communist candidate, Gennady Zyuganov (Mitofsky-CESSI, 1 July 1996).

There is a painful truth in Russian comedian Mikhail Zhvanetsky's sarcastic remark made during one of his television performances: there are no capitalists or communists in Russia. There are people who have adapted and people who haven't.[5]

The character of the Russians who were born between 1950 and 1970, in short, was formed in the later phase of the old cultural system, with all the deceptions, deeply rooted collectivism, and cultural enlightenment. As mature adults today, they operate in a dynamic system, that values highly individualistic and competitive behavior. A few from this generation now provide leadership for the new order. But most mind their own business, not knowing what to do with the problem of where the Russians, as people, go from here.

THE YOUNGER GENERATION

Young adults between 18 and 30 years old are not caught between the old and the new in the same way as their elders.[6] This generation experienced changes in values relatively early in the socialization process. Most of them have never been brainwashed by the official doctrines. For them, Khrushchev's promise to build communism in 20 years was a tale from a dusty school textbook. As they move into the twenty-first century, most of them will have perhaps only scattered and fragmented memories of the Soviet Union. Indeed, Russian political psychologists Leonid Gozman and Alexander Etkind (1992) suggested that the youngest Russians do not suffer from the conflicts between the old and new that their parents do.

What they lack, however, is the guidance provided by stable social institutions and solid norms anchored in past experience. Their parents had role models and books that promoted *vospitanie*—the process of a deliberate instillation of the society's positive values and appropriate rules of conduct. Their adolescent years, however, have been spent in a country torn apart by social, political, and economic turbulence. No surprise that joy and frustration, inspiration and anger, enthusiasm and apathy, as well as many other extremes, have become clearly detectable birthmarks of the entire generation (Shiraev & Bastrykin 1988).

Politically, when they express an opinion, the young were among the most distinct supporters of Boris Yeltsin in his presidency, as well as in his 1996 presidential bid against the communist opponent. More than forty-six percent of them cast their ballots for the president, and only sixteen percent voted for Zyuganov (*Time,* 1 July 1996). Only 3 percent of the communist supporters were people under 25 (Izvestia, 11 November 1995). More than 70 percent of the young supported private property (Wyman 1997, 206).

At the same time, Russian radical and ultra-nationalist groups are comprised primarily of young people under 30. For example, the Liberal Democratic Party of Russia (LDPR), the second largest opposition force in the country after the Communist Party, has the youngest electorate among the existing parties. The result is that Yeltsin supporters feared trying to accelerate turnout efforts toward the young (Ferguson 1996, 44). In a poll taken in April 1995 by the Obshestvennoe Mnenie Foundation, almost one-half of the adult respondents mentioned "socialism" as a desired possibility. More than two-thirds of the surveyed supported one of the fundamental assets of socialism: free higher education (Chuprov & Zubok 1996).

But whatever their political orientation, most of them see the country as in being in crisis. Seventy six percent of young people between 15 and 22 considered the situation in 1994 to be as "worrying" or "in crisis." Only 6 percent said that everything was normal. Research conducted by the Russian State Committee on Youth Affairs in 1994 suggested that by the age of 30, the vast majority of Russian young people had negative attitudes toward the central government and showed extremely low levels of political efficacy (Sharonov & Ruchkin 1996, 144, 149).

The result is that most young people show no real interest in politics. Voting is at the 20 percent level, and students are repeatedly labeled "categorically apolitical" (Olshansky 1995). Sociologists describe the emerging social behavior of post-Soviet youth as including a lack of confidence in political institutions, political passivity, and self-realization in the sphere of private life (Titarenko 1995). Indeed, in the elections of March 1990, the year of deep political crisis, the vote in some districts heavily populated with students was declared invalid because there was less than 50 percent electoral turnout (Gozman & Etkind 1992, 73).

All political parties kept admitting the lack of support from the Russian youth during the political crisis of 1990–91. By the mid-1990s only 33 percent of men and 12 percent of women under age 30 expressed very strong and strong interests in politics (Wyman 1997, 215). More than one-third couldn't identify their position in terms of political orientation, and only 23 percent could name a political party or leader of their choice (Sharonov & Ruchkin 1996, 147–48). Almost 78 percent of the young said that there was no possibility for them to influence the actions of the government. Among the students there were 79 percent who suggested they would not engage in any strike activity or other forms of civil protest (Chuprov & Zubok 1996, 134, 137).

Several publications shed light on young Soviet indifference to social participation (Kharchev & Alekseev 1977), disappointment in the social system (Shiraev & Bastrykin 1988), individualism (Umansky & Lutoshkin 1975), and other characteristics. In a survey conducted in the mid-1980s (a period when Mikhail Gorbachev enjoyed overwhelming support of the population), only 6 percent of the young respondents believed in "collectivism," one of the essential virtues of the "Soviet man." They also placed little value on responsibility. Indeed, the vast majority of these respondents have agreed that characteristics such as "being responsible, active, optimistic" were more typical for their fathers and grandfathers (*Sotsiologicheskie Issledovaniya,* #1, 1988, 52).

Equally important in explaining young people's political apathy is their emphasis on private activities. During the initial phases of the transformation, many of them rushed into private enterprise. About one-half of the young people questioned by the Sociology and Youth division of the Russian Academy of Sciences in 1990 said that business and commerce were their primary goals. At first, many exercised their entrepreneurial skills in the black market. In the mid-1990s, when "speculation," "ownership," "business," and "profit" were made legal, thousands of the young Russians jumped into new entrepreneurial opportunities. Many of these young entrepreneurs entered into the low-profit areas of retail trade, delivery, repair, custom manufacturing, and small brokerage operations. Indeed in the middle of the 1990s, from 60 to 80 percent of the city youth reported being engaged in business activities (Chuprov & Zubok 1996, 132). The more successful entrepreneurs entered financial business, wholesale trade, and related operations (*Sotsiologicheskie Issledovaniya.* #1, 1995, 40).

With the growing monopolization of economic activity in Russia, however, interest in the entrepreneurial activities has declined. Fewer young people are inspired to take chances in life—11 percent in 1994 as contrasted to 26.5 percent in the beginning of 1990 (Chuprov & Zubok, 132). In another study, only 47 percent wanted to work for a private enterprise. The professions, however, do not really offer them other opportunities. As Egor Stroev, a former chairman of the Chamber of Federation of the Federal Assembly has indicated, scores of young people do not obtain any professional training. Others lose the qualifications necessary for such a position (Stroev 1996).

Even more problematic has been the overall decline in the work motivation of this generation. In one survey, only 20 percent of the young individuals showed high levels of work motivation. The remaining 80 percent showed motivation on either low or very low levels (Sharonov & Ruchkin 1996, 145–46). Vladimir Chuprov and Yulia Zubok (1996, 130) suggested that the level of the work indifference among Russian youth was the highest in Europe. This trend, however, was also present in young Russians 20 years before perestroika. Official statistics of the 1970s suggested, for example, that the younger Soviet workers were causing more trouble at work and showing less professional motivation than the representatives of the older generations. According to the journal *Sotsiologitcheskie Issledovania* (#4, 1976), among the violators of so-called work discipline (those who showed up drunk, consumed alcohol at the workplace, missed a workday without a justified reason, took part in physical clashes with coworkers, etc.) 30 percent were between the ages of 20 and 25.

The result is evident in the economic status of these young people. In 1994, more than 82 percent of them were below the poverty level. Almost nine out of ten young people were relying on parental support (Chuprov & Zubok 1996, 129–32). According to the Moscow Institute of Youth Studies, the contemporary generation of young Russian people is worse off than the previous one in terms of health, and intellectual and spiritual development. Crime and poverty were the top two concerns of the surveyed young people in 1994 (Sharonov & Ruchkin 1996, 144).

Some observers have noted the psychological flexibility of the young. Generally they are less hesitant than their elders to change their lifestyles, habits, or occupations. For example, Russian adults under the age of 20 were among those who believed that they could easily become private farmers, if necessary, and could start an entirely new business unfamiliar to them. Men and women under 30 years of age made up about one-third of Russians who would be willing to emigrate. Only 7 percent of those who were older than 50 expressed the same willingness (*Sotsiologicheskie Issledovaniya,* 1, 1994, 27).

The psychological flexibility of the young, however, may not be all that adaptive when it is coupled with the lack of stable values. *Bespredel* is a word in the Russian language that generally means a bizarre and uncontrolled development of events, an "off the charts" situation. A more precise meaning of this word is found in the prisoners' lexicon, according to which a *bespredel* is a prison riot. It is a word that can be applied to many of the young. The "absence of self-imposed restraints" is a frequently mentioned characteristic of the youngest sector of this generation (USIA 1994, 1992).

A lack of restraint, when it is combined with a fluid social order, can have serious social consequences. As Moscow's *Izvestia* has reported, 60 percent of Russian racketeers are young people under 30 years of age. Generally, they are very well trained physically, are poorly educated, and have very few, if any moral principles at all. The same newspaper in August 1994 gave even more frightful figures. Young people under the age of 18 are likely to commit more crimes than adults: There were 2,612 registered cases of youth crime and 2,572 cases of adult crime per 100,000 people (1993). Alexander Solzhenitsyn has suggested that "the young today are astonishingly deluded and fooled by the propaganda of perversion, of living at someone else's expense. The generation is captured by a spirit of profiteering" (Solzhenitsyn 1996). Approximately six out of ten Russian young people do not mind engaging in illegal activity in order to solve their financial problems (Chuprov & Zubok 1996, 132).

The adaptation of people to the transition from a totalitarian regime to one that is more democratic and committed to the free market, in short, has been influenced by their age and experiences in both the old and the new order. Those born during the Stalinist period are torn between the values in which they were socialized and the requirements of life in the new Russia. Those who were socialized and advanced their careers during the Brezhnev regime have become the leaders of the new regime; many of them are inclined to embrace the new order, though some of the old socialist values continue to have an impact. Russian youth who have come into their adult lives during the transition are less ambivalent about the past, enjoying their freedom of expression and a virtually unrestricted freedom of action. But unanchored in values of the past and pessimistic about their futures, they seem to believe in nothing. Paradoxically, the political commitments of these three generations are inversely related to their acceptance of the new regime. The oldest generation—that generally opposes the changes—is the most politically active, the in-between group less so, and the youngest generation least active of all.

NOTES

1. Denial of evil in one's life is a very powerful psychological mechanism of self-protection. As Alexander Solzhenitsyn suggested, most would be unwilling to admit their guilt and repent (Solzhenitsyn 1996). That would not only be personally painful, it would also deny their real accomplishments (Gozman & Edkind 1992) "Life is given to us only once. And you have to live this life so that afterwards you will not experience a painful grief for the years spent purposelessly," said a literary hero of this generation, Pavel Korchagin.
2. This generation of Russians produced such noteworthy figures as A. Chubais, E. Gaidar, S. Shakhrai, B. Nemtsov, G. Yavlinski, and S. Kirienko, and scores of other young politicians, economists, and public figures.
3. Grigory Yavlinsky voiced an opinion during a televised interview, referring to Russian people's electoral behavior: "Our citizens will not vote according to the polls of the Public Opinion Foundation. . . . They will vote as their own conscience tells them. And the situation then will be completely different from one you are imagining" (Yavlinsky 1996). In other words, what people say in opinion polls has little relevance, because the real substance of their opinions is revealed when people cast their ballots according to their "true" thoughts and feelings.
4. Almost every fifth adult below the age of 44, however, cast his or her ballot for the communist candidate, Gennady Zuganov (*Time,* 1 July 1996).
5. For those who embraced the new order, many would have difficulties in

coming to terms with their own past accommodation to the communist system. Positions occupied in the Soviet years, works published, and words spoken are considered by many as one's liability today. There was guilt for being obedient to the old system, for saying and writing things that were politically correct and safe to express. This is guilt for accepting and believing in the values, which were proven to be totally bankrupt in the new social environment of the 1990s.

6. The young generation represents 20 percent of the overall population and 35 percent of the country's labor force.

Chapter 11

Attitudes toward Political Parties (Measured by Psycho-Semantic Methods)

Olga Mitina and Vladimir Petrenko

This chapter examines Russian people's attitudes about political parties. These attitudes can be described through opinion polls and analyses of opinion leaders' beliefs. Another useful and interesting method used by Russian political psychologists is called a psycho-semantic approach. This approach is a relatively new field for political psychology and aims to construct and describe so-called individual systems of meanings through which an individual perceives the physical and social world. These meanings, however, while reflecting the individual's naive and "everyday" mentality, may often be unidentifiable by that person. In the world of politics, for example, individuals may use political terminology and express attitudes toward various political topics without adequate reflection on and understanding of the subject. Psycho-semantics, using various methods of gathering and interpreting information, examines these individual meanings at the level of symbols, communications, rituals, and—very often—word constructs. Different statistical methods are then used to compare the individual political meanings and put them together into a more comprehensive picture, which may reflect various cognitive trends at the group or societal level.

Political parties, as unions of politically active individuals who pursue comparable political goals and maintain relatively similar political attitudes, play a role as collective carriers of particular ideologies. Psychologically, Russian political parties may be seen as the groups that convert various interests of different social groups into the language of political demands and programs available for rational comprehension and contemplation. Furthermore, through the struggle of ideas, political parties could stimulate creation of new cognitive constructs, new systems of meanings in individuals. Analyses of both individual and collective meanings (in other words, the semantic space) of political parties could provide a specialist with an opportunity to predict the dynamics of attitudes and their formation, and forecast some of the society's political developments.

Several models could be used for the construction and investigation of the semantic space of political parties. The first model is the direct interpretation or explanation of the parties' positions. The group matrix is formed from "within"—based on the answers of the party members to specially designed questions related to political and economic problems of the society. The factorial and cluster analyses of the party matrix allows the positioning of the parties within a multidimensional space, helps visualize the society's "political map," describes political groups and political interests, and predicts some political developments.

Another model of measurement is based on analyses of the parties' images—the evaluations given to the parties by average voters acting as "experts." The experts, in these cases, use particular scales for the evaluation of the parties' political and economic activities. For example, Perenko and Mitina (1997) conducted a study of the parliamentary elections in December 1995. The respondents were city dwellers with college educations and students who were interested in politics and paid attention to the media. The individuals surveyed were asked to evaluate each party eligible to participate in the elections, on a seven-point scale. The respondents were also asked to predict each party's success in the forthcoming elections. The results, in general, proved that nonexperts could evaluate various political developments quite adequately, even better than political scientists and public opinion experts. The external evaluation of political parties requires that participating subjects have particular abilities to reflect and explain and also have a certain knowledge of politics. Based on the factorial analysis of the answers, it is possible to create the semantic space and identify the respondents' political mentalities. The objects of study here could be categorical structures of individuals, larger samples, and the entire society. This method reliably predicts electoral results and allows us to build a multidimensional ranking of the political parties among the electorate. This model could be also effectively used when the respondents are professional policy experts, or highly educated and politically knowledgeable individuals. However, political consciousness of the vast majority of Russians, even if they have their opinions about the economy, culture, religion, and other issues, is not conceptualized and structured.

Certainly, the "internal" and "external" models yield very different results. Predictably, declarations made by politicians about their actions and their parties do not generally match their real actions, and this is reflected in public consciousness. There is a third model, however, which juxtaposes political parties' positions (based on the party members' answers) with attitudes of voters about the parties. Within the frame of reference of this method, one cannot create an individual semantic space. However, it is possible to compare the respondents' attitudes within already-created political parties' spaces. In other words, one can determine how close an individual's positions are to positions of a particular party. (A computer program, which allows an individual to conduct his or her political self-identification, was developed by V. Petrenko, M. Gambaryan, and O. Mitina.) This method of projection of individual political attitudes upon political position of major parties, used on a larger representative sample, allows researchers to identify potential electoral support of particular political parties. The results could also allow political parties and leaders to either adjust or keep their political opinions, based on the desire to widen their electoral support.

This method of prognosis of electoral results has a lot in common with various methods of indirect questioning in psycho-diagnostic procedures. In personality inventories, the subject is never asked directly about the presence in him or her of a particular trait: The subject may not be aware of its existence. Moreover, the individual could be unfamiliar with professional terminology. In addition, some traits may be seen as negative, not socially desirable, and therefore they could be consciously or unconsciously rejected or denied. However, sociologists and political psychologists, while making their forecasts, often rely on respondents' answers to direct questions, like "What party are you going to vote for in the forthcoming elections?" In a state with a century-old party structure, and with political preferences passed on from one generation to another, the answers regarding two, three, or even four political parties could be effectively analyzed. However, in Russia, where the age of political parties does not exceed ten years (the multiparty system was legally established in 1989) and voting bulletins contain several dozen party names, the pollsters quite commonly get the "I don't know" answer. Indeed, people cast their votes and make other judgments, but often these decisions seem not to be based on a logical analysis.

First of all, the names of the parties are confusing. For example, there are parties with almost-identical names: the Democratic Choice of Russia, the Democratic Party of Russia, the Social-Democratic Party of Russia, and the Liberal-Democratic Party of Russia. Very often, the average voter, who tries to support the democratic changes, does not know which party he or she is supposed to support, and often makes a decision based on chance. Secondly, political attitudes of most Russians are clearly contradictory and unbalanced. For example, a person could often vote for two political foes at the same time (Petrenko & Mitina 1997). Therefore, asking direct questions may not always be productive in attitude measurement. The above limits may give psycho-semantic methods particular advantages. Below there are several examples of how these methods were used in examination of political attitudes between 1991 and 1997 (with the support of the Russian Foundation of Fundamental Studies).

Two surveys took place in the early 1990s. The first was conducted in August of 1991, prior to the coup and the collapse of the Soviet Union. The second took place in the fall of 1993, before the dismantling of the Supreme Soviet of the Russian Federation and the armed confrontation between the government and the opposition (the method and procedures are described in Petrenko & Mitina 1997).

The respondents, national leaders of various political parties, were given questionnaires that contained statements and assertions regarding different aspects of the social and political developments taking place in the country. The statements were direct quotes from speeches and interviews of Russian political leaders of different political orientations. Among them were democrats and fascists, nationalists and communists, monarchists and greens. There were some additional statements in the questionnaire taken from the Declaration of Human Rights and other international documents. The list of statements was selected so that it reflected the most frequently discussed problems of the Russian society. The representatives of different political parties, without knowledge about the source of the assertions, were supposed to express their agreement (+1), disagreement (-1), or absence of opinion (0). The final matrix displays general views of the surveyed members of each party participating in the study. Tables 11–1 and 11– 2 contain some data (average scores for each party) gathered in 1991 and 1993 studies.

SELECTED QUESTIONS FROM THE 1991 QUESTIONNAIRE

1. It is necessary to legally guarantee the right of the military not to follow orders which contradict domestic or international law (Program of Moscow People's Front, *Grazhdanski Referendum*, #1, 1989). . . .

5. Such realities are being created that one-sided disarmament will resemble stupidity or crime (General Makashov, V.A, *Izvestia,* 16 March 1990). . . .

10. Military service is an honorable duty and sacred responsibility of every citizen of the USSR (Constitution of the USSR). . . .

13. Boris Yeltsin could be identified as a right-winger. Also, he created "Yeltsinism:" risky, half-democratic, half-authoritarian politicking (N. Andeva. *Moscow News* #2, January, 1989). . . .

18. KGB, the political police, should be dissolved (Democratic Union Party, documents of the Second Congress). . . .

24. Some Soviet editions are filled with poison directed against the USSR and socialism. It seems that there is a hand of imperialism, reaction, and counter-revolution behind this (Fidel Castro, *Socialism or Death,* Havana, 1989). . . .

36. There should be control of working people over the media (First Congress of the United Front of Working People of the USSR, Documents and Materials). . . .

38. Lenin's ideas, free from dogmatic interpretations, enriched with modern thinking and by the experience of the socialist and the world construction, serve as a reliable foundation of perestroika (V. Kryuchkov, KGB Chairman, *Soglasie,* #19, 1989). . . .

39. We are being fooled by the media. A mass rehabilitation has begun, and under the cover of Glasnost, Zionism is being rehabilitated (D. Bolashev, member of the Central Committee of the Communist Party, *Moscow News,* #10, 1989). . . .

42. If our leader and founding father has founded something, that was massive terror and violence which became principles of

TABLE 11.1

Distribution of Answers. Party Activists. 1991

Name of the Party or Movement	Democratic Russia	Democratic Party of Russia	Party of Constitutional Democrats	"Memorial"	Republican Party of Russian Federation	Social-Democratic Party	Christian-Democratic Union	Democratic Union	Anarchists	Russian Green Party	Union of People's Socialists	Socialist Party
Resondents (n)	95	19	13	14	15	10	12	13	13	9	5	12
Internal Agreement	1.6	2.0	2.1	1.7	2.0	2.6	1.8	1.7	1.4	1.7	2.0	1.8
Question #												
1	0.7	1.0	0.8	0.7	0.4	0.6	0.4	0.5	0.7	0.7	1.0	0.6
5	−0.5	−0.5	−0.6	−0.4	−0.6	−0.9	−0.0	−0.7	−0.3	−0.8	−0.8	−0.1
10	−0.6	−0.5	−0.8	−0.5	−0.2	−0.9	−0.7	−1.0	−0.5	−0.8	−0.6	−0.5
13	−0.7	−0.7	−0.7	−0.5	−0.9	−0.9	−0.5	0.3	0.6	0.5	0.4	0.0
18	0.6	0.6	0.7	0.7	0.2	0.4	0.6	0.5	0.6	0.3	1.0	0.0
24	−0.8	−0.8	−1.0	−0.8	−0.7	−1.0	−0.6	−0.2	−0.2	−0.7	−0.4	−0.6
36	−0.5	−0.2	−0.3	−0.7	−0.6	−0.8	−0.4	−0.5	0.6	−0.1	−0.2	−0.6
38	−0.8	−0.6	−0.9	−0.8	−0.7	−0.9	−0.7	−0.4	−0.1	−0.2	−1.0	0.0
39	−0.6	−0.3	−0.6	−0.9	−0.6	−0.6	−0.5	−0.6	−0.4	−0.7	−0.4	−0.5
42	0.8	0.8	0.8	0.7	0.8	0.9	0.9	0.9	0.2	0.0	1.0	0.0
65	−0.7	−0.7	−0.6	−0.7	−0.8	−1.0	−0.3	−0.6	0.1	0.1	−0.6	−0.6
67	0.3	0.1	0.4	0.6	0.7	0.7	0.3	−0.1	−0.2	0.4	0.2	0.4
73	0.4	0.4	0.4	0.7	0.3	0.6	0.3	0.3	0.5	0.6	1.0	0.3
80	−0.5	−0.4	−0.4	−0.7	−0.4	−0.8	−0.1	0.0	−0.5	−0.7	−0.8	0.5
81	0.8	0.9	0.6	0.5	1.0	1.0	0.5	0.3	−0.0	0.6	0.8	0.6

Communists for Democracy	CPSS-Bolsheviks	CPSU - Marxist Platform	CPSU - Neutral	Communist Party of Russian Federation	CPSU - Center	Liberal-Democratic Party	"Civil Consent"	OOPIK	United Front of Working People	Christian Rebirth	"Pamiat"	Fellows Internal Affairs Academy	World War II Veterans	Disperse
12	13	12	10	9	7	13	13	6	11	8	6	26	10	
1.4	1.7	1.7	1.4	1.3	1.5	1.7	1.5	1.7	1.6	1.8	2.3	1.2	1.5	
0.4	−0.3	−0.4	0.4	−0.3	0.2	0.5	−0.1	−0.1	−0.4	−0.5	−0.3	0.1	−1.0	0.61
0.0	0.6	0.7	0.1	1.0	0.7	0.1	1.0	1.0	0.9	1.0	1.0	0.3	0.8	0.71
0.2	0.7	0.9	0.0	0.7	0.4	−0.4	1.0	1.0	0.8	0.5	0.6	0.5	1.0	0.74
−0.2	0.9	1.0	−0.4	0.8	0.2	−0.3	0.6	0.8	0.7	0.5	0.0	−0.2	0.8	0.69
0.0	−0.8	−0.7	−0.2	−0.4	−0.2	−0.2	−0.6	−0.5	−0.6	−0.6	−1.0	−0.1	−0.6	0.64
0.0	0.5	0.7	−0.1	0.6	0.1	−0.5	0.9	1.0	0.8	0.5	0.3	−0.1	1.0	0.72
0.0	0.7	0.6	−0.3	0.5	0.7	−0.3	0.7	0.8	0.7	0.3	0.3	0.1	0.5	0.66
0.0	0.3	0.9	−0.7	0.2	0.7	−0.6	−0.5	−0.5	0.7	−0.6	−1.0	−0.0	0.8	0.58
−0.4	0.3	0.4	−0.5	0.3	−0.2	−0.3	0.8	0.7	0.8	1.0	1.0	−0.3	0.6	0.69
−0.1	−0.9	−0.8	−0.1	−0.3	−0.5	0.6	0.5	0.2	−0.7	1.0	1.0	−0.2	−1.0	0.68
−0.1	0.6	0.8	−0.4	0.6	0.1	−0.0	1.0	1.0	0.9	1.0	1.0	−0.1	0.9	0.74
0.3	−0.2	0.0	1.0	0.4	1.0	0.4	0.0	0.1	−0.0	−1.0	−1.0	0.3	0.3	0.51
−0.1	−0.3	−0.3	0.2	−0.3	0.0	0.3	−0.5	−0.5	0.0	−1.0	−1.0	−0.2	0.0	0.54
−0.9	−0.6	−0.8	−0.2	−0.1	−0.5	−0.3	0.4	0.7	0.3	1.0	0.6	−0.6	0.0	0.61
0.8	0.4	0.7	0.8	0.8	0.8	0.9	0.1	0.2	0.5	−1.0	−1.0	0.8	1.0	0.57

Table 11.2

Distribution of Answers. Party Activists. 1991

Party Name	Democratic Choice	Democratic Russia	Moscow Liberals	Moscow Tribune	Republican Party of Russian Fed.	Economic Freedom Party	Rus. Mov. of Dem. Reforms	Bloc New Russia	Communist Party of Russia	People's Party of Russia	Russian Green Party	Social–Democr. Party of Russia	Anarchists	National Salvation Front
Q#														
3	0.62	0.65	0.9	0.67	0.73	0.42	0.83	0.46	0.67	−1	−1	0.31	−0.7	−0.7
4	−0.66	−0.72	−0.8	−0.83	−0.69	−0.37	−0.67	−0.63	−0.33	−1	−1	−0.86	−0.9	−0.26
7	−0.57	−0.72	−0.8	−0.83	−0.62	0.11	−0.5	−0.58	−0.33	0.67	0.83	−0.69	0.2	0.51
8	0.2	0.3	0.4	0	0.12	−0.21	0.17	−0.13	−0.33	−0.33	−0.5	0.03	0.1	−0.69
12	−0.83	−0.99	−1	−1	−1	−0.47	−0.67	−0.58	−1	0.67	−0.33	−0.9	−0.2	0.48
16	0.57	0.61	0.8	0.25	0.58	0.21	0.67	0.5	0.67	−0.33	−0.83	0.21	−0.9	−0.98
23	0.43	0.4	0.9	0.83	0.04	0.21	0.5	0.5	0.67	−0.33	0.33	0.76	−0.7	−0.68
28	0.64	0.76	1	1	0.65	0.11	0.5	0.5	1	0.33	−0.33	0.45	−0.5	−0.84
30	−0.8	−0.9	−1	−0.75	−1	−0.47	−0.33	−0.75	−1	−0.33	−1	−0.72	−0.6	0.73
36	0.64	0.66	0.6	0.67	0.77	0.26	0.83	0.71	0.67	1	0.5	0.76	0.1	0.03
40	−0.11	−0.37	−0.6	−0.42	−0.23	0.16	−0.17	0.29	1	1	−0.5	−0.14	−0.5	0.37
45	0.38	0.43	0.6	0.42	0.27	−0.11	0.5	0.54	0	0.67	−0.33	0.45	0.7	−0.3
46	0.01	−0.13	−0.2	−0.08	−0.12	0.26	0.83	0.08	0.67	0.67	−0.83	−0.24	−0.9	0.88
49	0.48	0.55	0.9	0.67	0.15	0.32	−0.33	0.67	−0.33	0.33	1	0.59	0.9	−0.7
50	0.3	0.27	0.1	0.08	0.35	0.32	0.67	0.25	0.67	0.33	−1	0.31	−0.9	0.81

the state policy. (Y. Afanasiev, a leader of the Democratic Russia Movement, *Izvestia,* 14 March 1990). . . .

65. Some of our nation's pseudo-leaders, who didn't pour their blood or sweat in our land, now trade our territory, while on their foreign voyages. This is happening when the NATO countries do not reduce but increase their military potential, when with encouraging praises from the West we conduct the conversion of the defense industry in such a hurry, when with the dis-

National–Republican Party	Rebirth Party	People's Freedom Party	Russian National Forum	Officers Union	Working Russia	Russian All–National Union	Communist Party of RF	Working P. of Communists of R	Liberal–Democr. Party	All–Russian Monarchist Cent.	Civil Consent	Democratic Party of Russia	People's Party of Free Russia	Union of Russia's Rebirth
0.58	-0.5	-0.67	-0.71	-0.5	-1	-0.59	-0.89	-1	0.72	-0.71	-0.08	0.07	-0.53	-0.5
0.11	0.1	-0.33	0.86	-1	-0.92	-0.41	-0.79	-0.91	-0.17	1	-0.77	-0.6	-1	0.5
0.32	0.7	0.58	0	0.75	0.73	0.41	0.63	0.68	-0.11	-0.21	0.35	0.47	0.33	0.17
-0.58	-0.8	-0.83	-0.71	-0.75	-0.81	-0.82	-0.95	-0.82	0.06	0.29	-0.56	-0.4	-0.87	-0.17
0.37	0.4	0.25	0.57	0.75	0.58	0.41	0.53	0.5	-0.22	-0.71	-0.69	-0.87	-0.67	-0.67
-1	-1	-0.83	-1	-1	-1	-1	-1	-1	-1	-0.64	-0.77	-0.93	-0.8	-0.5
-0.58	-0.6	-0.5	-0.29	-0.75	-0.77	-0.82	-1	-0.86	-0.06	-0.64	-0.33	-0.53	-0.2	0.33
-0.95	-1	-0.83	-0.86	-1	-0.69	-0.88	-0.89	-0.64	-0.28	0.21	-0.4	-0.6	-0.2	0.17
0.53	0.8	0.67	0.57	0.75	1	1	1	1	0.89	-0.21	0.1	0.27	0	0
-0.05	0.1	-0.25	0.14	-0.38	0.08	-0.41	0.11	0.18	0.22	0.21	0.77	0.73	0.93	0
-0.11	0.6	0.25	0.14	0.38	0.77	0.41	0.47	0.73	0.44	0.57	0.25	0.4	0.47	0
-0.26	-0.6	-0.25	-0.43	-0.5	-0.12	-0.41	-0.42	-0.23	-0.33	0.29	0.21	-0.07	0.4	-0.83
1	1	1	0.86	0.75	0.62	1	0.74	0.55	1	1	0.63	0.8	0.73	0.83
-0.79	-0.8	-1	-0.86	-0.75	-0.5	-0.94	-0.47	-0.41	-0.78	-0.57	-0.08	-0.47	0.2	-0.67
1	0.8	0.83	0.86	0.63	0.58	0.82	0.84	0.5	0.94	0.86	0.73	0.87	0.6	1

mantling of our armed forces of our allies and withdrawal of the Soviet troops from Eastern Europe, the strategic world balance is changing (General I.N. Kozhedub, *Izvestia,* 15 March 1990). . . .

67. Let us not push out the kind hands stretched out to us from across the ocean—because through Gorbachev's personality many people over there realized that we are not the Evil empire (Y. Drunina, *Izvestia,* 15 March 1990). . . .

73. Pacifism is a path to peace. . . .
80. The authoritarian regime within the Orthodoxy was not such a bad thing (A. Solzhenitsyn, *Sovetskaya Molodezh,* 9 January 1990). . . .
81. I think that a democratic path of development is the only favorable one for any country (A. Sakharov, *Sovetskaya Molodezh,* 9 January 1990). . . .

SELECTED QUESTIONS FROM THE 1993 QUESTIONNAIRE

3. I agree that the Russian Federation should become a presidential republic (Question placed for the referendum of 1993, Vechernyaya Moskva, 9 March 1993).
4. I support a solid state authority, which wholly serves the interest of the nation; for Russia it is a monarchy (V. Soloukhin, Den, #40, 1992). . . .
7. To fight against the Soviets is to ruin the foundation of democracy. (R. Khasbulatov, speaker of the Russian Supreme Soviet, Narodny Deputat, #5, 1992).
8. It is necessary to gradually restrict the roles of the Supreme Soviet (L. Ponomarev, Narodny Deputat, 10, 1992). . . .
12. I think that we need a congress, not a two-chamber parliament because the multi-party system has not been formed yet. The congress would provide wider representativeness of different social and political groups and would be less dependent in decision (I. Konstantinov, Moscow News, 21 March 1993). . . .
16. I trust President Yeltsin (Question placed for the referendum of 1993, Vechernyaya Moskva, 9 March 1993). . . .
23. I agree that the new Constitution of the Russian Federation should be adopted by a constitutional assembly, which would represent the multi-national people of the Russian Federation (Question placed for the referendum of 1993, Vechernyaya Moskva, 9 March 1993). . . .
28. It is necessary to dissolve the National Salvation Front as an organization which in its statements calls for the overthrow of the legitimate power, tries to destabilize the situation in the society, and sets people against each other (Yeltsin, Vechernyaya Moskva, 30 October 1992). . . .

30. Judicially, I do not recognize the collapse of the Soviet Union. I will never accept the destruction of the Soviet Union (M. Astafiev, Narodny Deputat, 10, 1992). . . . .

36. I think that preservation of the unified economic space as well as a confederation among the independent, sovereign states which used to comprise the USSR, in a great measure reflects the interests of all peoples (People's Party of Free Russia, Materials of the First Congress). . . . .

40. It is necessary the CIS to have unified armed forces (Civil Union's program). . . . .

45. I think that the Georgians and Abkhasians should find a reconciliation themselves without Russia's help (E. Shevardnadze, Izvestia, 11 March 1993).

46. I stand for the rebirth of united and unbreakable Russia (Russkii Vestnik, Appendix 4). . . . .

49. I feel calmly about the issue of autonomy, sovereignty of republics within Russia; this process is inevitable (G. Satrovoitova, Vechernyaya Moskva, 28 January 1992).

50. All the attempts to dissect Russia must be prevented by the lawful but strong means. (V. Aksyuchits, Moscow News, 16 August 1992).

Examining the answers of the representatives of each party, the investigator is able to form a generalized impression about the political positions of the parties. There is an interesting trend seen here, and that is the most parties' proximity to each other in terms of their attitudes. On the other hand, there is a very high diversity of the answers given by the Communist Party members in 1991 (the party was near its collapse at that time). There is also a high dispersion of answers given by the fellows of the Academy of Internal Affairs and the veterans of World War II. For the answers of these samples there could be a reasonable explanation. Unlike political parties formed according to their members' political views, both the samples of veterans and Academy fellows were comprised according to social status.

One of the forms of the data display could be an attempt to construct the "similarity tree" of the analyzed parties (Duran & Odel 1974). The structure of attitudes, while being a cognitive reality, could reflect political realities, such as positions of various political groups and coalitions of political parties.

The results reflected many close similarities among the parties' polit-

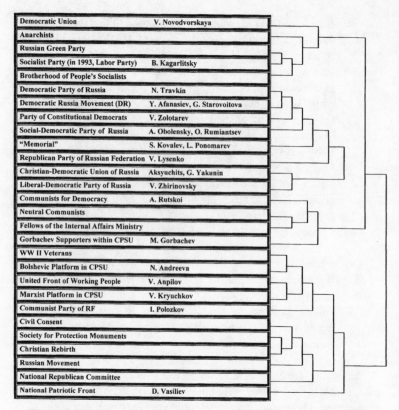

Figure 11.1 Cluster Structure of Russian Political Parties, 1991

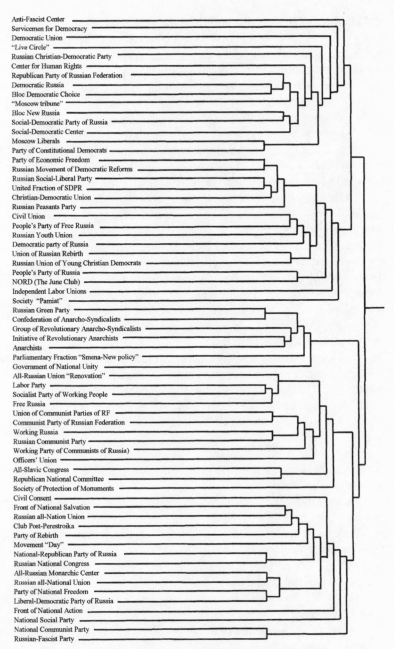

Figure 11.2 Cluster Structure of Russian Political Parties in 1993

ical platforms. The diagrams also show that the views of the Communist Party members in 1991 reflected the actual situation in the party. There was a strong commitment of the democratic wing of the party (Communists for Democracy) and its center (Gorbachev supporters) to the "democrats"; whereas traditional communists were leaning toward "national patriots" and supporters of statehood. Along with other factors, this polarization, perhaps, could have stimulated the dissolution of the party.

A factorial analysis of the data (the procedure has been described in Petrenko & Mitina 1997) shows that among the most significant factors splitting political parties in 1991 were the "de-centralization of the state" (for the democrats), the "unified socialist state" (for the communists), and "undivided Orthodox monarchy" (for the nationalists). The weight of the factor "denial or acceptance of the Communist ideology" was unexpectedly less significant compared to these other factors. It is also worth mentioning that the members of the Liberal Democratic Party (LDP) in 1991 supported the de-centralization of political power, contrary to the statements made by the party leader, Vladimir Zhirinovsky. This contradiction perhaps reflects a phenomenon common in many young Russian political parties: political platforms may fluctuate significantly based on the changing political credo of the parties' leaders. Thus, most of the interviewed members of the LDP resigned from the party and were replaced by individuals who maintained views similar to Zhirinovsky's.

In order to compare the results of the 1991 and 1993 surveys, only those political parties that participated in both surveys were selected. As a result of a factorial analysis and rotation, six major factors (which identify the dynamics of the semantic space of the examined political parties) have been identified:

Factor 1. Democratic freedoms and liberal values versus totalitarianism and nationalism

Factor 2. Decentralization and independence versus unitarian socialist statehood

Factor 3. Plurality of ideologies and growth of religion's role versus the communist ideology and atheism

Factor 4. Support of the president and the cabinet versus opposition to the president and the cabinet

Factor 5. Emphasis on self-governance versus accentuation of governmental power

Factor 6. Priorities of economic development versus priorities of ecological security

A comparison of the results of the 1991 and 1993 surveys shows that within factor 1, the struggle against totalitarianism has been reoriented. The data reflect diminished societal interests in this problem partly because of its relative resolution, and partly because of the decline of people's interest in politics. On the other hand, totalitarianism has been replaced on the attitudinal level with militant nationalism. Another finding that proves the trend of the decline of people's interest in politics could be a change in factor 3 over the observed period. The absence of a leading ideological doctrine of the transitional society and the diminishing interest in religion may cause further de-ideologization of the society. Analyses of factors 2, 4, 5, and 6 indicate an increased diversity of the answers in 1993 compared with the earlier survey. Problems such as support for the incumbent government, self-governance, and ecological concerns were not as divisive as they became by 1993. The growth of the general diversity in the answers may also suggest the increased importance of these problems for the surveyed individuals. The results also showed that the changes in public consciousness take place in time but also may depend on the location of the surveyed subjects.

The 1993 survey was conducted both in Moscow and in Samara, a relatively large and "typical" Russian city. The comparison showed a significantly low differentiation and lower cognitive complexity of attitudes on the local level compared to the Moscow sample (Petrenko, Mitina, & Brown 1995).

In a study conducted before the parliamentary elections of 1995 (Petrenko & Mitina 1997), there was an attempt made to use the factorial analysis method to identify particular types of political attitudes and describe social and demographic characteristics of the following discovered types. These six types of attitudes represent Russian ideological pluralism, with the first type conveying ideas of the state regulations over the economy, and the other five diverse types representing market-based relationships.

The semantic space of the respondent of the first type is characterized by the lowest cognitive complexity. They support a planned economy and are convinced that only the old party nomenclature will be able to revive the economy and take care of politics. The most significant attribute of this group is its age. Most people in this cluster are over 40, and most of them evaluate their material situation as poor. Among them are engineers, retirees, housewives, blue-collar workers with few qualifications, and those who voted for the Communist Party of the Russian

Federation. The respondents of the second type are characterized by their market-oriented attitudes. These are people of an average income, politically active scientists, artists, and those who voted for democratically oriented politicians. The third type resembles the previous one; however, this type has a higher cognitive complexity, and the individuals within this group are also less categorical in their judgments. There is a relative prevalence of men in this category who assess their income as very high, and Muscovites who have their own business. Generally, this group is apolitical. Those who voted in this group preferred to support Gaidar or Yavlinsky. The attitudes of the fourth group are both market-oriented and negative toward the contemporary political reforms in the country. The ideal reform path is seen by them as going from "the bottom to the top." They believe that democracy copied after the Western models is wrong for Russia. Their ideal is the Orthodox collectiveness (*sobornost*). The church is regarded very highly. The most typical representatives of this group could be such renowned Russian movie directors as Stanislav Govorukhin and Nikita Mikhalkov, with their nostalgic desire to restore the "lost" Russia. This type is comprised of people between the ages of 25 and 40, primarily men; most of them have high incomes. They negatively evaluate all political parties, but consider themselves supporters of the democrats. Individuals of the fifth type show attitudes, which in part resemble the market-oriented attitudes of the second type. But contrary to the second type, these attitudes are less influenced by a particular ideology. In general, the attitudes convey support of greater regional independence. People who express these attitudes are mostly women, students, and recent college graduates. The sixth type also represents market-oriented attitudes. Most people in this group are over 55, mostly women with college educations, who evaluate their income as low, and who work primarily in academia, education, and health-care fields.

In another study, political attitudes were examined through the evaluations of political leaders. In the summer of 1997, the respondents, who represented 18 Russian regions, described their opinions about top Russian leaders on a seven-point scale (the study was carried out by a center of political studies, Image-Contact). The sample of respondents represented a wide variety of social attitudes and personal political affiliations. Therefore, the average scores yielded by the survey require additional interpretation because of the diversity (disperse rates) of the answers. As expected, the most contradictory and dispersed evaluations have been received by the most popular political leaders. The less-known leaders received more neutral evaluations, and the answers about them were less dispersed. The factorial analysis of the data identified four basic factors, which could be used to interpret how the respondents form their perceptions of political leaders. These factors are: (1) positive or negative evaluation of the politician, (2) liberal values and orientation toward a market economy versus socialist values and a state-regulated economy, (3) populist behavior versus absence of such, and (4) "iron arm" values versus absence of such. Based on the analysis, a cluster structure of the most prominent leaders of 1997 was created. It shows the relative "proximity" and "distance" of political leaders to one other based on people's evaluations.

In another study conducted in 1997, several semantic models were constructed to describe the respondents' evaluations of both economic and political reforms. More than one thousand respondents from eight different regions were asked to evaluate various parties, their leaders, and different social events in terms of their impact on the major economic and political changes in Russia. As a result of the analysis, a typology of Russian people's attitudes toward the transformation and the reform process was created. There have been six major factors underlying people's attitudes about political transformations identified: (1) morality versus lack of morality, (2) totalitarianism versus democratization, (3) economic benefits versus lack of such, (4) dependency on developed countries versus independence from them, (5) criminalization of the economy versus absence of such, and (6) defense capability versus absence of such. In general, the study revealed an interesting phenomenon of mismatch among several of the expressed attitudes. Realizing the importance and usefulness of the economic reform (privatization, transition to a market economy, and private property), the respondents also evaluated these changes negatively, primarily in the categories of ruined morality and lack of social justice.

This discrepancy, a split in attitudes about the reforms, could be explained by at least two arguments. First of all, people's understanding of moral issues has been formed during the period of socialism, with its Marxist views on exploitation and private property, free health care and education, and social protection in general. These perceptions also have deep roots in Russian history and are based on the communal way of thinking, and a mentality of abstinence from the time of the Orthodox reformation. Secondly, "nomenclature privatization," corruption among many government officials, and active participation of criminal structures in the process of the redistribution of property, cause negative evaluations from most Russian people.

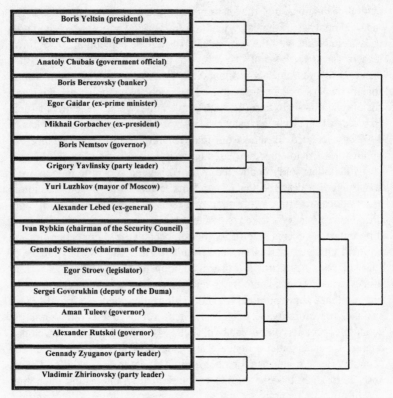

Figure 11.3 Political Proximity of Various Russian Leaders

According to Max Weber, the Protestant ethic paved the way to economic reforms in the West. To the contrary, in the Russian Christian Orthodoxy, there has always been a spirit of abstinence and detachment from the difficult realities (you cannot take clothes from a naked person). Communalism and collectivism are at odds with the spirit of liberal individualism found in entrepreneurs. The period of dominance of the Communist ideology based on serfdom and dictatorship of the proletariat has left deep marks in social attitudes and collective archetypes of many Russians. Traditionally, Russian society has always been influenced by a particular ideology, and the Russian man was supposed to obey, not make decisions. Perhaps under the layer of rational attitudes and preferences, there is an underlying layer of unconscious moral and religious values, the further examination and description of which is definitely needed.

Chapter 12

Gender Roles and Political Transformations

Eric Shiraev

Russian gender roles in the transition period are difficult to understand without placing them into a broader historical context. Prerevolutionary Russian society and its underlying peasant culture were patriarchal and paternalistic, and males officially and unconditionally governed the community. Different criteria were applied to the behavior of women and men, and in virtually all spheres of Russian life, priority and advantage were given to men (Kerig et al. 1993). Husbands and wives had different required rules of conduct within the family. According to the old Russian law, the wife must obey her husband, who is the head of the family, and she must love and respect him by showing him her readiness to serve and her attachment (Set of Russian Empire's Laws, St. Petersburg, 1857).[1]

Politics was viewed as an exclusively male occupation. Indeed, up until 1917, women had no official right to be elected in a local public office, though women could vote in local elections. In the beginning of the twentieth century, 20 to 40 percent of people qualified to vote in local elections were women. The vast majority of these women were described as someone's wife, widow, or daughter. In other words, women's electoral rights could be exercised in most cases through their male relatives. Moreover, women were denied the right to run for deputy seats.[2]

Powerful cultural stereotypes and pressure from their referent groups kept women from challenging these mores. For example, in the 1917 local elections there was significant resistance from many peasant women to voting. In some regions women apparently thought voting would actually be sinful and regarded the elections as devil's work. It was easier for them to leave problems up to village male elders and go about their own business. Not surprisingly, by the end of the nineteenth century only 4 percent of Russian women worked in education and health-care sectors (Rosenberg 1982, 398–399).

The Russian Orthodox Church conducted more subtle discrimination against women. Women were not allowed to step inside the altar. During baptisms, boys were carried by the priest through the altar, but girls had to remain outside. The vast majority of the local saints canonized by the Russian Orthodox Church are also men. The institute of priesthood is still a men-only establishment. The church today will not even consider suggestions that women be admitted into Russian religious seminaries and academies.

In the Soviet Union the commitment of the communists to the Marxist idea of equality between the genders led to an attempt to change these older discriminatory customs. Laws guaranteed political rights and equal opportunities with men to all women in Soviet Russia.[3] A high level of literacy for women was reached by the 1940s, and many new occupations opened up for women in the Soviet society. In the political realm rigorous quotas were introduced to maintain the ideologically required gender balance on all levels of the Soviet governmental and social system. Practically all of the Russian elected assemblies, legislative bodies, and committees in all government branches had a female membership level between 30 and 50 percent.

Soviet policies, however, did not radically change underlying attitudes toward women. Generally, Russian women were considered to be a kind of "second sex." In the Soviet regime women did not reach the top politically. For many years the highest governing body of the Communist Party, the Politburo, was an institution virtually closed to women. Lyudmila Furtseva, the culture minister under Brezhnev, was a rare exception. The vast majority of the mayors and local party bosses were still men. Though new occupations were opened to women under the Soviet regime, the individuals at the top were still predominantly male (Smith 1976). Even in intellectual circles the issue of gender equality was of little real concern. Indeed, Raisa Gorbachev's sociological treatise dealing with the hard life of women on the collective farms in parts of Russia was rather radical for the time.

Since the demise of the Soviet Union many of the older attitudes have become more explicit. Inequality today is no longer camouflaged by ideological doctrines of socialist equity among social groups. Patriarchal customs and sex discrimination are overtly present and viewed by many Russians as natural processes inevitable in a market society. Those who are concerned about gender equality are often viewed as either out-of-fashion conservatives or left-wing radicals (Young 1996).

Moreover, the position of Russian women has worsened in some respects during the transformation. Soviet-era quota policies have been dropped. The result is that in the first free national parliamentary elections of 1989, only 10 percent of elected deputies were women. The number of elected female officials did not exceed 10 percent in most central and local legislatures (*Bulletin* of the St. Petersburg Center for Gender Problems, #1–2, 1993, 60–70).[4] By 1995, there were 46 female Duma members, a small fraction of the Russian Parliament. Things were not better in the executive branch. By 1995, of the 89 people named by President Boris Yeltsin as his personal representatives to Russia's provinces, only one was a woman (Young 1996).[5]

The contemporary media buttress the notion that women are not suited for politics. For example, Igor Popov mockingly described in *Argumenty i Facty,* the leading weekly newspaper, all the misfortunes and bloopers that could occur if a woman were elected president of Russia (Popov 1996). Leading businessmen and politician Konstantin Borovoy (1998) explained why there were so few women in politics in the *Ogonyok* weekly: "Non-female traits are needed in politics: analytical skills, ability to make an expert opinion. . . . I even wrote a little poem (*chastushka*): I will never cast a ballot / For a Russian woman / I would rather pull this Russian woman / Into my bed." *The Moscow Times* (7 March 1998) reports numerous sexist remarks made by Duma speakers Ivan Rybkin and Gennady Seleznev during parliamentary debates. During the 1996 presidential campaign, a prominent sociologist and deputy of the Duma, Galina Starovoitova, wrote that in Russia a woman couldn't become president because of a negative stereotype against women in politics. She noted that the media persistently express the propagandistic idea that women are the inferior part of humanity. The image of active women is commonly depicted with insulting sarcasm or even open condemnation (Starovoitova 1998).

Economically the position of women also declined during the transition. Russian women are better educated than their male counterparts. In 1989, 47 percent of women and only 34 percent of men had completed four or two years of college (World Bank 1993). Yet female earnings have declined relative to men's. As the Moscow Center for Gender Studies reports, Russian women in 1991 earned on the average 75 percent of what men earned. By 1995, the figure had fallen to 40 percent (Young 1996).[6] By the mid-1990s, men owned 83 percent of Russian private business. The situation on the Russian market required constant negotiation of obstacles and "heroic" efforts to succeed, which made it extremely difficult for most women to start their own business (Perepelkin 1995). Only 7 percent of women who weren't entrepreneurs expressed wishes to start their own business someday (Committee on Labor and Employment, St. Petersburg, 1993).

Moreover, women generally hold positions that require lower skills. Some occupations are completely closed to women. They cannot serve in the military except for a few specified positions. With rare exceptions, they cannot study at government-sponsored military colleges or military academies, cannot drive buses or trucks. The most painful, however, is subtle discrimination, which some specialists call epidemic (Sillaste 1994). According to a report of the St. Petersburg Committee on Labor and Employment, in 1993, one-fifth of women looking for jobs were refused by their potential employers simply because they are women. Theoretically, an employee can take legal steps to avoid being discriminated against. But employers make their decisions on the basis of personal connections and contacts. Selection committees exist in very few companies, and résumés, in the form they are submitted in the United States, are typically not required. Job interviews have not become common practice. It is even common in job advertisements to include a "men only" phrase. The result is that of every ten unemployed people, seven were women (Sillaste 1994). The same ratio of unemployment between men (38 percent) and women (62 percent) remained in the mid-1990s (Katulski 1996, 175).

Sexual harassment is also rife in the workplace. Businesses commonly place advertisements for secretarial or assistant positions, clandestinely suggesting that the job description could include sex. One study found that half of the surveyed women say their bosses have made sexual overtures to them (Jansen & Shiraev forthcoming). A 1996 report said that men in one-third of all Moscow firms practiced sexual harassment (*The Baltimore Sun,* 1 February 1998). Moscow's Center for Gender

Studies surveyed women in several Russian cities and found that at least one in four women had been victims of sexual harassment at work (Young 1996). Yet sexual harassment in today's Russia is not considered to be worth much public attention. Institutions, both public and private, do not identify sexual harassment as a problem and have no established rules for acceptable contacts between men and women at work. The Russian language doesn't even contain an appropriate translation for this term. It is usually translated as "annoying begging," "sexual aspirations," or "intimidation." Surprisingly, many women don't view sexual harassment as an important topic for discussion. Sarcastic remarks about the "excessive" focus on sexual harassment in other countries, especially in the United States, are common (*Argumenty i Facty,* #2, January 1991, 6).[7]

Support for these gender role distinctions in the workplace is commonly displayed in the media. For instance, the journal *Semya* justified women's unemployment because it supposedly strengthens the family (*Semya,* March 1993).[8] In a magazine interview, K. Borovoy (1998), whose other sexist remarks have been mentioned earlier, said: "Business is a heavy thing, it is physically tiresome, not every woman is able to hang on. I met such businesswomen, primarily in the West: from the outside, they are taken care of, they are beautiful, but in reality they are men [*myzhiki*]."[9]

Even within what should be the haven of personal relationships, many women are subjected to violence and systematic harassment. In a series of in-depth, focused interviews, collected between 1992 and 1998 with 132 Russian women who represented a wide range of ages, professions, and social orientations, 74 of them mentioned that at least once in their lives they had had sex against their will. According to the interviews, lack or absence of men's respect toward women in personal relationships is a common trend (Jansen & Shiraev forthcoming). Data obtained by the St. Petersburg Institute for Social Research in 1996 (unpublished) suggests that nine out of every hundred Russian women were physically abused by their partners in the family; 38 percent were sexually assaulted, and 25 percent were raped outside of the family. These figures appear to be low, because Russian women use different, narrow interpretations for such words as "rape", "abuse" and "violence" (*Bulletin* of St. Petersburg Center for Gender Problems, #1–2, 1993, 61–72; Shiraev & Jansen 1999). According to estimations, only one out of ten women reports domestic violence against themselves, and only one out of five Russian women would report a rape case against themselves (*The Women's Dialogue,* #8, 1993).

Accompanying the above trends has been an increase in the "sexualization" of the mass media. Fifteen years ago it was socially unacceptable to promote anything sexual. Today one will be accused of being retrograde when he or she raises concerns about unlimited sexual freedom. Sexually explicit publications are openly sold by street vendors. There is practically no enforceable law to protect minors from exposure to pornography. The Russian media often take a "blame the victim" position in analyzing rape cases (see for example, *Argumenty i Facty,* #6, February 1996). With development of market relations, various ideas and theories of "natural" aspects of relationships between sexes and among people in general have replaced Marxist-Leninist dogma. Social Darwinism, losing many scholarly battles in the West (Schubert 1991), reappeared in Russia as a justification of current policies and practices regarding the sexes. From this perspective the attitudinal and behavioral traits of men and women are grounded in nature and as such cannot be significantly changed by new social rules.

One of the distinctive gender-related features is the division of responsibilities in the Russian family. The traditional Russian family starts with a courtship in which the man takes the lead in a struggle to "conquer" his partner's affection. In the Russian language the verb *to marry* has two gender-based versions. The first is used to describe men's behavior, and the other one is saved for women's. In the former the meaning is "active": Men marry women—they take them. The other version, reserved to describe women's behavior, is "passive": the woman is being taken by her man. It would be grammatically incorrect to use the stronger and active version of the verb while describing the woman's marriage. Even when working outside the home, women take care of the routine problems and chores such as shopping, cooking, cleaning, and taking care of children. In the 1990s, the average Russian woman worked 40 hours a week more than a man as a result of her duties at home and for the family, including shopping, child care, and housework (Juviler 1991).

The stress that women experience may help explain, in part, the declining marriage and birth rate. The birth rate in the country is down 30 percent since 1989. According to the state Statistics Committee of Russian Federation, the number of children in Russian preschools dropped from 9 million in 1990 to 5.1 million in 1996 (*Argumenty i Facty,* #10, March 1997). According to one poll, the "ideal" number of children a family is willing to have has dropped from 2 to 1.5 and is still declining (Matthews 1995). The average family size was 3.2 in 1989. It dropped to 2.6 in 1995. The marriage rate also has dropped from 9.7 per 1,000 in

1985 to 6.7 in 1995. Within the same period the divorce rate has risen from 4 to 4.7 per 1,000 (Zhuravlev et al. 1996, 61). The fact that adult children continue to live with their parents and share housing with them may have contributed to these figures. As could be expected, lack of privacy increases interpersonal tensions and conflicts.

The life expectancy of women, though it is still higher than it is for men, has also gone down during the transition. The life expectancy for women dropped from 74 in 1989 to 72 years seven years later. That is almost ten years less than the life expectancy in most of the world's developed countries. Deteriorating medical services contribute to the dramatic drop. Fifty percent of Russian medical facilities do not have hot water, 25 percent lack a sewage system, and up to 20 percent have no tap water at all (Feshbach 1995).[10] Persistent frustration based on an inability to provide normal living conditions for themselves and for their families may lead to serious psychological and other health problems for both women and men.

Despite these difficulties, women do not look to the government for possible solutions to their problems. Russian women, compared to men, are less interested in political events and express little desire to take advantage of new opportunities to enter politics. Surveys conducted by the Institute of Applied Politics indicate that 60 percent of Russian women did not want to participate in any form of political activity. Only 12 percent of women below the age of 29 expressed a strong interest in politics, compared to 22 percent of men. A double-digit gap between men and women in terms of their interest in politics was common for every age group, with the exception of the 45–59 group, in which 45 percent of women and 49 percent of men indicated their strong interest in politics (Wyman 1997, 215). G. Sillaste (1995) reported that more than 25 percent of female respondents expressed the belief that women should not be elected to any government office.

This passivity has had political repercussions. The Women of Russia, a political party that actively engaged in defending women's rights, couldn't even get a minimum 5 percent of the vote threshold in the 1995 Duma elections in order to be represented in the Russian legislature (Williams 1996). According to a poll conducted in 1995, this party scored well (11 percent) in the July ballot test and appeared to be equally strong in other polls. Yet even the supporters of the Women of Russia were politically passive. They expressed less interest in politics and government than other parties' supporters and were the least likely to vote (Ferguson 1996).[11]

This passivity has been joined with a growth of conservative political attitudes in Russian women (Kharchev 1994).[12] Russian women are favorable to an authoritarian style of leadership, which represents "stable management," "order," and "protection for the weak." A compromise orientation is the leadership style least preferred by women (Sillaste 1994). In 1991, in accordance with traditional Russian authoritarian views, women expressed more negative attitudes toward freedom of emigration from the USSR than men did. They were less favorable than men to the breakup of the republics of the former Soviet Union (35 percent of women were pro-independence, compared to 46 percent of men). Women in general were supportive of the "iron hand" in governing the country (58 percent of women against 42 percent of men). Moscow women as contrasted to Moscow men were also more negatively oriented toward newcomers. In 1992 the chauvinistic motto "Moscow is for the Muscovites" was supported by 73 percent of women and by 62 percent of men (*MMMM,* 1992).

Women tend to be more oriented than men toward local issues, especially those pertaining to schools and education. Men, in contrast, show greater interest in national and international affairs. This phenomenon of gender-related differentiation of interests seems to be cross-cultural (Jennings & Niemi 1981, McCourt 1977, Carroll 1989). Women's interests include primarily areas such as equality policies, environmental protection, disarmament policies, education, culture, and social and welfare policies. Men's interests include economic, industrial, and financial policies; energy issues, national security, and foreign affairs.

As might be expected, Russian women, especially in working-class families, express traditional views of gender roles and reaffirm that their most important commitment is to home and family (Zdravomyslova 1998). A survey conducted in 1992 shows the clear "traditionalist" view of Russian women: eighty-nine percent of urban women saw the family as the center and main interest of life; only 11 percent said that their career was their main goal in life.[13]

Still, the female support of traditionalism includes some attitudes that suggest their experience with communism has had some impact on their values.[14] Women are more often willing to say that the increasing gap between rich and poor is bad or unacceptable. Almost 60 percent of women of the youngest category surveyed (below 30) agreed, while only 33 percent of males accepted this view. Among senior respondents (over 60) 86 percent of women and 78 percent of men agreed with the statement.[15] Young women show less support (53 percent) for private property

compared to young men (61 percent).[16] In 1990, women were less supportive of Russia's transition to the market economy than men and
expressed a greater concern about a "moral and cultural crisis" in the
country, involving alcoholism, pornography, suicide, etc. (Wyman 1997
44, 179).[17]

Russian women also assume that they have the right to abortion.
Prohibited in the USSR for 20 years, abortion was again officially legalized by Khrushchev in 1955. Despite a number of regulations today, there
are no substantial legal obstacles to a woman's obtaining an abortion if
she wants it, provided the length of her pregnancy does not exceed the
established limits. Abortion remains the leading means of birth control
used by Russian women and recently constituted up to 25 percent of all
maternal mortality cases (Fong 1993). According to some sources the
number of legal abortions compared to births in the early 1990s was
approximately 10 to 13 (*The Women's Dialogue,* #8, 1993). A prominent
sociological journal (*Sotsiologitcheski Zhurnal,* #1, 1994) reports a much
higher ratio: 206 abortions per 100 births. *Argumenty i Facty* reports that
3 million Russian women have an abortion every year (#9, February
1996, 12).[18] Other sources indicate that every tenth woman in Russia has
at least one abortion yearly. In Moscow alone in 1992, there were 80 abortions per 1,000 women. This ratio does not include data from private clin-
ics (Zhuravlev, et al. 1996, 60). In Moscow there were 4,000 abortions
performed on girls who were 15 years of age and younger during one year
(*The Women's Dialogue,* #8, 1993).

Politicians generally stay clear of this issue in their speeches and
interviews. According to our own analysis of all the broadcast statements
major presidential candidates made in the 1996 campaign, not one raised
the issue of abortion in a campaign speech or interview. The topic is not
discussed in the media, partly because the people are either disinterested
or generally supportive of women's right to choose. Public condemnation
of abortions is often considered a sign of totalitarian violation of women's
rights. In addition, there are no strong and organized pro-life movements
in contemporary Russia.

As the data suggest, among women there is a widespread acceptance
of typical gender-based divisions of roles. The Center for Gender Problems reports that stereotypically, men are assumed to be occupied with
such concerns as the fight for power, money, and other resources; women
raise children, placate their husbands, support them, tend toward compromise, and wisely forgive their husbands for their weaknesses and sins
(Zdravomyslova 1998).

Women in Russia, as elsewhere, ordinarily accept the role into which they have been socialized. Thus young girls are told that they must sacrifice their interests to others. One young woman in a study done by the Center for Gender Problems recalls that adult family members repeatedly told her when she was a child that she had no alternative except to travel the sacrificial route: "What could be done? You have to be patient. To be a victim is normal and natural for a woman, you don't have to be angry about this." Another respondent somewhat ambivalently notes a similar theme: "My personal story is a story of a woman who must have helped her classmates, who must have served her husband, the elderly, the children—everybody at the same time. I should have forgotten about my own interests in order to help the more skillful and decent creatures (i.e., men) get all their benefits, help them be creative, make money and make decisions" (Khodyreva 1993).

The acceptance of most Russian women of their culturally assigned roles is but a manifestation of human beings' common need to maintain their positions as valued members of the communities upon which they depend for emotional and economic support. An open acceptance of a status of inferiority, however, is apt to be painful. To minimize that pain a variety of psychological maneuvers often are employed: denial, the exercise of power within the domain permitted, criticism of those who choose different paths, and the assertion of compensatory virtues. Thus in Russia suffering is not only seen as a natural consequence of being female, it is also seen as a manifestation of a unique characteristic of "soulfulness" (*dukhovnost*). American women provide convenient images for comparison. Almost 80 percent of the Russian women interviewed in a study (Jansen & Shiraev forthcoming) suggested that they have little in common with American women.[19] American women were viewed as too independent and therefore as having men's characteristics. The Russian women are considered "sensitive" and "touchy" while their American counterparts are seen to be "business-oriented," and "masculine."

Within the family, women in Russia often exert influence over matters such as family budgets and vacations. Some of them also find ways of using sex as a form of compensatory power. In the in-depth interviews mentioned earlier, one-third of the women surveyed saw the "female spell" (*zhenskie chary*) as essential to negotiating male-female relationships in the workplace and in the community at large. One of the respondents characterized this sexual bartering as follows: "If I need you for whatever practical reason, I will try to be close to you." Other women noted that their very dependency on men had its advantages. One of them explained the phenomenon this way: "Woman's destiny is to be dependent on men. In exchange for my sex, I get some perks, benefits, new opportunities, anything that men give me in exchange." Given this zeitgeist, sexual assault can easily be minimized and trivialized in terms of its impact on the victim. Such psychological maneuvers serve to reinforce the self-deprecatory perceptions as if they were the natural order of society (Jansen & Shiraev forthcoming).

The relationships between men and women described in the foregoing raise questions about the commonly held view in Russia about the "feminine nature" of the entire Russian people, men as well as women. The widely quoted philosopher Nikolai Berdyaev, for example, claims that the feminine part of the Russian soul is evident in the willingness of men as well as women to submit to God's will and abstain from violent action (1989, 80–93). Alexander Shatalov, a contemporary poet and journalist, employs a similar theme when he notes that Russian men, brutish in appearance but tender within, are complemented by fragile but strong-willed Russian women (Shatalov 1995).

Democracy was supposed to bring hope and inspiration to people. While it did so to some men, it did so too few women. Many women seem to be accepting as "natural" their roles of inequality, thus sheltering themselves inside the walls of traditionalism. Proclamations about the "true" and substantially different natures of men and women can obviate the need to address one's predicaments. In light of the overwhelming political and economic difficulties women face today, their reaffirmation of traditional gender roles is as understandable as it is tragic.

NOTES

1. The history of Western civilization documents only a few cases of women being in power and exercising that power successfully. Well-known examples are Elizabeth II and Katherine the Great, two legendary czarinas who ruled Russia in the eighteenth century.
2. When some liberals raised the question of women's right to be elected, this idea was adamantly opposed by an overwhelming majority of the elected deputies (*Moskovskie Vedomosti,* 7 October 1903, 1).
3. Three Soviet constitutions—1918, 1936, and the "Brezhnev" constitution of 1977—guaranteed equality for women.
4. Russian and Soviet cultural life was and still is heavily dominated by men. As Richard Stites notes (1992), of the people who have had a significant impact on Russian culture since 1900, 20 percent were females. Of the

names mentioned in *Who's Who in Russia Today,* a biographical directory of more than 2000 top government officials and political leaders, 10 percent are women (Saur 1994, 1996).

5. In former European communist countries, if a woman occupied a high post within the ruling party, there was a high likelihood that she was in charge of culture, education, or health care (Skjele 1991).

6. Worldwide, women perform nearly two-thirds of the work hours and get only 10 percent of the world's income and own less than one one-hundredth of the world's property. Even in Western countries women are paid less than 75 percent of men's income (*Women, Work, and Health: Stress and Opportunities.* 1991, 257).

7. When the Russian media first reported the allegations about President Clinton's sexual behavior, the Russian popular daily newspaper *Komsomolskaya Pravda,* collected 5,440 letters from Russian citizens telling him what they thought about those allegations. More than 90 percent of the letters suggested that Clinton should not pay attention to the "rubbish," keep doing what he is doing, and stay at his post (Transcript *CNN TODAY,* 25 February 1998).

8. Yet women have considerable influence over family decisions. Women are often responsible for such important decisions as the family budget, vacationing, and purchasing valuable items. In one survey conducted in the 1980s, in eight out of ten St. Petersburg families, wives had a crucial voice in planning the finances (Shiraev 1983).

9. Perhaps due to this cultural perception of gender roles, both men and women in Russia are strongly opposed to homosexuality. In 1989, for example, 31 percent of Russians believed that homosexuals should be executed, and 32 percent said gays and lesbians should be isolated. Only 12 percent suggested that "sexual minorities" should be left alone. The attitudes hadn't changed significantly by 1994. Almost 23 percent of Russians said homosexuals should be killed, 24 percent said they should be isolated, and only 29 percent said they have to be left alone (*The New York Times,* 8 July, 1995). This relatively strong antigay mood was partly based on law existing prior to 1993, which treated homosexuality as a crime. But even after the parliament repealed the Stalin-era law, millions of people remain hostile and prejudiced toward homosexuality. Many gays and lesbians complain about open discrimination, reporting acts of vandalism, job discrimination, and physical violence against them. *The Guardian* (24 June 1995) reported that the renowned Russian human rights activist Sergei Kovalev, who received world recognition for his efforts to stop the Chechen war, repeatedly refused to meet the gay and lesbian activists.

10. Life expectancy for men is 58 years (the shortest life span in the industrial world), a fall from the 62.5–year level in 1980 and the 64–year level in 1989 (*Argumenty I Facty,* #32 August, #18 April, 1997; see also Zhuravlev et al.,

1996, 63). The gap between men and women is considerably wider than the world average. The high smoking and alcohol consumption rates among men contribute to the problem. Men may suffer disproportionate stress, suggests gender specialist O. Zdravomuslova (1998), because more is expected of them in terms of social accomplishment.

At the same time, the suicide rate in Russia increased 67 percent from 1990 to 1994. Despite a minor decline of suicides to 58,000 in 1996, according to the State Committee on Statistics, the level remained abnormally high. Russia's suicide rate is triple that of the United States (*Chicago Tribune,* 16 March 1998).

11. Support for women in political roles in the United States remained low throughout the decades prior to the 1970s. For example, only 36 percent of Americans believed that there should be more women in politics. Less than a third of Americans in the 1930s and 1940s favored the appointment of a woman to the cabinet. Even in the late 1960s, only half of Americans supported the idea of a woman candidate for the presidency (Erskine 1971). The situation in the United States has changed dramatically since the beginning of the 1970s. A 1984 Gallup poll found that nearly nine out of ten Americans would vote for a woman mayoral, gubernatorial, or congressional candidate (Gallup, 1985).

12. Despite the fact that Russian political conservatism is quite different from American and Western European models, many elements in those ideologies remain similar. Among them are the importance of moral and religious values, tough attitudes on crime, support of the death penalty, attitudes on self-support, negative attitudes toward gays, and strong emphasis on the family.

13. Moreover, a third of respondents clearly expressed the wish to quit working altogether and become housewives, and only 6 percent of women said they wanted to make a career even if this meant they had to give up the interests of the family.

14. Age also could be a contributing factor to women's conservatism. Compared to men, more women agreed with the statement "democracy does more harm than good": The gap between males and females is within the 6 to 12 point range, with 17 percent of women younger than 29 and 32 percent of women 60 and older being in agreement with this statement (Wyman 1997, 218). The November 11, 1995, issue of *Izvestia* outlined some demographics of the main parties, including the Communist Party of Russia. In a sarcastic way, this organization was called a party of "retired women," as this party draws 55 percent of its support from pensioners. The majority of them are women because the current life expectancy of Russian males is significantly lower than that of females.

15. In general, support for private property declines with age, with men being more supportive in all age categories. Those who least advocate private

property in Russia are women and men over 60: 30 percent and 34 percent, respectively (Wyman 1997, 217–18).

16. Some opinion polls, however, do not support the suggestion about women's "traditionalism." Thus, women in the late 1980s and in 1990 expressed less confidence in the Communist Party (a traditional institute of power) than men did (Pichulin & Skokov 1990).

17. Traditionalism in thinking causes resistance to anything new. In November 1997, the New Social-Psychology Institute conducted a survey among 2,200 residents of central Russian cities. The study revealed that television viewers find advertisements for feminine hygiene products more disturbing than those for any other product. More than 60 percent of women respondents said they were bothered by the ads. Women explained their frustration that the topic was extremely private and sensitive, and therefore should have been banned from public viewing (*Moscow Times,* 31 March 1998).

18. To compare, Sweden has an abortion ratio of 30:100; Austria 17:100; and Holland 10:100.)

19. There are common cross-cultural perceptions of masculinity and femininity. The masculine person is expected to be independent, active, aggressive, rational, individualistic, and instrumental. The feminine person is expected to be passive, dependent, soft, emotional, oriented toward others, and expressive (Best & Williams 1997, 163–200).

Chapter 13

Pop Music as a Mirror of the Russian Transformation

Eric Shiraev and Sergei Danilov

In this chapter an analysis of changes in pop music is used to suggest some of the ramifications, both cultural and organizational, of the demise of governmental support and censorship of the popular arts. The authors have firsthand knowledge of the Soviet and Russian popular music industry. From the early 1980s to the early 1990s, we were part of the industry as producers and award-winning songwriters. We worked with many stars of Russian popular music. In this chapter, we occasionally refer to our own experiences and original interviews conducted in 1998.

We approach this topic from the perspective that popular culture was in many respects an adaptation to the transformational process in Russia. Two Russian performers, with different musical tastes, have expressed a similar view. In 1990, Yuri Antonov, one of the most successful Soviet pop singers and composers, suggested that Russian pop music perfectly reflected the state of anarchy in the Russian state (Antonov 1990). Seven years later, Pyotr Mamonov, an idol of the musical grotesque and shock, noted that the destiny of modern music is to express the chaos that rules in the society (Mamonov 1997). Indeed, music in Russia does seem to express for various people at various times their feelings about the ongoing social transformations. Music helps some people express a rebellion against the repression manifested in the old order. Some individuals, through music, reject the inhuman conditions of the new market system, and manifest a desire to escape from the turmoil of everyday life and even, perhaps, retain the good things of the past.

THE INITIAL PHASE

The musical tastes of the early perestroika period can be best understood as a reaction to politics of the old order. Before perestroika Soviet artists provided pleasant entertainment that did not disturb the political status quo. Rock music, with its anti-establishment themes, was subjected to severe restrictions and continuous threats of extermination. One of us, for example, who organized dozens of unofficial rock concerts in the beginning of 1980s, recalls that most of those events ended with the arrival of the police, detention of musicians and some spectators, and endless questioning by KGB officers. The other author almost fell victim because of his passion for rock music when he helped to organize a concert of the controversial punk group Strange Games (Stites 1992, 162) at Leningrad State University. As a result, he almost lost his professorship and was reprimanded by a local party official.

The government obtained its leverage, in part, because it provided the supports needed to perform in a technologically complex world. Without fine electronic equipment and instruments of decent quality, such as amplifiers, microphones, electric guitars, and sound systems, it was almost impossible to put together a show. The best equipment of the highest quality was made in the West and could be purchased only with hard currency. To secure the equipment they needed, most of the leading performing artists would spend countless hours in the offices of either local or central government officials responsible for culture. To record a song in a studio, the performers had to seek out contacts with the studio management, which was under the control of local or central radio and television headquarters (which, in turn, were under the direct control of the regional party office). One of the authors remembers that in the early 1980s he accompanied a popular singer, Edita Piekha, to the office of Pyotr Demichev, the Soviet culture minister and candidate Politburo member. After lengthy negotiations, the singer was granted a new set of German acoustic equipment for her concerts. And this was by no means an isolated case. Performers' status depended not only on their talent, but also on their acceptance by the ruling elites. Popular performers, such as Iosif Kobzon, Alla Pugacheva, Edita Piekha, and Sofia Rotary were all in this category of the "accepted."

With the elimination of censorship in the early years of perestroika the situation changed. Thousands of formerly banned rock groups and individual performing artists aired themes ranging from the condemnation of corruption to mockery of ideological dogmatism. Their works were embraced by the intelligentsia as expressions of social protest and as new ways of thinking. Rock bands and vocalists, such as Boris Grebenshchikov, Viktor Tsoy, and Yuri Shevchuk (Stites 1992, 193), began to sing about social injustice, the idiocy of the ruling elite, and freedom.

Audiences embraced these messages. Rock musicians performed to sellout crowds in ten-thousand-seat sports arenas. Newspapers were bombarded with letters from teenagers claiming that new rock idols, and not communist textbooks, teach real life and tell the truth about past and present (Shiraev & Bastrykin 1988). Rock singers began to give interviews to major media networks and newspapers in which they discussed politics and economics. Artists previously banned from the media began to appear in new and acclaimed television shows. One of these shows, *Vzglyad* (Outlook), was created at the behest of Alexander Yakovlev, a close adviser of Gorbachev. The show combined provocative political discussions with uncensored musical entertainment and quickly became extremely popular among viewers (Lysenko 1995).

As the rock idols prospered, their pop counterparts, with their politically correct and innocuous themes, languished. Artificially happy looking, most pop singers in the early days of the transformation found themselves at odds with their anxious and politically motivated audiences. With the appearance in Russia of relatively affordable VCRs, and access to video clips from Europe and America, millions of Russians were able to compare Western and Soviet popular music. They discovered that Western pop music was clearly more entertaining.

HOW POP SURVIVED

Some pop stars were able to persevere through the early phase of perestroika by adapting to the new situation. They departed from the stereotypes established by the Soviet state-run concert organizations. Short hair, suits, and bow ties for men, and long gowns for women were replaced by extravagant outfits, and sometimes no outfits at all. Such well-known artists as Valery Leontiev and Alla Pugacheva led the trend. Leontiev transformed himself into a Michael Jackson and Bruce Springsteen hybrid surrounded by female dancers wearing little more than combat boots and performing with a stage backdrop that cost tens of thousands of dollars (Daigle 1996). Alla Pugacheva, who has dominated Soviet and later Russian show business for almost three decades, also went through an astonishing metamorphosis. She boldly traded the official gown for a miniskirt outfit that eventually became just a jacket and pantyhose.

The transformation of the image was also evident in groups' new names. By the end of the 1980s all kinds of musical groups were adopting exotic, shocking, or deliberately meaningless names. Rock bands such as Automatic Satisfier (punk), Pop Mechanics (fusion avant-garde), and AVIA (Russian abbreviation for Anti-Vocal Instrumental Ensemble) exemplified this change. Pop singers later followed the trend, but in a less scandalous way. During the Soviet period they had appeared under names such as Friendship, Singing Hearts, and Happy-Go-Lucky Guys. New stage aliases clearly followed the Western style: Lada Dance, Kar-Men, Lika MC, Ivanushki International, and others.[1]

Perestroika marked the beginning of differentiation in pop music. New musical styles were borrowed directly from European and American groups. A wide range of disco, techno, reggae, rap, and other types of musical groups appeared during the 1980s. Many new bands, such as Forum, Zemlyane, Mirage, and August, were making crucial changes in style, sound, and visual effects on stage. What musicians ultimately adopted was a politics-free and "moderately" shocking entertainment.

NEW MUSIC BACKERS

Musical performers of the 1980s and '90s would also be influenced by the new kinds of sponsorship upon which they depended. During the Soviet period, musicians had looked to Moscow for support. "In Russia, Broadway, Tin Pan Alley, Motown, Nashville, and Hollywood were all in Moscow," Richard Stites (1992) noted. Popular performers (among them Alexander Morozov, Larisa Dolina, Alexander Serov, and Valeri Leontiev) found they had to move to Moscow in order to achieve success. Compared to performers in other cities, those in Moscow had better access to recording studios, television, and government officials. After perestroika, Moscow remained the center of the music business. One of the principal reasons for this situation was television. Even though the Central Television, which was the only Moscow-based Soviet network, has been broken up into several private companies, they remain the principal source of promotion of pop musicians. Unlike in the United States, where music is primarily played on major musical cable companies like MTV or The Nashville Network, Russian TV networks air a variety of talk shows with a substantial amount of musical clips. In virtually all occasions, performing artists pay to appear on television.[2]

Undoubtedly, an appearance on a major network is a significant event for any performer. However, obtaining nationwide popularity through TV appearances is only a first step that should be taken by a pop singer. The next step is to capitalize on this popularity. With the lack of a developed system for collection of royalties and enforcement of intellectual property rights, Russian pop performers depend almost entirely on profits they collect from concerts. But to organize a successful money-making tour across Russia, the performer needs substantial investments. During the Soviet era, the local government was responsible for employing artists, and advertising and organizing their concerts. Only a few popular performers managed to make their initial success without any help from the government. Some of them, like Mashina Vremeni and Zemliane, relied on the money they earned throughout several years of unofficial concerts. Others, like Alexander Morozov, obtained the initial capital through hefty royalties paid for their popular songs.

After the government system collapsed, musicians were left on their own. Seeking new sponsors, they found them, again, in Moscow. After Russia formally proclaimed its independence in 1991, Moscow quickly became the center of gravity with Russian money and power. Like banking and oil exports, show business soon became dominated by new Russian tycoons. According to insiders, the music market by the end of the 1990s was divided among a handful of Moscow magnates, including Sergey Lisovsky, who controls Russia's most powerful concert and advertising agencies, and Igor Krutoy, a songwriter who became an owner of the largest musical production company. Capitalist relationships replaced the old governmental support system of popular culture and pop music.[3]

MARKET-DRIVEN MUSIC

Under pressure from their new backers, performers had to attract large audiences. Scores of nice-looking, polished, and shining individuals began to appear on the made-in-Moscow assembly line of popular music. They perform almost-identical songs with identical beats and cliché lyrics. The "ompa-ompa" style melodies and repetitive, well-rhymed assertions (Daigle 1996) fill hours of airtime on the radio and TV. A song with the refrain "Russian vodka, you have destroyed me," arranged in disco-pop, with elements of Gypsy folk melody, became a hit almost overnight. A popular series of 24 audio tapes entitled "Soyuz" presents an endless parade of faceless bands and individuals singing almost-alike songs (Soyuz, Moscow, copyright 1998).

The most egregious of such bands in the 1990s is Na-Na, a group of four handsome male lip-syncers accompanied on stage by a couple of dozen semi-naked and dancing girls. This group was created by Bari Alibasov, a well-connected manager of Soviet-era popular music who has made no secret of his desire to make as much money as possible. The band's repetitive bubble-gum lyrics and thoughtless music became a recurring topic in Russian musical publications (See for example, *Argumenty i Facty*, #11, March 1998, 16). Another example is Ivanushki International, a creation of the popular producer Igor Matvienko, who doesn't hide the fact that two sins dominate Russian show business: "conceit and vanity" (Silunas 1997, 19). Borrowing some elements of their stage image from Russian fairly tales, Ivanushki International, three happy-looking scaramouches, reached their ultimate success by triumphantly appealing to their audience's regressions.

Not all of the performers agreed to sell themselves out to the new musical establishment. Their fate is both sad and illustrative, like the rise and fall of Igor Kornelyuk, one of the top popular artists in the 1980s. Unlike most pop performers in Russia, Kornelyuk received a formal musical education: he graduated from the St. Petersburg Conservatory. He had an unmatched passion for synthesizers and other new electronic keyboard instruments. His extraordinary melodic talent, coupled with the new sound and sophisticated orchestrations, quickly made him a very popular performer and assured his catapulting to the highest echelons of the musical elite. He was admired by the establishment for his beautiful melodies and the "acceptable" contents of his songs. In several years Kornelyuk became a household name. In 1989, his ten-concert series in the four-thousand-seat St. Petersburg's Oktiabrsky concert hall were sold out in a few hours.

At the beginning of the 1990s, Kornelyuk faced the dilemma of whether he should be an independent performer or accept financial sponsorship from the Moscow music magnates. By that time, the country's profitable concert halls and stadiums had become dependent on Moscow-based production companies that represented most of the popular artists. At the same time, the privatization of television and astronomical cost of video clips meant that an outsider had practically no means to ensure his or her appearance on a major TV show because so much money was needed to buy the airtime.[4]

Kornelyuk chose to be independent, and this decision immediately cut him off from the main commercial pipeline. Like Tom Jones and Donna Summer in the United States, Igor Kornelyuk in Russia is still remembered by many and receives occasional invitations to perform in fashionable nightclubs in Moscow and St. Petersburg. But his old glory days and unlimited success are long gone.

PRISON-STYLE MUSIC

Another genre of Russian pop music that crested in the 1990s had deep roots in prison-style inmate folklore (*blatnaya muzyka*). This kind of musical expression was not entirely new to Russian society. Even before the Bolshevik revolution and terror of Gulag, the Russians felt inexplicable sympathy toward prison inmates. One of the most popular Russian proverbs is: "Do not dare to think to escape from the beggar's bag and prison." Multitudes of old Russian folk songs described life in *katorga,* the prison-like labor camps in Siberia, where both notorious criminal and political prisoners were sent to work under unbearable conditions. Soviet culture has never recognized the existence of the inmate folklore, but the songs from or about the criminal world remained very popular among at least two generations of Russians. Some of the most popular bards, such as Vyssotsky and Galich, contributed to this genre between the 1960s and 1980s (Stites 1992, 157–58).

Alexander Rosenbaum was one the first Soviet "official" artists to understand the commercial potential of the songs attributed to the criminal world. He took the risk and released an uncensored audiocassette, which contained songs whose lyrical heroes were thieves, bandits, prostitutes, and other troubled individuals. The tape became an instant hit. In order to keep his job at a state concert organization, Rosenbaum had to lie that he wrote those songs for a theatrical play. When this trick did not work, he publicly admitted that the tape was a result of his error in judgment. He apologized and promised never to sing those songs again. Through the humiliation of apology, Rosenbaum was able to continue performing. But the more important strategic goal was achieved: He became popular across the country, not as a singer but rather as a bard who romanticized the criminal world.

Today, many performers employ a stage image and lyrics that associate them with the criminal world. A quick look at pictures on Russian CDs and tapes reveals countless broken noses, buzz cuts, tattoos, and other inmate attributes. The popular band Lyube (whose leader used to sing for a mainstream Soviet pop group) derived its name from one of the first countrywide-known gangs from the Moscow suburb Lyubertsy. In their songs, Lyube, like many other groups of this type, used prison slang and a wide variety of criminal topics. In an obvious attempt to boost his ratings, a rather mediocre singer, Fyodor Stolyarov, who had spent seven years in prison for insurance fraud, appeared on St. Petersburg television with the songs he had written in jail. One of the most popular albums released in 1997 was "The Fate of a Thief" by Ivan Kuchin, an "inmate" music hero.

CRIMINAL FEEDBACK

The criminalization of Russian private business (see chapter 7) has promptly metastasized into the newborn private show business. Criminal bosses gladly embraced the emerging musical industry. Wherever a new source of profit appeared in the new Russia, criminal business arrived on the scene and attempted to control the process (Dolgova & Diakova 1993). Though not as profitable as banking operations, gambling, or raw materials exports, popular music could generate substantial income. Typically, the revenue from the concerts is collected in cash. There are many illegal and easy ways to hide substantial amounts of money received from ticket sales. The lawlessness caused performing artists to seek reliable protection, which was readily offered by criminal groups. As a result, musical performers, like thousands of enterprises and ventures, found themselves almost entirely dependent on mobsters (Shlapentokh 1996; *Moscow News,* 1 October 1993).

Bribery, violence, and extortion became common characteristics of the music business. Methods of "stepping on the throat" employed by criminal investors are brutal and merciless. Several years ago the manager of a popular female band, Kombinatsiya, was killed because he reportedly refused to join a show-business conglomerate led by the famous Russian tycoon Sergey Lisovsky. Lisovsky later denied the allegations, but some show-business sources indicated that they would not be surprised if, in fact, Lisovsky was the man behind the murder. When the first concert tour of Demis Roussos, a Greek crooner widely popular in Russia in the 1970s, turned out to be a financial fiasco, the Russian producer of the singer's tour was forced to hide in a high-security clinic. One of the authors of this chapter learned that the dramatic escape was deemed necessary because of an unpaid debt of $60,000 to the mob. "It seems like everything, from the door of your home to the highest agencies and Kremlin offices, is under criminal roof," a popular Russian newspaper bitterly proclaimed (*Izvestia,* 18 October 1994). Producer and songwriter Vadim Tsyganov agrees: "Before we had the government, now we have both the Mafia and money controlling the industry"(Daigle 1996).

SHOCK BY POPULAR DEMAND

Popular demands influenced the image of the hero in Russian popular culture, and moved it toward general vulgarization and sexism. Shock messages permeated not only the pop stage and television, but also theater, exhibition halls, and even conservatory classrooms. Frontal nudity is commonplace on television. The television show *In Bed With . . .* features pop stars and celebrities of different ranks, including politicians, who share their sexual secrets with millions of viewers (*Aida* December 1997, 3). Major newspapers do not hesitate to publish articles about masturbation, pornography, sexual addictions, and perversions. The popular *Argumenty i Facty* weekly, winner of the best newspaper title awarded by the Union of Journalists in 1995, began one of its articles on condoms by asking: "Who is this lad leaking from his end?" Below appeared a picture of a man holding a poster "Rubber condom is for the people and serves to the people!" (*Argumenty i Facty,* #6, February 1996, 12). Alice in Wonderland was staged nude by body-art director Kirill Ganin in the popular Mir movie theater in Moscow. Pop artist Alexander Brener once inspired an act of public masturbation over the Moskva swimming pool, then defecated in front of a Van Gogh painting in the Pushkin Museum of Arts in Moscow (Vardenga 1996). The newspaper *Express Gazeta* (July 1998, #28, 24) announced a performance of a "nudist group" at the newspaper headquarters (a photo near the announcement showed a little girl and two adult men dancing together naked).

Pop singers did not wait too long to follow the trend. During a concert dedicated to International Women's Day in March 1998, the leader of the rock band Krematoriy (Crematorium) wished the female audience physical, platonic, and any other kind of love. He expressed hope that men will not "hit the dirt with their faces and other body members." These remarks were reviewed positively by the media. One reporter wrote, "[Crematorium] sang about sexual kitten in the sky, about bitches playing the fifes [a Russian allusion to oral sex], and about those who liked strawberry with ice; in short, they sang about women" (*Argumenty i Facty*, #11, March 1998, 16). The leader of another popular rock band, Chaif, said in an interview to a major weekly newspaper that the band wanted to have sex with the audience, and "as long as the gals saw that the singers were real men, everything would be fine" (*Argumenty i Facty*, #33, August 1997, 13).

Sexual confessions and various sexual innuendoes conveyed by performers became familiar to Russian audiences. During a televised Christmas Eve show (1994), singer Alexander Buinov sang to persuade his wife not to touch him and let him sleep because no sex is better than bad sex. Valery Leontiev, as well as many younger performers, appears on stage wearing only revealing tights. The pop singer Volkova, known to the Russian audience as Lada Dance, confessed in a newspaper interview that her dream was to be featured in *Playboy*. "When I am 60 I don't want to regret about the missed opportunity," she said (Volkova 1998). She finally fulfilled her dream by posing for a Russian edition of the magazine in 1998. The *Playboy* experience was shared by other famous female singers, such as Irina Saltykova, Natasha Korolyova, and the Blestyashchie (Shining) quartet.

REMEMBRANCE OF THINGS PAST

Recently, as Russians have felt the full force of their political and economic hardships, they have tended to glorify aspects of the past. This trend is evident in the recent interest of Russian audiences in old music. Soviet musical hits of ten, twenty, or more years ago returned to radio and television and easily became profitable items. Several years ago one of the principal Russian TV networks produced *Old Songs about the Essential* a musical show staged as an old Soviet movie and packed with popular performers singing the songs of the fifties. In spite of the obvious lack of any dramatic talent in most of the singers, the show was an enormous success and, due to popular demand, was aired again several times. Inspired by their success of the first try, the producers created *Old Songs 2* and *Old Songs 3*. The main idea of the spectacle remained the same:

Some characters from popular Soviet movies (played by popular singers) stage several scenes from those movies and sing the old songs attributed to that time period. The last show was produced for New Year's Eve 1997 and was based upon an early 1970s movie about the adventures of Ivan the Terrible in Soviet Russia. Accordingly, the songs performed in the show were the hits of the seventies, but the audience expressed great interest and the program became a champion of the widespread nostalgia for the symbols of the past.[5]

An interesting episode is indicative of this nostalgia. In May 1998, RTV, one of the most popular TV networks in Russia, broadcast a live show called *Musical Ring*. The show presented two competing composers and pop singers, Igor Kornelyuk and Victor Chaika. After every round of a three-round show, each singer would get votes from television viewers across Russia by telephone. During the show, when both performers introduced their most recent songs, Kornelyuk trailed his challenger by a wide margin. In the third round, evidently losing, Kornelyuk barraged the audience with an avalanche of the hits that made him famous in the 1980s. As a consequence, he won. As one of his producers mentioned in an interview, Kornelyuk prevailed because he sang what the millions of audience members wanted to hear: their favorite songs from old and pre-sumably better times.

THE SONG REMAINS THE SAME

The broad picture of pop music in Russia resembles the overall political and social landscape. As in politics, many of the new people who emerged on the wave of perestroika have vanished or just found better things to do. Pyotr Mamonov, a shock-rock singer and actor, moved with his family into a remote and secluded country home. Andrei Makarevich, a rock idol of the 1970s and 1980s, became a host of a popular TV cook-ing show. Boris Grebenshchikov, a "living legend of Russian rock," com-poses lyrical songs for movies. Nikolai Fomenko, an actor and member of a very popular band in the 1980s and 1990s, the Secret Beat Quartet, con-ducts a TV talk show.

At the same time, a lot of old performers have survived the cata-clysms of the transitional period and have come forth even more powerful than before. Like the "Old Guard" in the political world, many former Soviet stars have been able to adapt to the new market conditions, remain-ing among the handful of performers who enjoy mass recognition, wealth, and popularity. Alla Pugacheva, the most famous Soviet pop star was named by the press "woman of the year" in 1997. Her success in the polls matched the popularity of Boris Nemtsov, former first deputy prime minister (Levada 1998). Not surprisingly, Pugacheva was considering running for the State Duma (Shulyakovskaya 1998). Pugacheva is not the first pop performer to look for a public office. Crooner Iosif Kobzon, who first appeared on the Soviet stage in the mid-1960s, was a member of the Duma and earned his reputation as a wealthy power broker between the criminal world and government establishment.

Other stars of the past preferred to stay away from politics, but their popularity has not diminished. Singer and songwriter Alexander Rosenbaum celebrated his fiftieth anniversary by performing a special show in one of the most prestigious concert halls in Moscow. The show was attended by the quintessence of the Russian elite: artists, financial tycoons, and politicians. Ilya Reznik, one of the best known Soviet poets and songwriters, who enjoyed almost 30 years of fame, marked his sixtieth birthday with a performance in the Rossiya concert hall in front of the Kremlin. The top-ranked *Ogonek* magazine has featured a front-page story about Reznik. Edita Piekha, a singer who has had perhaps the longest successful career in the history of Soviet and Russian pop music, celebrated her sixtieth birthday by giving a free concert on the central square in St. Petersburg with thousands of people in attendance. Valery Leontiev, who was not as open as others about his age (he was over 50 in 1999), kept giving sold-out concerts in practically every Russian city. He continues to fill the Red Square in Moscow with thousands of fans during his open-air shows.

When a star of yesterday's Russian popular music, Pyotr Mamonov, was asked about why he lost his popularity and decided to live in seclusion, he replied: "I do not want to come back and sing my old songs. I want to be free. I do not want to be for sale" (Mamonov 1997, 108). His remark proves, perhaps, that success in Russian popular music today comes to those who are for sale: those artists who are able to function in a new capitalist system of supply and demand while trying to satisfy many of the audience's tastes inherited from yesterday.

NOTES

1. Before perestroika a trend of changing stage names also existed. For example, some Jewish performing artists would change their real names for more

appropriate Russian pseudonyms to accommodate the covert anti-Semitism of local officials. Thus, a guitarist named Schneider became Dobrov when he was promoted by music officials to his band leader position. Jazz critic Feiertag changed his name to Popov. Alexander Rosenbaum for a long time was known as Ayarov. Comedian Eugene Alper, a winner of the all-union competition in 1988, announced his decision to change his name to Alperin (he emigrated from the country in 1989).

2. Oleg Kvasha, a popular composer and performer, said in a telephone interview on October 5, 1998 that one should pay from $3,000 to $10,000 for a single broadcast of his or her musical clip on television.

3. For example, in 1996, prime-time advertising on ORT Russian public television ranged from $17,500 to $30,500 a minute based on the exact time reserved. Daytime rates ranged from $3,500 to $16,500 per minute. Rates for RTR ran from $8,500 to $25,000 a minute in prime time, and from $1,100 to $9,000 during the day. The channel NTV put the price tag between $14,500 and $23,000 for prime-time commercials (*The Moscow Times,* 27 September 1996).

4. Nostalgic feelings may be reinforced by the loss of many famous and beloved musicians and singers who were just barely in their thirties when they passed away. Viktor Reznikov, a stylish songwriter and performer, died after a road accident. Viktor Tsoy, a musical hero of millions, was killed in a car accident. Singer Igor Talkov, a sincere fighter for truth, was fatally shot by a mobster. Sergei Kuryokhin, a talented musical innovator, died of terminal illness. Scores of talented performers have emigrated.

Chapter 14

The Post-Soviet Orientations toward the United States and the West

Eric Shiraev

Russia's victory in World War II, possession of nuclear power, and successes in space exploration and sports gave the Soviet people the feeling that they were strong and unique. In addition, Marxism reinforced the old belief that Russia had a special moral destiny (Smith 1989, 65; Zubok & Pleshakov 1996, 4). Dividing the world into two huge antagonistic groups, communism provided clarity as to the nature of Russia's friends and enemies. Some political psychologists suggest that the battle against the external enemies helped hold the nation together (Volkan 1988, Koenigsberg 1992). In the same way, Leonid Abalkin argues that the collapse of the Soviet Union was partly caused by the disappearance of the external enemy (1995, 41).

With the dissolution of the Soviet Union, many Russians have gone through a soul search often seasoned by frustration, nostalgic sentiment, and pragmatic calculations. In place of communist ideology, Russians were left with an unstructured set of attitudes. In 1995, 81 percent of the population wanted to see Russia as a great power once again (*Izvestia,* 13 October 1995, 6). Some have embraced a Russia-centered isolationism and feelings that the Russian people have sacrificed too much for the benefit of other countries. As Alexander Solzhenitsyn noted in a telephone press conference, "we create national advantages for small nations at the expense of the Russian nation" (Solzhenitsyn 1996). In one of his early speeches, Boris Yeltsin also expressed this point of view: "Russia feeds everybody, Russia sacrificed for everybody. Russia has always been giving. Let us improve the lives of our own people first, because the situation cannot be tolerated any longer" (Yeltsin 1990).

For most Russians, the loss of superpower status has been accompanied by the growing feeling of inferiority toward Western countries (Gorbachev 1994, Urban 1994). The collapse of the Soviet Union was commonly perceived not as a new beginning, but as a bitter failure. People were increasingly inclined to think that all treaties completed or negotiated in the 1990s were disadvantageous to Russia (Surikov 1997). In an analytical article on foreign policy published by *Izvestia* in 1994 (Kondrashov 5 March 1994) a renowned journalist angrily protested against the American illusions of superiority over Russia, and the false American belief that Russia would disregard its national interests in order to serve those of the United States. The leaders of the nationalist and communist blocs have attributed these negative developments to an external enemy. Thus the nationalist leader Vladimir Zhirinovsky has stated on television, "We had democracy for the communists, nowadays we have democracy for the fifth column, for the Zionists, and for the CIA" (Zhirinovsky, 14 June 1996). The communist leader Gennady Zyuganov was absolutely certain that a deep animosity toward the United States resides in the Russian soul (Zyuganov, 15 June 1996). General Lebed predicted the inevitable victory of Russian culture against American "chewing gum" (Lebed, 13 May 1996). Great-power nostalgia has begun to penetrate newspaper publications in the early 1990s, especially pro-communist and nationalist newspapers (Fadeyev, 11 August 1993).

Yet the majority of Russians have not paid much attention to foreign-policy issues in their everyday lives (Mikulski 1995). Other problems have preoccupied them: the breakup of the Soviet Union in 1991, the parliamentary coup of 1993, the war in Chechnya, the parliamentary elections of 1993 and 1995, the presidential elections of 1996, the frequent political assassinations, and the unpaid salaries. "The average Russian thinks about his salary and prices. He's not in a position to think about foreign policy," said Viktor Kremenyuk, deputy director of Moscow's USA/Canada Institute (*The Moscow Times,* 8 February 1997). Indeed, according to *Izvestia* (13 October 1995, 6), 72 percent of citizens attach priority to domestic problems, and only 18 percent to prioritize foreign ones. The neighboring former Soviet republic of Ukraine, for example, was viewed as more important than the United States. Only Zyuganov's electorate shows a stable pattern of rejection of American movies, music, and lifestyle, and Western democratic principles in general.[1]

Russian foreign-policy elites, however, do debate foreign-policy issues; in this chapter we focus on their point of view. Today, as in the past, there are three primary orientations toward the West. First, there is the nationalist-chauvinist platform, which is articulated by a wide and diverse mixture of politicians, policy experts, and opinion leaders who hold negative opinions of the West and the United States in particular. Vladimir Zhirinovsky has been the leading representative of this perspective in the mid-1990s. Second, the earlier Yeltsin government contained some members who sought partnership with the West on some fundamental economic and foreign policy-issues, including security in Europe and a reduction in U.S. and Russian nuclear forces. "The West is a natural ally of Russia," stated Russia's foreign minister in 1992 (*Izvestia,* 16 January 1992). The major nonpartisan press in the early 1990s expressed predominantly pro-Western and pro-American attitudes. For example, between 1990 and 1993, *Argumenty i Facty* published 54 articles about the United States. Thirty-two (59 percent) contained clearly sympathetic and positive information about U.S. policies, business, and domestic situations. Seventeen (32 percent) were gossip stories and reports about American celebrities. Only five stories (9 percent) were critical, covering some social problems in the United States. A third, Eurasian perspective reflects Russia's geopolitical position straddling the two continents and its historical role as a great power. Most frequently, this outlook was discussed among academic and intellectual elites (Rubtsov 1995, Kara-Murza et al. 1995, Pechurkov 1995, Gozman & Etkind 1992, Peresvet 1992). Some politicians, like Ruslan Khasbulatov, also expressed this point of view (*The Economist,* 15–19 June 1996, 19–21).

Running throughout these orientations, to a greater or lesser degree, is a "typical" ambivalence toward the West (Carr 1958, 10). Traditionally Russians have singled out one Western country to either reject or employ as a model for imitation (Shlapentokh 1988, 158). At different times the Netherlands, Germany, England, and France filled such roles. Since

World War II this role was assigned to the United States. Admired and envied as a model, the United States is also feared and mistrusted as a potential enemy (Dobson 1996; see also Kliamkin & Lapkin 1996).

Recent American policies have contributed to this ambivalence. The tough stance the United States took in its negotiations with Mikhail Gorbachev over the Intermediate Nuclear Forces (INF) treaty and the future of Germany led many in the Soviet military and diplomatic establishment to feel that the United States had exacted too many concessions from the USSR in the final days of the Cold War. The decision to expand NATO and the American intervention in Bosnia in 1994, created even greater concerns. The result has been a substantial decline in the number of "pro-Western" experts and specialists (Survey undertaken by Germany's Ebert Foundation, May 2, 1997, *Swiss Review of World Affairs*). The *Derzhavniki*—supporters of the "great state"—began to increasingly replace *Zapadniki*—pro-Westerners (Umbach 1996, 477). The overall picture of the Russian political situation has become not one of a liberal administration under pressure from nationalists, but one of a nationalist government struggling to fend off other, more decisive, nationalists (*The Guardian*, 21 October 1995).

The Russian military was particularly unhappy about the appearance of the United States and its allies near Russia's borders (*Novaya Yezhednevnaya Gazeta*, 15 January 1994, 2). Some media reported in early 1997 that Russia's top generals had a secret petition in which they insisted on re-aiming some Russian nuclear missiles on Warsaw, Prague, and Budapest, as a symbol of their dislike of the U.S.-sponsored NATO expansion.

The communists and nationalists have been particularly vehement in their opposition to U.S. foreign policies (MacWilliam 1997). In 1992, *Pravda* compared the sanctions against Yugoslavia to the U.S. blockade of Cuba in the 1960s, calling both these policies "imperialistic" (20 November 1992; see also *Pravda*, 2 June 1992, 3; *Pravda*, 16 September 1992, 3; *Pravda*, 19 November 1992, 7). The American intent in Bosnia was to defeat Russia (*Pravda*, 3 March 1994, 3). In an article published by *Izvestia* in 1994, the American government was accused of disregarding Russia's national interests in Bosnia (Kondrashov 5 March). The author, in a typical post-Soviet "explicit" journalistic style, complained of the public degradation of Russia that had been "spreading its legs" for the Americans. Moreover, *Pravda*, in its issue of June 28–July 5, 1995, presented statistical figures supporting its view of a military threat coming from the United States. During the 1996 election campaign, Zhirinovsky repeatedly suggested the United States' main objective is to destroy Russia (Zhirinovsky, 10 June 1996).

These same groups also argue that American policies have been aided and abetted by the passive role of the Yeltsin government. As early as June 1992, newspapers complained of the absence of an "independent foreign policy" for Russia (Bogomolov 1992). Others charged that the Russian government was guilty of "100 percent subordination" to the interests of the United States and the NATO bloc (Kondrashov 1994). Russia's diplomacy was claimed to be "led around by the nose" and said to have "fewer and fewer chances to defend its independence and their chosen political course" (Bolshakov, 2 March 1994).

The U.S. decision to expand NATO even alarmed moderates. Mikhail Gorbachev accused NATO of expanding far beyond its historical borders (1994). Yegor Gaidar, former acting prime minister and the leader of Russia's Choice Party, repeatedly criticized NATO's expansion decision. Grigory Yavlinsky's faction issued a statement that the NATO bloc's involvement in regional conflicts in Europe went "beyond the bounds" of its responsibility, that it could lead to the disruption of the military-political equilibrium in Europe, and that it is contrary to Russia's national and state interests (Mikheev 1994). General Lebed commented sarcastically, "America and its western allies continue to think that they can push Russia aside and keep it away from competition." (Lebed, 13 May 1996). Even the centrist newspaper *Negavisimaya Gazeta* (15 January1997) suggested that the expansion of NATO contributed to the development of mistrust and hostility between Moscow and Washington. The West and NATO were charged with creating a "cordon sanitaire" around Russia's borders (Volkov 1994). The United Nations was repeatedly accused of being a "tool for NATO's policies," which, in turn, gets its inspiration directly from across the ocean (Fadeyev 1994). By 1995, it was rare to encounter a politician who could risk calling himself or herself a "Westerner."

The U.S. involvement in the Balkans has also been a matter of concern and frustration (Shiraev & Terrio forthcoming). At first the theme was sounded in such radical opposition newspapers as *Pravda* (Volobuev & Tyagumenko 1992). The Bosnian conflict was considered to be a major rehearsal of the West for future battles with Russia. "Remember, if they destroy the Serbs today, they will move against us tomorrow" (*Pravda* 21 January 1993, 5). The air strikes against the Serbian positions in Bosnia were labeled "the laws of the jungle" (Fadeev 11 August 1993). In 1995, former Gorbachev top advisor Alexander Tsypko saw the U.S. intervention as having a clear anti-Russian motivation—the establishment of a "better relationship with the Muslim world, Turkey in particular" (*Ogonyok*, #25, June 1995, 73). Others accused the U.S. of conducting an anti-Serbian policy under the UN flag, with minimal cost in dollars and possible American casualties (Kondrashov 20 April 1994; see also Peresvet 1995). The Russian press was also very critical of the 1994 cancellation—allegedly under pressure from the United States—of Moscow's ill-fated cryogenic rocket sale to India (the deal personally guaranteed by Yeltsin to the Indian government).

Since the early 1990s, some members of the Russian foreign-policy elite complained that Russia was being treated as junior partner in the world political system. Yevgeny Ambartsumov, chairman of the Joint Committee on International Affairs and Foreign Economic Relations of the Russian parliament, stated that it would hardly seem obligatory that Russia "duplicate the U.S. position in all respects" (*Izvestia*, June 29 1992, 3). Andrianik Migranyan (1992), director of the CIS Center of the Russian Academy of Sciences' Institute of International, Economic and Political Research, suggested that one cannot fail to see that Russia's national and state interests cannot constantly coincide with the interests of the west, let alone of the United States.

The Yeltsin government has not been averse to using these anti-American feelings in its dealings with the United States. Quite common were warnings that the Russian "reds" and "browns" were eagerly waiting in the wings to destroy democracy (Arbatov 1992). Speaking in Prague against NATO expansion, former acting prime minister Gaidar said that the alliance expansion would play into the hands of Russian hard-liners and would help the Russian radical nationalists. It would be much safer for the democrats in power in Russia without NATO, he argued, than with an enlarging NATO and the fascists in power in Moscow (*Reuters World Service,* 16 January 1995). Political scientist and deputy to the Duma Yevgeny Ambartsumov (1994) implied that Washington's actions were certainly compromising Russia's cooperation with the West and providing grist for the mill of the nationalists and radicals in opposition to the Kremlin.

Gradually, the Yeltsin Administration began to adopt some elements of the opposition's rhetoric regarding foreign policy. Beginning in December 1993, Yeltsin and the Foreign Ministry could no longer ignore the opinion of the opponents, especially the new national legislature, the Duma, with its strong anti-American and anti-Western platform supported by most of the Communist, Liberal-Democratic Party of Russia, and scores of unaffiliated members. Since 1993, the differences between the arguments of the "pro-American" government and "anti-American" opposition became increasingly blurred. "For some time now, it has been difficult to determine the origin of various statements made in the field of foreign policy—Kozyrev or Zyuganov," commented *Izvestia* in March of 1994 (Yushin 1994). For example, President Yeltsin openly singled out and criticized America for its foreign policy course and accused European countries of allowing their actions to be dictated by the United States (Press Conference with Boris Yeltsin. Official Kremlin International News Broadcast, 8 September 1995). In an interview to French television, Yeltsin also said he was reluctant to place Russian troops under NATO command in Bosnia (MacKenzie 1995).

The harsh criticism of the Kremlin's foreign policies has induced members of the Yeltsin government and its allies in the media to show that they would not simply dance to U.S. tunes (see interview with Viktor Kremenyuk 1994). Russian intervention in Chechnya revealed Moscow's increasing willingness to flex its muscles. *Krasnaya Zvezda,* a daily publication of the Defense Ministry, demanded that Russia should be accepted as a great power and an equal partner in deeds as well as words (Sidorov 1994). In February 1994, Foreign Minister Kozyrev declared that Russia "has no intention of listening to lectures on the rules of good behavior from Western politicians" (Abarinov 1994).[2] Yeltsin's special envoy in the former Yugoslavia, Vitaly Churkin, warned that NATO's policy against the Bosnian Serbs could have negative consequences for Russian public opinion and other dangerous repercussions in Russia (*Chicago Tribune* 11 February 1994).

Yeltsin's opponents argued that the West was consciously trying to turn Russia backwards (Pushkov 1994). The U.S. pressures for Russian adoption of a free market have also created resentment in many Russians (Kremenyuk 1994). As early as 1992, the specialist on U.S.-Russian relations, Georgy Arbatov, noted that Russia's massive economic failure, after all, discredited the United States because of its inaction. In addition to the negative fallout from the financial crisis, anti-American and anti-Western statements in the 1990s were on the rise. In 1998, a top Russian economic planner said that the International Monetary Fund was partly responsible for Russia's financial collapse in that year (Powell & Matthews 1998, 52). For financial reasons, the Russians announced they would no longer be a key partner with the United States in NASA's international space station program. The Russians were also unhappy with the Clinton administration's policy of trying to get U.S. oil companies to build a major pipeline—through Azerbaijan and Georgia—to Turkey, a NATO ally. The Russians viewed this as a manifestation of an anti-Russian policy. Bill Richardson, U.S. secretary of energy, said, "We have difficulty convincing the Russians that we're not trying to edge them out. They see the area as their sovereign virgin territory" (Goldberg 1998). There is no surprise that NATO's campaign in Yugoslavi in 1999 a caused serious problems in U.S.-Russian relations.

The institutionalization of Russian anti-Americanism, however, should not be regarded as final and irreversible. Most Russian critics of the United States and its policies understand possible negative consequences of an open conflict between nuclear powers. A vast majority of educated Russians are not prepared to sacrifice their political liberties for the sake of xenophobic and isolationist ideas. With some notable exceptions, most opinion leaders admit that the main blame for what happened to Russian economy and society should be laid at the door of Soviet and post-Soviet rulers. However, anti-American sentiments in Russia will continue to have an impact on the policy climate and, if the 1990s' trends persist, will continue to grow. Historically, this development should not be regarded as a simple legacy of Soviet communist experience and cold war confrontation, but rather as a new complex phenomenon with its own origins and dynamics.

Freud argued in his very prescient *Civilization and its Discontents* (1930) that leaders can unify a people by turning their frustration and rage outwards. Certainly Hitler did this with a profoundly demoralized German people in the 1930s. Most Russians do not want to return to a situation in which their lives are controlled as they were under the Soviet regime. The Russian people as a whole do not dislike the United States. But if the present political and economic paralysis continues in Russia without any hope for change, even a long-suffering people could seek out an authoritarian leader, particularly if he seems to have a realistic program for a more prosperous and orderly future. The danger for the United States is that such a leader could hope to unify the people and provide them with an answer to their problems by directly playing upon their ambivalence toward the West. The direction of all anger upon an external enemy could be a useful tool for restoring pride and unity to the Russian people. A people who are hopeless and rudderless, as Harry Stack Sullivan's 1953 work on demoralization indirectly suggests, are inclined to search out a spectrum of possible solutions to the impasse in which they find themselves.

NOTES

1. A survey conducted by Vox Populi service in August and September of 1995 showed that altogether 52 percent of Russians view the influence of Western culture as negative (*Izvestia,* 13 October 1995, 6).

2. As early as January 1994, the largest faction of the Duma threatened that if the Ministry of Foreign Affairs failed to take a clearly "pro-Russian" position within one week, the LDPR would demand the foreign minister's resignation (Rodin 1994). The faction leader Vladimir Zhirinovsky recounted how he had told Prime Minister Chernomyrdin that he would not rest so long as Kozyrev is a minister: "My mission is to remove him from the Russian government," he said in February (Baturin & Gryzunov 1994). Widely considered "soft" (Kremenyuk 1994), Kozyrev couldn't overrun the growing political opposition because of his allegedly pro-Western and pro-American position (Mlechin 1994).

Part IV

Conclusions

Chapter 15

Russia's Open-Ended Transition: toward an Integrated Research Model

Andrei Melville

The Soviet/Russian transformation between 1985 and 1998 was an important and in some respects a unique event in human history. As a turning point in the flow of political and cultural development in an important part of the world, it deserves the kind of endeavor undertaken in this volume. To even attempt to understand such a complex process, a holistic approach employing concepts from several different disciplines is almost a necessity. The contributions of each author to what may be a partial understanding of this process is provided in the introduction to this volume and will not be repeated here. Rather, I shall deal in this chapter with some of the broader methodological issues related to building a more inclusive, integrated theory of transformational politics.

Two distinct approaches in comparative politics and area studies have emerged during recent years, each offering a different model for understanding what happened in Russia during the last turbulent decade.

Russia's transition from communism is understood by some authors as an example of a larger generic case—a transition from authoritarianism to democracy (Di Palma 1990, Bova 1991, Huntington 1991-92, Schmitter with Karl 1994, Linz & Stepan 1996). From this point of view, Gorbachev's perestroika, the disintegration of the USSR, the collapse of communism, and the subsequent transformations in post-communist Russia and the former socialist countries are all part of one global process—the "third wave" of the "global democratic revolution."

A quite different understanding of post-communism has emerged in recent years, according to which post-communism is, to a large degree, a specific phenomenon (in regard to initial conditions, tasks, political actors, and the like). The assumption is that there is no reason for comparing it with the processes of democratization that are characteristic of southern Europe and Latin America (Terry 1993; Bunce 1995, 1998). In line with this approach there is also an understanding of post-communism as a "peaceful revolution" (McFaul 1995, Fish 1995), differing from other processes of democratization because of the political and socioeconomic tasks it introduces. The complexity and difficulty of these tasks make post-communist transitions fundamentally different from the mainly political transitions from authoritarianism to democracy.

It appears to this author, however, that the time for a general and integrated theory of post-communism is yet to come. Post-communism as a metaphor still needs to be developed into a comprehensive theory, which would provide the conceptual tools to analyze the full variety of transformations in Russia and in other former Soviet-type societies. What is missing today in the methodological arsenal of both comparativists and area specialists is an integrated theory that enables us to conceptualize the multitude of political, social, economic, psychological, ideological, and other phenomena that have emerged out of the rubble of communism.

It should be admitted that those who stress a specific post-communist transition process point to some very real features not present in most other types of post-authoritarian transitions. Among them are the simultaneous tasks of political democratization and economic marketization; the need for the dismantling of a great part of existing production capacities for the sake of modernization and restructuring of others; the appearance of a nationalist (and nondemocratic) reaction to the communist collapse; and the lack of a civil society consisting of a system of ties within civil society itself and between civil society and the State. This list of differences between post-communist and post-authoritarian transitions can easily be extended.

One should add to this list of post-communist transitions the possibility that the result may not be a consolidated democracy but a type of hybrid regime that uses the democratic rhetoric as a smoke screen for a de facto restoration of various and even pre-communist forms of authoritarianism. By way of illustration, we can consider a recent survey undertaken by Freedom House that rates countries according to evaluations of the state of political processes, including free and fair elections; the evolution of civil society; the status of an independent media; rule of law, including constitutional, civil, and criminal law reform; governance and public administration, including transparency and government accountability; privatization; and economic reform. According to these criteria, only seven among the newly independent states (the Czech Republic, Hungary, Poland, Slovenia, Estonia, Lithuania and Latvia) are considered to be consolidated democracies. Fourteen (Russia, Moldova, Slovakia, Bulgaria, Romania, Ukraine, Macedonia, Croatia, Albania, Armenia, Kyrgyzstan, Georgia, Kazakhstan and Azerbaijan) are transitional, while four (Belarus, Tajikistan, Uzbekistan and Turkmenistan) are consolidated autocracies (Karatnycki 1997).

This data suggests that it is probably more beneficial not to use a notion of "transition to democracy" (which implies that the final result of the process of transition is democracy in its Western sense) but a broader and more neutral notion of democratic transition. The role of unpredictability in such transitions is widely recognized (Przeworski 1991). In spite of the extensive use of democratic rhetoric, these transitions may very seldom meet democratic standards, even in a minimally procedural (a la Schumpeter or Dahl) sense of the word. A consolidated democracy is not necessarily the final result of such a process.

Even the establishment of formal democratic institutions and procedures of either "electoral democracy" or "illiberal democracy" (Diamond 1996; Diamond, Plattner, Chu, & Tien 1997; Zakaria 1998) in no way guarantees a particular outcome of the transition. Therefore, there is a widely accepted distinction between two major phases in the practice of democratic transition: (1) the formal inauguration of democracy and (2) its consolidation (Mainwaring, O'Donnell, & Valenzuela 1992; Gunther, Diamandouros, & Puhle 1995; Linz & Stepan 1996; Merkel 1998).

We may go even further, raising the following question: Do democratic transitions really have one predominant direction from the initiation of democratic reforms to consolidated democracy at the end of the process? The answer could imply that different types of illiberal democracies may emerge and some of them may represent not an intermediate stage in a democratic transition but quite different phenomenon—a transition from one type of non-democracy to another type of non-democracy.

All this leads to important theoretical and methodological problems related to current comparative research on post-authoritarian and post-communist transitions: Are we able to trace a causal relationship between a multitude of factors which are at hand at the beginning of transition, as well as during the transitional process, to its political, economic, and social outcomes? Why do democratic transitions begin earlier and proceed more smoothly in some countries than in others? Why do some non-democratic regimes initiate a gradual democratization themselves, while others resist it until they collapse? Why do only a few transitions result in consolidated democracies while many others stumble while in a non-consolidated phase or stagnate as consolidated autocracies?

In an effort to answer these questions, some authors (Almond & Verba 1963; Rustow 1970; Inglehart 1988; Lipset 1959, 1996) emphasize structural factors—socioeconomic and cultural conditions—as prerequisites of both democracy and democratization. Others stress procedural factors, such as the sequence of specific choices, decisions, and actions taken by actual political actors upon whom the process of democratic transition rests (O'Donnell & Schmitter 1986, Linz 1990, Di Palma 1990, Przeworski 1991, Schmitter with Karl 1994, Karl & Schmitter 1994).

It appears that these two methodological approaches, the structural and the procedural, do not mutually exclude each other. Moreover, there is apparently no insurmountable contradiction between them. It must, however, be admitted that at present even a preliminary theoretical synthesis of these two methodological approaches has not been achieved. Such a synthesis would be equally important for the elaboration of an integrated theory of contemporary post-communism. And what is more important, there may very well be other significant but unnoticed factors, that may in different ways influence the democratic transition at its different stages. In the absence of an integrated theory of democratic transitions (and post-communist transitions in particular) it may be a useful preliminary step to try to structure and systematize all major factors—from macro to micro—that may influence such transitions (Melville 1998). Post-communist Russia may provide us with a good case study within the frame of reference of this approach.

Such an endeavor makes it necessary to reveal both general and specific elements of the process. Keeping in mind all the differences between Russia's post-communist transformation and the transitions from right-wing authoritarianism to democracy in Southern European and Latin

American countries, it can still be suggested that these processes were influenced at least partly by some similar factors. Analogies between the Russian and the classic post-authoritarian transitions are often dismissed on the grounds that Gorbachev's coming to power was not the result of a split in the Soviet elite into reformers and conservatives. It is argued that he initiated reforms by using purely Soviet apparatus methods (from top to bottom). In reality, even if Gorbachev's way to power was ensured by traditional nomenklatura methods, his subsequent reform initiatives caused the Soviet elite to split.

As in most cases of democratic transition, the initiation, first of a liberalization and then of a partial democratization of the regime, was taken from above by the leader-reformer. As a centrist reformer, Gorbachev was initially inclined to gradual and evolutionary reforms within the framework of the existing system. He appealed for support to the radical democratic opposition forces outside the regime in order to strengthen his position in the confrontation with conservatives and fundamentalists within. However, the legalization and then the institutionalization of the radical democratic opposition (for example, the Interregional Group of Deputies of the USSR Supreme Soviet and the "Democratic Russia" movement) caused a defensive reaction from the conservatives, who pulled their ranks more closely together and subsequently institutionalized themselves as the Communist Party of the RSFSR, and as the "Unity" bloc in the Supreme Soviet. For a time Gorbachev succeeded in balancing between these two groups by pursuing a policy of zigzags. However, the gap between the two political poles, both of which assumed their own speed and logic of development, was constantly widening. As a result, political centrism as a method of reforming the system suffered a complete collapse. The unsuccessful conservative coup in August 1991 aimed at saving the system resulted in a successful countercoup staged by the radical democrats.

One can easily see that almost from its outset the transition pattern in the Soviet/Russian case differed profoundly from classic types of democratic transitions. What, then, are the macro- and micro-factors which may be responsible for these peculiar aspects of the Russian transformational trajectory?

Starting our analysis at the macro-factor level in accordance with our research model, we should direct attention to international (geopolitical, strategic, economic, political, and cultural) factors that stimulated the efforts of reforms in the USSR. It seems that these external/international factors, while creating a stimulus for perestroika-type reforms in the Soviet

Union, were neither crucial nor determining. However, the analysis of these international factors of Soviet/Russian transformations is still on the research agenda. External factors may come to be seen as presenting conditions and obstacles to democratic consolidation in Russia in the future.

We should also mention the fact that in the Soviet/Russian case one basic precondition for democratization—i.e. the existence of a state integrity and national identity—was and is missing. The multiethnic composition of both the USSR and Russian Federation and the rise of the centrifugal forces of nationalism that led to the disintegration of the USSR continue to be a threat to Russia. During the disintegration of the Soviet Union, calls for national self-determination were used to give meaning and substance to the program of anti-communism. However, in the post-communist context the desire for national revival began to assume forms hardly compatible with democracy. In some places, nationalism assumed the features of openly ethnocratic and imperial forms.

The crisis of national identity, which is clearly felt today in post-communist Russia, cannot be found, as a rule, in other cases of democratic transitions. From a long-term perspective it may prove to be the most difficult task. At present, there is no clear answer to the following questions: What is today's Russia like? Did it really inherit the status of the USSR? Is it a successor to the last great empire of the world? Or is it only one of the empire's 15 splinters? Is it true that post-communist Russia represents a fundamentally new type of statehood, which emerged out of the rubble of the old empire? Or is today's Russia a continuation of the framework of that Eurasian geopolitical entity which existed first in the form of the Russian empire and then in the form of the USSR? There is still no answer to the question of whether it is possible to achieve a different—democratic and non-imperial—regime that could govern and organize these territories which historically have been structured in an autocratic and imperial paradigm. Until answers to these questions are found, until the problem concerning territorial integrity within the framework of a voluntary federation is solved and the new national identity of Russia established, it is difficult to predict not only the results but also the progress of Russia's democratic transit.

The economy provides additional obstacles to democratization in Russia. Unlike most democratic transitions of the third wave, the processes of democratization in the USSR and Russia were initiated as attempts at revitalizing the economy and society. Moreover, in the Soviet Union, unlike several post-authoritarian transitions to democracy, there were not even simple elements of a market economy, an absence that complicated and continues to complicate transformation processes.

Still some authors (Starr 1988, Lapidus 1989, Lewin 1991) argue that behind the facade of the Soviet regime there were gradually emerging forces of modernization. These forces resulted from accumulated social change—including urbanization, professional differentiation, increased educational level, and the emergence of the "embryonic" middle class as the carrier of new values and attitudes. There is another line of argumentation, according to which transformation processes initiated by perestroika were caused not by the gradual modernization of the Soviet society but, quite the contrary, by its decay and devolution (Malia 1990, 1992; Janos 1991; Jowitt 1992). This debate certainly should be continued.

Narrowing our focus further, we should consider the lower structural level of social and class factors. First, we need to integrate into our argument the absence of an adequate social base for democracy. From the standpoint of political democratization and its tasks, the transition to a market economy is not an end in itself but a means of creating a middle class as a mass basis for democracy. The processes of transformation in the Soviet society, at least since the 1960s, created a kind of early analogue of a middle class. With the disintegration of the Soviet state, the deepening economic crisis, and the initiation of market economy reforms, this embryonic Soviet "old middle class" was actually washed away as the society split up into two poles (a process also typical for Third World countries). One extreme represented a zone of mass poverty, the other a narrow stratum of wealth, with socially amorphous elements between them. As for a "new middle class," it has not yet appeared in Russia. The problem of shaping an adequate mass social basis of democracy, based on private property relations as opposed to relations vis-à-vis the state, remains unsolved in post-communist Russia.

Another specific feature of Russia's transition is the maintenance of the old ruling class in power. In cases of successful transition, a pact between parties competing with and confronting each other during the process of democratization provides for the old ruling class guarantees of political and economic security (Glad 1996, Glad & Blanton 1997). As a result of this process, the old ruling class can take part in the democratic political process. In Russia, however, there was a lack of a social agreement. The old nomenklature retained its political and economic status by the camouflaging of apparent administrative changes made by the new authorities—for instance, by the relabeling of official positions, while filling these positions with the same personnel. This was accomplished without any rhetorical explanations of what had transpired (Khryshtanovskaia 1996; for a different argument see Lane & Ross 1998).

It is partly for this reason that the uncompleted democratic transition in Russia became not so much a radical break with the past Soviet system, but rather a particular metamorphosis of it. The nucleus of the old nomenklatura (which included the old party apparatus and economic pragmatists) joined the new career professionals from democratic ranks as part of the renewed ruling class under slogans of democracy and anti-communism (Shevtsova 1995). This renewed ruling class held on to power and acquired private property. It became the winner in the large-scale processes of redistribution of state property and of the transfer of this property to private hands. Hidden behind a smoke screen of so-called public privatization, the redistribution took place among clans and cartels that were and still are part of the ruling class. As a result, corporate interest groups created a base for the oligarchic political system that is presently being established in Russia. At the same time, the interests of the masses are still poorly articulated and the lower layers of society do not have adequate political representation.

The present situation is one in which an elite employs the formal procedures of democracy for nondemocratic purposes. This situation is the result of a superficial democratization that provides virtually no mechanisms of democratic control over the actions of the authorities (Shevtsova 1997). According to the terminology of Schmitter and Karl (1994), it is a hybrid, a kind of "democradura," a regime that drastically limits the possibilities for an effective mass participation in politics, but at the same time allows competition for power at the elite level. Still, the "democradura" in Russia is a relative one, at least because at the elite level, the rules of the game are not based on open political competition. They consist of clan and corporate laws structuring the "under-the-carpet" struggle for power. Characterizations such as "delegated democracy" (O'Donnell 1994), "authoritarian democracy" (Sakwa 1997), or "hybrid regime" (Shevtsova 1997) can also be applied in many respects to the key features of the current Russian regime. On the other hand, the present hybrid regime in Russia inherited much of the old Soviet political genotype, and it resembles, to an ever-greater extent, a closed corporate and profoundly corrupt political structure of the Latin American type.

The issue of the nature of the current political regime in Russia is related to a more general methodological problem. This problem arises in the first place within the context of a large variety of post-authoritarian regimes, which are referred to as "democracies with adjectives" (for example, "authoritarian democracy," "neopatrimonial democracy," "military-dominated democracy," "protodemocracy," "illiberal democracy," "electoral democracy," etc.). One can only agree with Collier and Levitsky (1997, 450) that this issue still needs conceptual clarification: "Diminished subtypes are useful for characterizing hybrid regimes, but they raise the issue of whether these regimes should, in fact, be treated as subtypes of democracy, rather than subtypes of authoritarianism or some other concept."

At the level of cultural factors we need to address the following problem. Both in the USSR and in Russia, the democratic transition was not preconditioned by a civic culture that supported democratic values and orientations. The functioning of new, formally democratic political institutions, however, influences the dynamic of public values and orientations. As a result, the latter start to develop and acquire a dynamic of their own, which in turn begins to influence political institutions and processes. Empirical evidence shows the tendency toward consolidation of some dispersed and uncoordinated democratic values, habits, and practices in Russian mass consciousness (Melville, 1998a). Still, in Russia today, according to various public opinion polls, normative support of democracy is lower and normative support of authoritarianism is higher than in many other current cases of democratic transition. The analysis of cultural and value-attitudinal dimensions of transition processes in Russia and in other countries in transition remains a challenging task for political scientists and comparativists.

Since at the level of structural factors we are not able to develop a comprehensive explanatory model of Russian democratic transition, we should also consider procedural factors. It has become almost trivial to speak about the unprecedented task of carrying out both democratic transformations of the political system and economic reforms aimed at creating a market economy in post-communist Russia. The latter task presupposes a dismantling of the command economy and the creation of new foundations for market economy relations. It is believed that, ideally, both tasks should not only condition each other but also, in the end, mutually support each other: Democratization facilitates an advancement towards the market, while the market creates the economic and social basis of democracy. In classic post-authoritarian transitions the problem concerning the simultaneous nature of political and economic reforms does not arise because a market economy already exists in some form. However, in the Soviet Union and then in Russia, these two tasks proved in many respects to create obstacles for each other.

This is not to claim that quite painful economic structural transformations, including the privatization of state property, were not on the agenda of other democratic transitions. Nevertheless, successful political and economic reforms, including those taking place in the countries of Central and Eastern Europe, were not carried out simultaneously. Nor were they carried out in the way they are in China, where economic reforms not only precede but actually replace political reforms.

In most successful democratic transitions a consistent political democratization was carried out first, and then effective democratic institutions were built and consolidated. Next came the establishment of what Linz and Stepan (1996) call an "economic society," that is, a system of social guarantees and mediating institutions between the state and the market. Only after these political developments were painful economic transformations were carried out. Other authors (Brzezinski 1993, McFaul 1995) draw attention to this circumstance. Following such a sequence of events, persistent political democratization helped ensure mass support for democracy during heavy economic reforms on one hand, while a social contract was provided to facilitate the economic transition on the other.

Neither of the above happened in Russia. After 1991 the state disintegrated, for Yeltsin created neither democratic political institutions that could have supported the economic reforms, nor institutions of state support for the market economy and the social security system. The impact of extremely painful economic reforms, which were not accompanied by any social contract and were not supported socially or politically, fell upon the socially unprotected population.

When analyzing these developments, one ought to go beyond the framework of the Western-style free market's opposition to the command administrative system in transition. This should be done for analytical and comparative reasons. None of the countries that have undertaken processes of successful democratic transition during the last two decades was entering the market in its pure form per se, a prerequisite of, or a guarantee for, democracy. Here lies the source of one of the fatal errors of the early strategists of Russia's transition, who acted out of the belief that a free market (even if it is "wild") can provide the economic and social basis needed for political democracy. The economic and financial collapse in Russia on August 17, 1998, signaled the end of seven years of Russia's post-communist political reform and the "virtual economy" (Gaddy & Ickes 1998), conducted only formally and superficially according to monetarist models. In fact, the privatization of the state with the help of state mechanisms turned out to be a mere prikhvatizatsia (robbery, confiscation), with the subsequent flow of capital out of the country. This strategy, seen from today's perspective, was based on a false premise that the most important thing for successful marketization is appropriation of big capital by whatever means possible.

A comparative analysis of successful democratic transitions shows that nowhere in Southern Europe, Latin America, or Central and Eastern Europe did the transition to democracy rely solely on the reconstruction of the classic ideal of a free market under a state functioning as a "night watchman." Contrary to some widespread misconceptions, both the logic and actions of successful "democratizers" were quite opposite: First radical political transformations (the building of effective institutions of democracy); then social reforms, which provide some sort of a social safety net and a social basis of support for democracy; to be followed by profound structural transformations of the economy (the establishment of a modern free market).

The ideological opposition to state interventionism of the now globalized and Western-centered market does not apply to the present situation in Russia. The Soviet administrative system of economic management, which had disintegrated by the end of the Gorbachev epoch, was completely crushed by the reformers. At the same time, many key levers of administrative influence continue to exist. As a result, there has evolved a political-criminal market in which bargaining between political and economic clans in key positions, combining power and property, takes place. Today, as distinct from what was going on in the recent past, these cartels have become all the more vigorous and powerful. They no longer enter politics by delegating the representation of their interests to authorized persons, but are themselves becoming the most influential political players. These players do not need free market competition. They have already adjusted the state they privatized to their own personal and corporate needs. Now it is the state that is propped up by shadowy political bargains and government subsidies, no matter how insubstantial, that are needed to preserve the monopoly and domination of certain economic cartels.

An analysis of procedural factors also points to the continuation of traditional administrative methods of carrying out political and economic reforms. The almost complete subordination of social groups, classes, and strata to the paternalistic vertical arrangement of state power was always a characteristic of pre-Soviet Russia and the USSR. It was not society that was creating the state, but state power itself that was shaping society. In other words, social and economic relationships were a creation of the state. The Soviet state was not a creation or product of pre-existing social and economic relationships. In post-Soviet Russia, embryonic signs of democracy and its representative institutions began to emerge on a flat social landscape in which there were few historical patterns or infrastructures of diverse socioeconomic interests (McFaul 1993).

Moreover, the new authorities in Russia followed the Russian tradition of carrying out reforms and transformations according to a vertical, top-down power structure. In most successful democratic transitions the reform initiative comes from above. However, an important and fundamental difference between Russia and other cases is that in the latter a reform impulse from above acts only as the primary catalyst of broader and profounder processes that emerge and develop in society. The functions of the authorities are usually reduced to providing institutional support for these processes in accordance with generally accepted democratic procedures.

In Russia, the political processes were different. The new authorities' approach to reform was consistent with traditional administrative methods (mainly due to the new political elite's ties with the old nomenklatura). This, in turn, created a split between the authorities and the society, a split that is pernicious for democracy and leads to a growing alienation of society from the government. Public disappointment and indifference increases. Certainly, positive factors can also be observed in the available data. For example, the "privatization" of one's personal sphere is about to replace a sense of traditional statism according to which an individual is only partly subordinate to the state. However, private interest is perceived in the mass consciousness not merely as independent of the state and the authorities, but in direct conflict with them. This does not in any way provide favorable conditions for the development of the forms of political participation needed for effective functioning of democratic institutions.

The lack of a pact between reformers and conservatives is also revealed at the procedural level of analysis. After renouncing the compromises that Gorbachev sought, albeit inconsistently, and as part of the bid for a full and unconditional victory over the Soviet regime, Yeltsin and the radicals supporting him dismissed the possibility of compromising with their adversaries. In other cases such a pact helped formulate the rules of the democratic game, ones that were subsequently adhered to by the main political forces of the system. As there was no such pact in Russia, quite a big political segment of society was artificially excluded from the democratic process for a long time, until the 1993 elections, which legalized the opposition.

It should also be noted that the lack of a formal pact in no way prevented the second and third echelons of the Soviet nomenklature from successfully becoming part of the new system of authority. Today, there is reason to believe that some elements of a pact after all did take place de facto. One of the elements of this partial pact was the recognition of formal elections as the only acceptable method of legitimization of power by the nation-wide political forces of Russia. However, as distinct from the logic of classic transitions to democracy, this pact was not a phase that preceded the democratization of an authoritarian regime. It was a stage of post-communist transformation at which a new ruling class had already emerged and different ruling groups had already "adjusted" to each other, determined their interests and zones of intersection, and agreed upon the "rules of the game." They did not take into account the overwhelming mass of the population. As a result, the pact, which appeared de facto but in a limited form and among the most influential groups within the present Russian elite, only deepens the gap between the authorities and the society and keeps society from participating in politics.

The Russian democratic transition is also characterized by the lack of founding elections that could have legitimized the new order in social and political life. Relying on his charisma as a people's leader who enjoys the support of everyone and therefore does not need an additional legitimization, Yeltsin refused to hold the first free elections. Thus he failed to lay the foundations for a legitimate democratic power which would have facilitated a smooth and gradual development of a multiparty system in the country. It should be noted that Yeltsin refused to hold these first free elections in a situation where radical democrats would have had the best chance of obtaining a powerful majority in the parliament. This majority might have provided popular support for the radical economic reforms he initiated. The lack of this most important initial institutional phase in the process of Russia's democratic transition largely explains (or at least makes it less unexpected) the results of the parliamentary elections in December 1993, which shocked most observers in Russia and abroad. These parliamentary elections were only formally and chronologically the "first" and founding ones.

The initial shock stage of market economic reforms, in short, was forced on the population by an executive power already associated in mass consciousness with the radical democrats. It does not come as a surprise that the result of this short and agonizing stage of shock therapy was the growth of mass discontent with the democratic authorities and their policies. This has been the case in practically all similar of democratic transitions. Reforms have inevitably caused a public reaction, and the pendulum of mass sentiment has swung against them. It happened in Russia during the first free parliamentary elections in December 1993, which according to the general logic of democratic transitions fulfilled the function of the second elections—the "elections of disappointment."

When dealing with the characteristics of Russian democratic transition, we have almost accomplished our methodological descent to the level of micro-factors that relate to personal and individual factors—decisions and actions of the key political actors. It seems only one factor can more or less convincingly explain Yeltsin's refusal to hold free parliamentary elections in the autumn of 1991. It was his reluctance to share the laurels of victory with persons who only recently had become his close associates in the democratic movement. As a result, only some of the Russian democrats were co-opted into the new structures of authority. A large section of the democratic movement remains out of business, in a position of disappointed observers who are becoming ever more critical.

The role of individual and personal factors (to put it bluntly—Yeltsin's personality) had its influence upon the general trajectory of the transition. Here we would like to refer to what Breslauer outlines as a fundamental contradiction in Yeltsin's approach to managing the transition—a contradiction between his personalism (patriarchal familialism), on the one hand, and the need for institution building, on the other. "Yeltsin put far more energy into establishing and developing the formal structures of a capitalist democracy than he did into creating the regulatory institutions and organizational infrastructure required to make such a system function effectively" (Breslauer 1998, 6). To summarize, individual micro-factors need to be taken into account as important ones in the analysis of different cases of transition and in the attempts to conceptualize them.

Is the research framework presented above suited for the analysis of the democratic transitions in the Russian case and in general? Ideal methodologies, we must admit, do not exist but it seems that this research model of gradual descent from macro- to micro-factors may be considered a fruitful one. Certainly it does not provide a full explanation. It does provide one possible route toward the broader explanation of the "mystery" of democratic transitions.

As for the particular Russian case, the author of these remarks believes that at this moment we are dealing with an open-ended transition and cannot yet see its directions or its outcome. Meanwhile an important analytical task may consist in the continuation of our efforts first to systemize and take into account relevant factors to the Russian transition, and then on this base try to develop conceptualizations of post-communist transitions as a very specific and diversified phenomenon.

Contributors

Carol Barner-Barry is a professor of Political Science at University of Maryland. Her books include *Contemporary Soviet Politics* (1991), *Psychological Perspectives on Politics* (two editions), and *The Politics of Change* (1995). She has also published numerous articles for different academic journals. Her works are widely used as college textbooks in political psychology, comparative politics, and Russian politics classes.

Serge Danilov is a former Russian music and film producer, one of the founding insiders of the Leningrad "Rock-Club" in the 1980s. He graduated from Leningrad Institute of Culture.

Carolyn M. Ekedahl is Chief of Public Communications on the Public Affairs Staff at the CIA. She is the author of *Moscow's Third World Policy Under Gorbachev* (Westview, 1990), and coauthor of *The Wars of Eduard Shevardnadze* (Penn State University Press, 1997).

Betty Glad is the Olin D. Johnston Professor of Political Science at the University of South Carolina. She is the 1997 recipient of the International Society for Political Psychology's Harold B. Lasswell Award for Distinguished Scientific Contribution to Political Psychology. She has served as president of the International Society for Political Psychology and Vice President of the American Political Science Association. Her works include biographies of Jimmy Carter, Charles Evans Hughes, Key Pittman, and many articles on American presidents and foreign leaders. Her IPSA presidential address, "Passing the Baton: from Gorbachev to Yeltsin, from DeKlerk to Mandela," was published *in Political Psychology* in 1996.

Melvin Goodman is Professor of International Security Studies at the National War College (Washington DC). His books include *Gorbachev's Retreat: The Third World (1991), The End of Superpower Conflict in the Third World* (1992), and *The Wars of Eduard Shevardnadze* (1997).

Patricia Karl is Research Associate at the Richard L. Walker Institute of International Studies at University of South Carolina. She served in the CIA between 1986–1991. Her work in the Directorate of Intelligence included a stint in the Political Psychology Division. She has also taught courses in comparative politics and international relations at Vassar College and Louisiana State University.

Brian Kuns is currently is a graduate student at the University of South Carolina, where he is specializing in Russian politics. He spent a year in Novgorod, Russia teaching high school English and traveling the country.

Andrei Melville is Professor of Political Science and Dean at Moscow Institute of International relations. His academic interests include research of transformational politics, public opinion, Russian-American relations, and comparative politics. As a research and exchange professor, he worked at several American universities, including University of California at Berkeley.

Gordon Smith is Professor of Political Science at the University of South Carolina. He has written several books on law in the Soviet Union and Russia and is now researching public opinions, voting behaviors, political attitudes and their change in the contemporary Russian society.

Olga Mitina is a political psychologist at Moscow State University. Over the last five years, she has published numerous articles on the nature and development of political attitudes in contemporary Russian society. Based on a solid empirical approach, she provides both quantitative and qualitative testing of people's opinions on a wide spectrum of social and political issues.

Vladimir Petrenko is Professor of Psychology at Moscow State University. He is one of the leading political psychologists in Russia and conducts research in the fields of elite and mass opinion, as well as public perception of political parties and political leaders. His research papers regularly appear in the leading Russian scholarly journals.

Eric Shiraev was on the faculty at Leningrad State University from 1986 to 1992. He is now at George Washington University where he teaches political psychology. He has published several books and articles in both Russian and English. His specialty is cross-national research in political psychology. His first book, *Fashion, Idols, and the Self* (1988) was one of the initial attempts to analyze many cultural and political transformations of the Russian youth. He is a coeditor of a book on international public opinion and the Bosnia crisis (Pennsylvania State University Press), and a textbook on cross-cultural psychology (Allyn and Bacon).

References

Abarinov, V. 1994. "Bosnia: Moskva Ne Otritsaet Vozmozhost Ispolzovania Sily s Vozdukha" [Moscow Doesn't Rule Out The Use of Airpower]. *Sevodnya,* February 15.

Abalkin, L. 1995. *Ekonomicheskaya Reforma: Zigzagi Sydby i Uroki na Budushchee* [Economic Reform: Zigzags of Fate and Lessons for the Future]. Moscow: Institute of Economics, RAS.

Agutin, L. 1998. Interview in *Argumenty i Facty,* 12.

Ahdieh, R. B. 1997. *Russia's Constitutional Revolution: Legal Consciousness and the Transition to Democracy, 1985–1996.* University Park, PA: Pennsylvania State University Press.

Alliluyeva, S. 1967. *20 Letters to a Friend.* New York: Harper & Row.

Allison, G. 1996. "Update on the Current Russian Political Scene after Russian Duma Elections." Harvard University: JFK School of Government WWW Homepage, January 26.

Almond, G. & S. Genco. 1977. "Clouds, Clocks and the Study of Politics." *World Politics,* 40.

Almond, G. A. & S. Verba. 1963. *The Civic Culture: Political Attitudes and Democracy. Five Nations.* Princeton, NJ: Princeton University Press.

Alter, P. 1989. *Nationalism.* London: Edward Arnold.

Ambartsumov, E. 1994. "In the World: Echoes of the Bosnian Bombings." *Moskovskie Novosti,* April 10–17.

Antonov, Y. 1990. Interview in *Argumenty i Facty,* 31.

Arato, A. 1985. "Some Perspectives of Democratization in East Central Europe." *Journal of International Affairs.* 38 (Winter).

Arbatov, G. 1992. "Rescue Russia, or Else!" *Newsday,* October 25.

Arendt, H. 1968. *Totalitarianism: Part Three of the Origins of Totalitarianism.* New York: Harcourt, Brace & World.

Asiand, A. 1989. *Gorbachev's Struggle for Economic Reform.* Ithaca, NY: Cornell University Press.

Associated Press. 1989. "Soviets Convene Legislature." *The State* (Columbia, SC). June 4.

Baker, J. 1995. *The Politics of Diplomacy: Revolution, War and Peace, 1989–1992.* New York: G.P. Putnam's.

Barner-Barry, C. & C. Hody. 1995. *The Politics of Change: The Transformation of the Former Soviet Union.* New York: St. Martin's Press.

Barringer, F. 1988. "Soviet Ousts Yeltsin from Ruling Body." *The State,* August 19.

Barsukov, V. 1996. "Perspektivy Postkommunisticheskogo Konservatisma i Presidentskie Vybory [Perspectives of Postcommunist Conservatism and Presidential Elections]." *Polis,* 2.

Bass, B. 1985. *Leadership and Performance Beyond Expectation.* New York: Free Press.

Bauman, Z. 1994. "A Revolution in the Theory of Revolutions." *International Political Science Review,* 15.

Baturin, A. & S. Gryzunov. 1994. "Tanets s Metloi v Ispolnennyi Zhirinovskogo" [Dance With a Broom, as Performed by Zhirinovsky]. *Izvestia,* February 1.

Berdyaev, N. 1989. "Istoki i Smysl Russkogo Kommunisma" [Origins and Meaning of Russian Communism]. Excerpts. *Yunost,* 11.

Berger, P. L. & T. Luckmann, 1966. *The Social Construction of Reality: A Treatise on the Sociology of Knowledge.* New York: Doubleday.

Best, D., & J. Williams, 1997. "Sex, Gender, and Culture." In J. Berry, M. Segall, & C. Kagitsibasi. *Handbook of Cross-Cultural Psychology,* Volume III. Boston: Allyne Bacon.

Blasi, J., M. Kroumova, & D. Kruse, 1997. *Kremlin Capitalism.* Ithaca, NY: Cornell University Press.

Bogardus, E. 1934. *Leaders and Leadership.* New York: D. Appleton—Century Company, Inc.

Bogert, C. 1990. "Yeltsin on the Record." *Newsweek,* July 23.

Bogomolov, P. 1992. Editorial. *Pravda.* June 2.

Bohlen, C. 1998a. "A Humble Yeltsin is Fading Away." *The New York Times,* September 20.

———. 1998b. "New Cabinet. Yeltsin Creates Inner Cabinet of Primakov and Six Deputies." *The New York Times,* September 23.

———. 1998c. "Ruble is on 'Tilt,' but Russians Keep Their Balance." *The New York Times,* October 6.

———. 1993a. "For Moscow, a Sigh of Relief Replaces Feelings of Outrage." *The New York Times,* October 5.

———. 1993b. "Two Survivors Describe Euphoria and the Fear." *The New York Times,* October 6.

———. 1993c. "Russia in Mourning for Moscow Dead." *The New York Times,* October 6.

———. 1992a. "Gorbachev Assails Yeltsin's Rule in Sharpest Attack Since Quitting." *The New York Times,* May 31.

———. 1992b. "In Bout with Yeltsin, Gorbachev Loses Office Space." *The New York Times,* October 9.

Boldin, V. 1994. *Ten Years That Shook the World.* New York: Basic Books.

Bolshakov, V. 1994. "Yugoslavia: Trevozhnoe Ozhidanie." [Yugoslavia: Tense Waiting]. *Pravda,* February 22.

"Boris Yeltsin" 1996. *Russia Today,* June. www.cs.indiana.edu\hyplan\dmiguse\Russian\bybio.html

Borisov, S. 1998. An interview. *Ogonyok,* 10.

Borovoy, K. 1998. An interview. *Ogonyok,* 12.

Bova, R. 1993. "Political Dynamics of the Post-Communist Transition: A Comparative Perspective." In F. J. Fleron, Jr. and E. P. Hoffmann (Eds.), *Post-Communist Studies and Political Science:* 239–263. Boulder: Westview Press.

———. 1991. "Political Dynamics of the Post-Communist Transitions." *World Politics,* (October).

Breslauer, G.W. 1998. *"Evaluating Yeltsin as a Leader"* (unpublished paper), December.

Brown, A. 1996. *The Gorbachev Factor.* Oxford: Oxford University Press.

Brumberg, A. 1991. "Russia after Perestroika." *New York Times Book Review,* June 27.

———. 1990. "Gorbachev: His Trials and His Errors." *New York Times Book Review,* August 12.

Brzezinski, Z. 1993. "The Great Transformation." *The National Interest,* (Fall).

Bunce, V. 1998. "Regional Differences in Democratization: The East Versus the South." *Post-Soviet Affairs,* (July-September).

———. 1995. "Should Transitologists Be Grounded?" *Slavic Review,* 54.

Bunich, P. 1992. *Zoloto Partii.* [The Party's Gold]. Moscow:

Burns, J. M. 1978. *Leadership.* New York: Harper & Row.

Caryl, C. 1998. "Only a Fool Pays Taxes in Capitalist Russia." *US News and World Report,* March 30.

Carr, E. H. 1958. *Socialism in One Country.* Vol. 1. London: Macmillan and Co.

Carroll, S. 1989. "The Socializing Impact of the Women's Movement." In R. Sigel (Ed.). *Political Learning in Adulthood.* Chicago: The University of Chicago Press.

Checkel, J. 1993. "Ideas Institutions, and the Gorbachev Foreign Policy Revolution." *World Politics,* (January).

Chernyaev, A. 1993. *Shest let s Gorbachevym* [Six Years With Gorbachev] Moscow: Progress-Kultura.

Chinyaeva, E. 1996. "A Eurasianist Model of Interethnic Relations Could Help Russia Find Harmony." *Transition,* 22.

Chronology of Russian Financial Crisis. 1998. *Russia Today,* October 12. www.RussiaToday.com\ rtoday\ special\ chrono.html

Chuprov, V. and J. Zubok. 1996. "Youth and Social Change." In C. Williams, V. Chuprov, and V. Staroverov (Eds.), *Russian Society in Transition.* Aldershot, England: Dartmouth.

CISS Index to International Public Opinion, 1993–94; 1994–95; 1995–96.

Clark, W. 1993. *Crime and Punishment in Soviet Officialdom.* Armonk: M.E. Sharpe.

———. 1989. *Soviet Regional Elite Mobility after Khrushchev.* New York: Praeger.

Clines, F. 1990 a. "Gorbachev Tries to Develop Radical Economic Program Perestroika." *New York Times,* April 15.

———. 1990b. "Challengers New and Old Nip at Gorbachev's Heels." *New York Times,* June 24.

———. 1990c. "Russian Party Elects Hard-Liner: Gorbachev to Keep Political Post." *New York Times,* June 24.

CNN broadcast, 1998. News. October 13, 9:30 AM.

———. 1991a. Meeting of Supreme Soviet of Russia. August 24.

———. 1991b. Gorbachev speech at Foros. August 23.

Coleman, F. 1990. "The People Want to Get Rid of Communism." *Newsweek,* May 14.

———. 1989. "Nikita Gorbachev?" *Newsweek.* September 11.

Collier, D. & S. Levitsky. 1997. "Democracy with Adjectives. Conceptual Innovation in Comparative Research." *World Politics,* (April).

Committee on Labor and Employment. 1993. Report. St. Petersburg.

"Congress of the Dead." 1990. *Newsweek.* 23 July.

Conway, M. M. 1990. *Political Participation In the United States.* 2d ed. Washington, DC: CQ Press.

Dahlburg, J. 1992. "Gorbachev's Travel Limited Until He Testifies." *Los Angeles Times,* October 3.

———. 1989. "Soviet Congress Gives Party Critic Seat with Gorbachev's Approval." *The State,* May 30.

Daigle, K. 1996. "Show Business Takes Its Toll on Freed Soviet Talent." St. Petersburg *Times online.* www.sptimes.ru\times\219–220\show-bus.html

Dallin, A. 1991. "Learning in U.S. Policy Toward Soviet Union in the 1980s." In G. Breslauer & P. Tetlock (Eds.), *Learning in U.S. and Soviet Foreign Policy.* Boulder: Westview Press.

Davis, C. L. & J. G. Speer. 1991. "The Psychological Bases of Regime Support Among Urban Workers in Venezuela and Mexico." *Comparative Political Studies, 3.*

The Democrat (online). 1998. Indiana University.

Denisov, Y. 1996. "Pochemy Rossiyane ne Priemlyut Zolotoi Serediny, ili Ob Umerennosti v Politike" [Why Russians Do Not Accept a Happy Middle, or on Moderation in Politics]. *Polis,* 1.

Desai, P. 1989. *Perestroika in Perspective*. Princeton, NJ: Princeton University Press.

Diamond, L. M. Plattner, Yun-han Chu, & Hung-mao Tien (Eds.). 1997. *Consolidating the Third Wave Democracies. Themes and Perspectives*. Baltimore and London: The Johns Hopkins University Press.

Diamond, L. 1996. "Is the Third Wave Over?" *Journal of Democracy,* (July).

DiFranseisco, W. and Z. Gitelman. 1984. "Soviet Political Culture and 'Covert Participation' in Policy Implementation." *American Political Science Review,* 78.

Di Palma, G. 1990. *To Craft Democracies: Reflections on Democratic Transitions and Beyond.* Berkeley: University of California Press.

Dobbs, M. 1997. *Down with Big Brother.* New York: Alfred A. Knopf.

———. 1990b. "Yeltsin Quits Communist Party." *Washington Post.* July 13.

Dobson, R. 1996. *Russians Choose a President: Results of Focus Group Discussions.* USIA, June 1996.

Dobrynin, A. 1995. *In Confidence: Moscow's Ambassador to America's Six Cold War Presidents (1962–1986)* New York: Random House.

Doder, D. & L. Branson. 1990. *Gorbachev: Heretic in the Kremlin.* New York: Viking.

Dolgova, A. & S. Diakova, (Eds.) 1993. Organizovannaya Prestupnost.[Organized Crime]. Vol 2. Moscow: Kriminologicheskaya Assotsiatsia.

Dunlop, J. B. 1997. "Russia: In Search of an Identity?" In I. Bremmer & R. Taras (Eds.), *New States, New Politics: Building the Post-Soviet Nations.* New York: Cambridge University Press.

———. 1989. "A conversation with Dmitri Vasil'ev, the leader of Pamyat." *Radio Liberty Report on the USSR* 1, no. 50 (December 15).

Duran, B. S. & P. L. Odel. 1974. *Cluster Analysis: A Survey.* New York: Springer-Verlag.

Ekonomicheskie i Sotsialnye Peremeny: Monitoring Obshchestvennogo Mneniya. 1994. 6.

"Russia's Nighmare." 1998. *The Economist,* August 22.

"Taxman in a tank." 1998. *The Economist,* June 13.

"Russia Survey." 1997. *The Economist,* July 12.

"Broken code." 1997. *The Economist,* October 25.

"Russian survey." 1995. *The Economist,* April 8.

Editors of *Time* Magazine. 1988. *Mikhail S. Gorbachev: An Intimate Biography.* New York: A Time Book, New American Library.

Ekadahl, C. M. & M. Goodman. 1997. *The Wars of Edward Shevarnadze.* University Park, PA: Pennsylvania State University Press.

Ekiert, G. 1991. "Democratization Processes in East Central Europe: A Theoretical Reconsideration." *British Journal of Political Science,* 3 (July).

Eklov, B. 1989. *Soviet Briefing: Gorbachev and the Reform Period.* Boulder: Westview.

Elster, J. 1998. *Institutional Design in Post-Communist Societies: Rebuilding the Shipping at the Sea.* Cambridge: Cambridge University Press.

Erlanger, S. 1992. "Yeltsin Transfers Gorbachev Foundation Property." *The New York Times,* October 8.

Erskine, H. 1971. "The Polls: Women's Role." *Public Opinion Quarterly,* 35.

Esman, M. J. 1994. *Ethnic Politics.* Ithaca, NY: Cornell University Press.

Etzioni, A. 1964. *Modern Organizations.* Englewood Cliffs, CA: Prentice-Hall.

Fadeyev, E. 1994. "Bosnia: Nato Nachinaet i . . ." [Bosnia: Nato begins and . . .]. *Pravda,* March 3.

———. 1993. "Yugoslavia Flash Point: Carrion Crows." *Pravda,* August 11.

Fainsod, M. 1958. *Smolensk Under Soviet Rule.* Cambridge: Harvard University Press.

Farmer, K. 1992. *The Soviet Administrative Elite.* New York: Praeger.

Fein, E. B. 1990. "Gorbachev Hints He Would Accept Multiparty Rule." *New York Times.* January 14.

Felshman, N. 1992. *Gorbachev, Yelstin and the Last Days of the Soviet Empire.* New York: St. Martin's Press.

Ferguson, G. 1996. "Parties and Politics in Russia." *The Public Perspective,* 2.

Feshbach, M. 1995. An interview. *Blue and Gray* (Georgetown University), October 10.

Finifter, A. 1996. "Attitudes toward Individual Responsibility and Political Reform in the Former Soviet Union." *American Political Science Review,* 90 (March).

Finifter, A. W. and E. Mickiewicz. 1992. "Redefining the Political System of the USSR: Mass Support for Political Change." *American Political Science Review,* 86 (December).

Fiorina, M. P. 1981. *Retrospective Voting In American National Elections.* New Haven, CT: Yale University Press.

Fish, M. 1995. *Democracy from Scratch: Opposition and Regime in the New Russian Revolution.* Princeton, NJ: Princeton University Press.

Fong, M. 1993. *The Role of Women in Rebuilding the Russian Economy: Studies of Economies in Transformation.* Paper number 10. Washington DC: World Bank.

Forbes, H. D. 1985. *Nationalism, Ethnocentrism, and Personality: Social Science and Critical Theory.* Chicago: The University of Chicago Press.

Gaddy, C. & B. Ickes. 1998. "Russia's Virtual Economy." *Foreign Affairs* (September-October).

Galuszka, P. & R. Brady. 1996. "The Battle for Russia's Wealth." *Business Week,* April 1.

Ganguly, R. & R. Taras. 1998. *Understanding Ethnic Conflict: The International Dimension.* New York: Longman.

Garthoff, R. 1994. *The Great Transition: American Soviet Relations and the End of the Cold War.* Washington, DC: The Brookings Institutions.

Gerasimov, V. 1992. "Za Spinoi u Lyudei i Protiv Serbov." [Behind the People's Back and Against the Serbs]. *Pravda,* November 20.

George, A. 1979. "Case Studies and Theory Development: The Method of Structured, Focused Comparison," in P.G. Lauren (Ed.), *Diplomacy: New Approaches in History, Theory and Policy.* New York: Free Press.

George, A. & T. McKeown. 1985. "Case Studies and Theories of Organizational Decision-Making." *Advances in Information Processing in Organizations* 2.

Gibson, J. L. 1996." A Mile Wide but an Inch Deep: The Structure of Democratic Commitments in the Former USSR." *American Journal of Political Science* 2 (May).

———. 1995. "The Resilience of Mass Support for Democratic Institutions and Processes in the Nascent Russian and Ukrainian Democracies." In V. Tismaneanu (Ed.), *Political Culture and Civil Society in Russia and the New States of Eurasia:* 53–111. Armonk, NY: M.E. Sharpe.

———. 1993. "Mass Opposition to the Soviet Putsch of August 1991: Collective Action, Rational Choice, and Democratic Values in the (Former) Soviet Union." Paper presented at the Annual Meeting of the American Sociological Association, August 13–17, Miami Beach, FL.

Gibson, J. L. & R. M. Duch. 1993. "Political Intolerance in the USSR." *Comparative Political Studies,* 26 (October).

Glad, B. 1996. "Passing the Baton: Transformational Political Leadership from Gorbachev to Yeltsin; from de Klerk to Mandela." *Political Psychology* 17, 1 (March).

———. 1991. "The Idiopathic Presidency: Contingency, Context and Synthetic Reason in Political Analysis." Presidential Address, Presidency Research Group, 1990. *Presidency Research Groups News Letter.*

———. 1973. "Contributions of Psychobiography." In J. Knudsen (Ed.) *Handbook of Political Psychology.* WA: Jossey-Bass Publishers.

———. 1969. "The Significance of Personality for Role Performances of Chairman of The Senate Foreign Relations Committee: A comparison of Borah and Fulbright." Paper presented at the APSA Annual Meeting.

Glad, B. & R. Blanton. 1997. "From de Klerk to Mandela: Transformational Changes in South Africa," *Presidential Studies Quarterly,* 17, 3 (Summer).

Glinka, S. 1998. "The Ominous Landscape of Russian Corruption." *Transitions,* 5 (March).

Goldberg, J. 1998. "The Crude Face of Global Capitalism." *The New York Times Magazine,* October 4.

Gorianinov, V. 1996. "Empiricheskie Klassificatsii Zhiznennykh Tsennostei Rossian v Postsovetskii Period." [Empirical Classifications of the Life Values of Russians During the Post-Soviet Period]. *Polis,* 4.

Gorbachev, M. 1998. "Russia Needs a Change." *The Nation,* October 5.

———. 1996. *Memoirs.* New York: Doubleday.

———. 1995a. *The Search for New Beginning: Developing a New Civilization.* San Francisco: Harper.

———. 1995b. *Soyuz Mozhno Bylo Sokhranit.* Moscow: Aprel-85.

———. 1994. "Opasno Kogda s Rossiei Obrashautsa Kak s Mladshim Partnerom" [It Is Dangerous When Russia is Treated as a Junior Partner]. *Nezavisimaya Gazeta,* February 22.

———. 1993. *Gody Trudnykh Resheniy.* Moscow: Alfa-Print.

———. 1992. *Moya Pozitsiya (My Position).* Moscow: Novosti.

———. 1987. *Perestroika: New Thinking for Our Country and the World.* New York: Harper and Row.

———. 1985a. Interview with *Time Magazine.* Printed in *Pravda,* September 1.

———. 1985b. "The Key Issue of the Party's Economic Policy." *Report to the Plenary Session of the CPSU Central Committee.* June 11. Printed in *Izbrannye Rechi i Stat'I* [Selected Speeches and Papers]. Moscow: Progress.

———. 1985c. Interview with the editor. *Pravda,* April 8.

"Gorbachev Appeals for Unity." 1990. *The State* (Columbia, SC), July 3.

"Gorbachev Reveals Soviet Defense Budget." 1989. *The State* (Columbia, SC), May 31.

Gorbacheva, R. 1991. *I Hope.* New York: HarperCollins.

Gordon, M. 1998a. "Russian Legislators Reject Prime Minister Candidate." *The New York Times,* September 1.

———. 1998b. "Russian Premier's Calming Words: He Has No Economic Plan." *The New York Times,* October 2.

Gozman, L. & A. Etkind. 1992. *The Psychology of Post-Totalitarianism in Russia.* London: Centre for Research Into Communist Economies.

Greenstein, I.F. 1969. *Personality and Politics.* Chicago: Markham Publishing Company.

Grilli di Cortona, P. 1991. "From Communism to Democracy: Rethinking Regime Change in Hungary and Czechoslovakia," *International Social Science Journal* 45 (May).

Grunt, V., G. Kertman, T. Pavlova, S. Patrushev, & A. Khlopin. 1996. "Rossiyskaya Povsednevnost I Politicheskaya Kultura: Problemy Obnovleniya" [Russian Everyday Life and Political Culture: Problems of Renovation]. *Polis* 4.

Grushin, B. 1994a. "Is Peace at all Possible in Today's Russia?" *Mir Mnenii i Mnenia o Mire,* December.

———. 1994b. "Does Fascist Dictatorship Threaten Russia?" *Mir Mnenii i Mnenia o Mire,* October.

———. 1994c. "Has Russia Entered an Era of Democracy?" *Mir Mnenii i Mnenia o Mire* September.

Gunther, R., R. Diamandouros, & H.J. Puhle (Eds.). 1995. *The Politics of Democ-*

ratic Consolidation: Southern Europe in Comparative Perspective. Baltimore and London: Johns Hopkins University Press.

Gyula, J. 1983. "Political *Seilschaften* in the USSR." In T. H. Rigby & B. Harasymiw (Eds.) *Leadership Selection and Patron-Client Relations in the USSR and Yugoslavia.* London: George Allen & Unwin.

Hahn, J. 1993. "Attitudes Toward Reform Among Provincial Russian Politicians." *Post-Soviet Affairs* 1.

Havel, V. 1986. *Living in Truth.* London and Boston: Faber and Faber.

Hendley, K. 1996. "Rewriting the Rules of the Game: Legal Development in Post-Soviet Russia." Paper presented at the 1996 Meeting of the American Political Science Association, San Francisco.

Hermann, M. G. 1980. "Assessing the personalities of Soviet Politburo Members." *Personality and Social Psychology Bulletin* 6.

Hewett, E. A. 1988. *Reforming the Soviet Economy.* Washington, DC: Brookings Institution.

Hitchings, T. E. (Ed) *Facts on File.* Selected Volumes 1985–1998. New York: Facts on File, Inc.

Hoffman, D. 1998a. "Russia's Robber Barons." *The Washington Post,* January 12.

———. 1998b. "Russia Accuses Data Collector of Corruption." *Washington Post,* June 10.

Hough, J. & M. Fainsod. 1979. *How the Soviet Union is Governed.* Cambridge: Harvard University Press.

Hughes, J. 1996. "Moscow's Bilateral Treaties Add to Confusion." *Transition* 19 (September).

Humphreys, B. 1998. "Why '1040' Tax Form is 13 Pages Long in Russia." *Christian Science Monitor,* January 28.

Huntington, S. 1991–92. "How Countries Democratize." *Political Science Quarterly* 106.

———. 1965. "Political Development and Political Decay." *World Politics* 3 (April).

Imse, A. 1990. "Soviets' One and Only is Gorbachev." *The State* (Columbia, SC), March 15.

Inglehart, R. 1988. "The Renaissance of Political Culture." *American Political Science Review* 82.

Institute of Applied Politics. 1993. *Ekonomicheskie i Sotsialnye Peremeny* 4.

International Affairs. 1998. (USSR.) 10 (October).

Irving, C. 1989. *Public Opinion, Polls, and Democracy.* Boulder: Westview Press.

Izvestia. 1989. January 7.

Izyumov, A. 1990. "Time to Wind Down the Party." *Newsweek,* June 27.

Janos, A. 1991. "Social Science, Communism, and the Dynamics of Political Change." *World Politics* October.

Jansen, L. & E. Shiraev, E. 1999. *The Pain of Illusion: Harassment and Discrimination Against Russian Women* (Manuscript under review).

Jennings, M. & R. Niemi. 1981. *Generations and Politics.* Princeton, NJ: Princeton University Press.

Jennings, P. 1998. *ABC Nighttime News,* October 19.

Jos, P. H., M. Tompkins, & S.W. Hays. 1989. "In Praise of Difficult People: A Portrait of the Committed Whistleblower." *Public Administration Review* November/December.

Joseph, R. 1991. "Africa: The Rebirth of Political Freedom." *Journal of Democracy* Fall.

Jowitt, K. 1992. *New World Disorder. The Leninist Extinction.* Berkeley: University of California Press.

Juliver, P. 1991. "Human Rights After Perestroika." *Harriman Institute Forum,* 4 (June).

Karatnycki, A., A. Motyl, & B. Shor (Eds.). 1997. *Nations in Transit.* New Brunswick and London: Transaction Publishers.

Kagarlitsky, B. 1997. Transcript of presentation. *Piat Let Posle Belovezhia* [Five Years After the Belovezh Agreement]. Moscow: Aprel-85.

Kampleman, M. 1991. *Entering New Worlds: The Memoir of a Private Man in Public Life.* New York: HarperCollins.

Karl, T. & P. Schmitter. 1994. "Democratization Around the Globe: Opportunities and Risks." In M. Klare & D. Thomas (Eds.). *World Security. Challenges for a New Century.* New York: St. Martin's Press.

Kara-Murza, S. 1996. Editorial. *Sovetskaya Rossia,* May 5.

Kara-Murza, A., A. Panarin, & I. Pantin. 1995. "Dukhovno-ideologicheskaya Situatsiya v Sovremenoi Rossii: Perspektivy Razvitiya" [Psychological and Ideological Situation in Contemporary Russia: Perspectives of Development]. *Polis* 4.

Karklins, R. 1994. *Ethnopolitics and Transition to Democracy: The Collapse of the USSR and Latvia.* Washington, DC: The Woodrow Wilson Center Press.

———. 1986. *Ethnic Relations in the USSR: The Perspective from Below.* Boston: Unwin Hyman.

Katulskii, Y. 1996. "Labor Policy." In C. Williams, V. Chuprov, & V. Staroverov (Eds.), *Russian Society in Transition.* Aldershot, England: Dartmouth.

Keller, B. 1990a. "Shevardnadze Stuns Kremlin by Quitting Foreign Ministry and Warning of Dictatorship." *New York Times,* December 21.

———. 1990b. "Gorbachev Urges a Fractious Party to Pull Together." *New York Times,* July 3.

———. 1990c "Gorbachev Jeered at May Day Rally." *New York Times,* May 2.

———. 1990d. "Democracy, Gorbachev's Way." *New York Times,* March 18.

———. 1989a. "Soviet Poll Finds Deep Pessimism Over Gorbachev's Economic Plan." *New York Times,* November 5.

———. 1989b. "In Soviet, Party Officials Rage at Changes Under Gorbachev." *New York Times,* April 28.

———. 1987. "Gorbachev Presses for Vote with Choice of Candidates." *New York Times,* February 20.

Kelley, J. 1994. "Frustrated Russians Cool to the USA." *USA Today,* January 12.

Kerig, P., Y. Alyoshina, & A. Volovich. 1993. "Gender-Role Socialization in Contemporary Russia." *Psychology of Women Quarterly* 17.

Key, V. O. Jr. 1961. *Public Opinion and American Democracy.* New York: Alfred E. Knopf.

Kharchev, A., & V. Alekseev. 1977. *Obraz Zhizni, Moral, Vospitanie* [A Way of Life, Morality, Socialization]. Moscow: Politizdat.

Khasbulatov, R. 1993. *The Struggle For Russia.* New York: Routledge.

Khodyreva, N. 1993. An interview. *Bulletin of the St. Petersburg Center for Gender Problems.*

Khrushchev, N. S. 1971. *Khrushchev Remembers.* New York: Bantam Books.

Kliamkin, I. & V. Lapkin. 1996. "Socialno-Politicheskaya Ritorika v Postsovetskom Obshestve" [Social-Political Rhetoric in the Post-Soviet Society] *Polis* 1.

Klugman, J. 1989. *The New Soviet Elite: How They Think and What They Want.* New York: Praeger.

Koenigsberg, R. 1992. *Hitler's Ideology.* New York: Library of Social Science.

Kolko, G. 1997. "Privatizing Communism." *World Policy Journal* 14 (Spring).

Kondrashov, S. 1995. "Rossia Mozhet Prodeshevit v Bosnii i Vobshe." [Russia Can Go Cheap in Bosnia and In General]. *Izvestia,* November 21.

Korchilov, I. 1997. *Translating History.* New York: Scribner.

Korobeinov, A. 1996. *Gorbachev: Drugoe Litso* [Gorbachev: Another Face] Moscow: Pressa.

Korzhakov, A. 1997. *Boris Yeltsin ot Rassveta do Zakata* [Boris Yeltsin From Dawn to Dusk]. Ribinsk: Ribinski Publishing.

Kotkin, S. 1998. "Disappearing Rubles, Omnipresent Rust Belt." *The New York Times,* October 5.

Kremenyuk, V. 1994. "Deputy Director of the Russian Academy of Sciences' Institute of the US and Canada, Comments on President Bill Clinton's Visit to Moscow." *Novaya Yezhednevnaya Gazeta,* January 15.

Kristov, N. 1998. "As Free-Flowing Capital Sinks Nations, Experts Prepare to 'Rethink System." *The New York Times,* September 20.

Kull, S. 1990. "Dateline Moscow: Burying Lenin." *Foreign Policy* 78 (Spring).

Lane, D. & C. Ross 1998. "The Russian Political Elites, 1991–95: Recruitment and Renewal." In J. Higley, J. Pakulski & W. Wesolowski (Eds.), *Postcommunist Elites and Democracy in Eastern Europe.* New York: St. Martin's Press.

Lapidus, G. 1989. "State and Society: Toward the Emergence of Civil Society in the Soviet Union." In S. Bialer (Ed.), *Politics, Society and Nationality: Inside Gorbachev's Russia.* Boulder: Westview Press.

Lebed, A. 1996. Interview. Radio Russia. Moscow, June 13.

———. Interview. Radio Russia. Moscow, May 24.

———. Interview. Ostankino Radio Mayak, Moscow, May 14.

————. Press Conference. Moscow, May 13.

Lebow, R. N. 1981. *Between Peace and War, the Nature of International Crisis.* Baltimore and London: The Johns Hopkins University Press.

Levinson, H. and S. Rosenthal. 1984. *CEO: Corporate Leadership in Action.* New York: Basic Books.

Levada, Y. 1998. An interview of VTsIOM director Yuri Levada to Itar-Tass, January 5.

————. (Ed.). 1993. *Sovetsky Prostoi Chekovek* [Soviet Simple Man]. Moscow: Nauka.

————. 1991. *Lest Mnenie!* [There is an Opinion!]. Moscow: Politizdat.

Levgold, R. 1991. "Soviet Learning in the 1980s." In G. Breslaur & P. Tetlock (Eds.), *Learning in US and Soviet Foreign Policy.* Boulder: Westview Press.

Lewin, M. 1991. *The Gorbachev Phenomenon.* Berkeley: University of California Press.

Liesman, S. & A. Higgins. 1998. "Seven-Year Hitch. The Crunch Points: How Russia Staggered from There to Here." *The Wall Street Journal,* September 23.

Ligachev, Y. 1996. *Inside Gorbachev's Kremlin.* Boulder: Westview Press.

Lind, M. 1998. "Marx, Smith—or List?" *The Nation* October 5.

Linz, J. 1990. "Transitions to Democracy." *The Washington Quarterly* 13.

Linz, J. J. & A. Stepan. 1996. *Problems of Democratic Transition and Consolidation: Southern Europe, South America, and Post-Communist Europe.* Baltimore: Johns Hopkins University Press.

Lipset, S. 1996. "The Social Requisites of Democracy Revisited." In A. Inkeles & M. Sasaki (Eds.), *Comparing Nations and Cultures. Readings in a Cross-National Disciplinary Perspectives.* Englewood Cliffs, CA: Prentice Hall.

————. 1959. "Some Social Requisites of Democracy: Economic Development and Political Legitimacy." *American Political Science Review* 53.

Lynch, A. & R. Lukic R. 1996. "The Russian Federation Will Remain United." *Transition* 12 (January).

Lysenko, A. 1995. Interview. *Komsomolskaya Pravda,* July 15.

MacKenzie, J. 1995. "High-Profile President Looks Like a Candidate." *The Moscow Times,* October 20.

MacWilliam, I. 1997. "Bread Impresses Russians More Than NATO." *The Moscow Times,* February 8.

Mainwaring, S., G. O'Donnell, & S. Valenzuela (Eds.), 1992. *Issues in Democratic Consolidation: the New South American Democracies in Comparative Perspectives.* Notre Dame: University of Notre Dame Press.

Malia, M. 1992. "From Under the Rubble, What?" *Problems of Communism* 41.

————. 1990. "To the Stalin Mausoleum." *Deadalus* 119.

Mamonov, P. 1997. Interview. *Playboy.* Russian Edition November.

Marlin, O. 1990a. "Group Psychology in the Totalitarian System: A Psychoanalytic View." *Group* 141.

———. 1990b. "Czechoslovakia's Gentle Revolution: Role of the Young." Paper presented at the International Psychohistorical Association Conference. New York City, June 6.

Martin, M. 1990. *The Keys of This Blood.* New York: Simon & Schuster.

Materialy Politburo. 1990. March 12. A special publication.

Mathers, J. 1995. "Corruption in the Russian Armed Forces." *The World Today* 51 (August-September).

Mathews, J. 1995. *The Washington Post,* January 31.

Matlock, J. F. 1995. *Autopsy on an Empire: The American Ambassador's account of the Collapse of the Soviet Union.* New York: Random House.

McCourt, K. 1977. *Working-Class Women and Grass-Roots Politics.* Bloomington: Indiana University Press.

McFaul, M. 1995a. "State Power, Institutional Change, and the Politics of Privatization in Russia." *World Politics* 47 (January).

———. 1995b. "Why Russia's Politics Matter." *Foreign Affairs* 1 (January/February).

Medvedev V. 1994. *V Komande Gorbacheva* [In Gorbachev's Team]. Moscow: Bylina.

Medvedev, Z. 1986. *Gorbachev.* New York: W.W. Norton.

Melville, A. 1998a. "Polititcheskyi Tsennosti i Orientatsii i Polititcheskyi Institouti [Political Values and Orientations and Political Institutions] In L. Shevtsova (Ed.), *Rossiya Polititcheskaya* [Political Russia] Moscow: Moscow Carnegie Center.

———. 1998b. "K Teoretiko-Metodologitcheskomou Sintezou Strouktournogo i Protsedournogo Podkchodov k Analizou Demokratitcheskikh Tranzitov" [Toward a Theoretical-Methodological Synthesis of Structural and Procedural Approaches to Democratic Transitions]. *Polis* 2.

Merkel, W. 1998. "The Consolidation of Post-Authoritarian Democracies: A Multi-Level Model." *Democratization* Autumn.

Meyer, S. 1998. "The Sources and Prospects of Gorbachev's New Political Thinking on Security." *International Security* Fall.

Migdal, J. 1988. *Weak States, Strong Societies.* Princeton, NJ: Princeton University Press.

Migranyan, A. 1992. "Realnye i Illuzornye Perspektivy vo Vneshnei Politike [Real and Illusory Guidelines in Foreign Policy]. *Rossiyskaya Gazeta,* August 4.

Mikheyev, V. 1994. "Nato Ultimatum s Ugrozami Vozdushych Udarov Protiv Serbov ne Pouchili Podderzhki v Moskve" [The NATO Ultimatum Threatening Bombing in Bosnia Gets No Support in Moscow]. *Izvestia,* February 1.

———. 1992. *The Rise and Fall of Gorbachev.* Indianapolis: Hudson Institute.

Mikulski, K.I. (Ed). 1995. *Elita Rossii o Nastoyashem i Budushem Strany* [Russian Elite About the Country's Present and Future]. Moscow: Vekhi.

Miller, A., V. Hesli., & W. Reisinger. 1996. "Understanding Political Change in Post-Soviet Societies: A Further Commentary on Finifter and Mickiewicz." *American Political Science Review* 90 (March).

———. 1994. "Reassessing Mass Support for Political and Economic Change in the Former USSR." *American Political Science Review* 88 (June).

———. 1990–91. "Public Support for New Political Institutions in Russia, the Ukraine, and Lithuania." *Journal of Soviet Nationalities* 1, 4 (Winter).

Mitofsky-CESSI. 1996. Survey results. *Time,* July 1.

Mlechin, L. 1994. "Moskva Sovershaet Oshibky Izbegaya Sovmestnykh s Zapadom Deistvii v Bosnii." [Moscow is Making a Mistake by Shunning Joint Actions with the West in Bosnia]. *Izvestia,* April 23.

MMMM *Mir Mnenii i Mnenia o Mire* [The World of Opinions and Opinions about the World]. (A monthly publication of Sluzhba VP, Moscow.)

Morrison, J. 1991. *Boris Yeltsin.* New York: New York Times Press.

Morrison, D. 1988. *Mikhail S. Gorbachev: An Intimate Biography.* New York: Time Books.

Moses, J. C. 1976. "Regional Cohorts and Political Mobility in the USSR: The Case of Dnepropetrovsk." *Soviet Union/Union Sovietique* 3, part 1.

Murray, D. 1995. *A Democracy of Despots.* Boulder: Western Press.

Murrel, G. 1997. *Russia's Transition to Democracy.* Sussex: Sussex Academic Press.

Nenashev, M. 1993. *Poslednee Praviteltsvo SSSR* [The Last Government of the USSR]. Moscow: Moskva

New Outlook. 1990. 1, 3 (Summer).

Nie N. H., V. Sidney & J.R. Petrocik 1976. *The Changing American Voter.* Cambridge: Harvard University Press.

Oberdorfer, D. 1991. *The Turn: From the Cold War to the New Era.* New York: Poseidon.

Odom, W. E. 1990. "The Soviet Military in Transition." *Problems of Communism* May-June.

O'Donnel, Guillermo. 1994. "Delegative democracy." *Journal of Democracy* 5.

Olshansky, D. 1995. Press Conference. Official Kremlin International News Broadcast, December 6.

Openkin, L. 1996. I Reka Vremeni Vspiat ne Techet [And a River of Time Doesn't Flow Backwards]. *Rossyiskaya Gazeta,* June 7.

———. 1996b. "Reka v Poiskah Beregov" [A River in Search for its Banks]. *Polis* 1.

Pankov, V. 1991. "*Propoved o Nashikh Grekhakh.*" [A Sermon About Our Sins]. *Nezavisimaya Gazeta,* December 12.

Parish, S. 1996. "Enter Lebed, Exit the Hard-Liners." *Transitions,* July 26.

Pechkurov, V. 1995. Article. *Ogonyok* 27.

Perepelkin, O. 1995. "Rossiiski Entreprener: Shtrikhi k socialnomu Portretu" [The Russian Entrepreneur: Some Sketches to Its Social Profile]. *Sotsiologicheskie Issledovaniya* 1.

Peresvet, A. 1992. An editorial *Nezavisimaya Gazeta,* July 14.

Petrenko V. & O. Mitina. 1997. "The Psychosemantic Approach to Political Psychology: Mapping Russian Political Thought." In D. Halpern, A. Voiskounsky (Eds.). *States of Mind.* New York: Oxford University Press.

Petrenko V., O. Mitina, & R. Brown. 1995. "The Semantic Space of Russian Political Parties on a Federal and Regional Level. *Europe-Asia Studies* 5.

Philps, A. 1998. "Russia Data Chief Held as Tax Dodger." *Electronic Telegraph,* June 10. www.telegraph.co.uk.

Pishculin, N. & S. Skokov. 1990. "Za-Protiv" [Yea-Nay]. *Dialog* 16.

Pomorski, S. 1978. "Crimes Against the Central Planner." In D. Barry, G. Ginsburg, & P. Maggs (Eds.), *Soviet Law After Stalin.* Alphen aan den Rijn, The Netherlands: Sijhoff & Noordhoff International Publishers.

Popov, I. (1996). "If a Woman Becomes President." *Argumenty i Facty* 10 (March).

Powell, B. & O. Matthews. 1998. "The Gray Men are Creeping Back." *Newsweek,* October 19.

Pravda. 1990a. July 3.

————. 1990b. July 14.

————. 1988a. July 26.

————. 1988b. December 8.

————. 1987. April 25.

"Primakov Says Government Must Stabilize Ruble." 1998. *Russia Today,* September 18. www.RussiaToday.com

Przeworski, A. 1991. *Democracy and the Market: Political and Economic Reforms in Eastern Europe and Latin America.* Cambridge: Cambridge University Press.

"Psyching Out Gorbachev." 1989. *The Washington Post,* December 17.

Pushkov, A. 1994. "Russia and America: The Honeymoon is Over." Part 3. *The Moscow News,* January 10.

Raig, I. 1984. "The Development of Private Supplementary Farming in the Soviet Countryside." *Istoriia SSSR* 5 (September.-October.).

Reber, A. S. 1995. *The Penguin Dictionary of Psychology,* 2nd ed. London: Penguin Books.

Remington, T. F. 1993. "Regime Transition in Communist Systems: The Soviet Case." In F. J. Fleron, Jr. and E. P. Hoffmann (Eds.), *Post-Communist Studies and Political Science:* 265–298. Boulder: Westview Press.

Remington, T. F., S. Smith, D. Kiewiet & M. Haspel. 1994. "Transitional Institutions and Parliamentary Alignments in Russia, 1990–1993." In T. F. Remington (Ed.), *Parliaments in Transition: The New Legislative Politics in the Former USSR and Eastern Europe.* Boulder: Westview.

Remnick, D. 1993. "The Hangover." *New Yorker,* November 22.

Rhodes M. 1996. *New Russian Barometer V.* Glasgow: Center for the Study of Public Policy, University of Strathclyde.

———. 1995. *New Russian Barometer IV.* Glasgow: Center for the Study of Public Policy, University of Strathclyde.

———. 1993. "Political Attitudes in Russia." *RFE/RL Research Report* 3 (January 15): 42.

Riasanovsky, Nicholas. 1984. *A History of Russia.* New York: Oxford University Press.

Rigby, T. H. 1970. "The Soviet Leadership: Towards a Self-Stabilizing Oligarchy?" *Soviet Studies* 2 (October).

Rivera, S. 1995. "Tendentsii Formirovania Sostava Postcommunisticheskoi Elity Rossii" [The Tendencies in Formation of the Structure of Post-Communist Elite in Russia]. *Polis* 6.

Rodin, I. 1994. "MIDu ne Nravitsia Proekt Podgotovlennyi Tremia Fraktsiami" [Foreign Ministry Doesn't Like the Three Factions' Draft]. *Nezavisimaya Gazeta,* January 22.

Rosenberg, W. 1982. "The Zemstvo in 1917 and Its Fate Under Bolshevik Rule." In T. Emmons & W. Vucinich. (Eds.), *The Zemstvo in Russia.* Cambridge: Cambridge University Press.

Rose, R. & C. Haerpfer. 1994. *New Russian Barometer III.* Glasgow: Center for the Study of Public Policy, University of Strathclyde.

Rozov, V. S. 1997. "A Transcript of a Comment." *Piat Let Posle Belovezhia* [Five Years After the Belovezh Agreement]. Moscow, Aprel-85.

Rubtsov, V. 1995. "Nakazanie Svobodoi" [Punishment by Freedom]. *Polis* 6.

"Russia's Future." 1994. USIA Qualitative research report.

"Russia's Nightmare." 1998. *The Economist,* August 22.

"Russia Tackling Crisis, Purges Tax Service." *Russia Today,.* 1998. June 10. www.Russiatoday.com.

Rustow, D. A. 1970. "Transitions to Democracy: Toward a Dynamic Model." *Comparative Politics* 3 (April).

Ryzin, J. V. (Ed.) 1977. *Classification and Clustering.* New York: Academic Press.

Sakwa, R. 1997. "Rezhimnaya Sistema i Grazhdanskoye Obsh'estvo v Rosii." [The Regime System and Civil Society in Russia]. *Polis* 1.

———. 1993. *Russian Politics and Society.* London: Routledge.

Sanger, D. 1998. "As Economies Fail, the I.M.F. is Rife with Recriminations." *The New York Times,* October 2.

Schlozman, K. L. & S. Verba. 1979. *Injury to Insult: Unemployment, Class, and Political Response.* Cambridge: Harvard University Press.

Schmemann, S. 1993a. "Ban on Opposition." *The New York Times,* October 5.

———. 1993b. "Yeltsin and Legislature Act to Oust Each Other." *The New York Times,* September 22.

————. 1991a. "Declaring Death of Soviet Union, Russia and 2 Republics from New Commonwealth." *New York Times,* December 9.

————. 1991b. "Gorbachev Now: Vilified But Still a Force." *New York Times,* August 27.

Schmidt-Hauer, C. & M. Huber. 1986. "Gorbachev: The Path to Power." Topsfield, MA: Salem House.

Schmitt, D. & Winter, G. D. 1998. "Measuring the Motives of Soviet Leadership and Soviet Society: Congruence Reflected or Congruence Created?" *Leadership Quarterly* 3.

Schmitter, P. with T. Karl, 1994. "The Conceptual Travels of Transitologists and Consolidologists: How Far to the East Should They Attempt to Go?" *Slavic Review* 53.

Schubert, G. 1991. *Sexual Politics and Political Feminism.* Greenwich: Jai Press.

Schweitzer, A. 1984. *The Age of Charisma.* Chicago: Nelson Hall.

Scott, J. C. 1972. *Comparative Political Corruption.* Englewood Cliffs, CA: Prentice Hall.

Sergeyev, V. 1997. *The Wild East. Crime and Lawlessness in Post-Communist Russia.* Armonk: M.E. Sharpe.

Sharonov, A. & B. Ruchkin. 1996. "Young People, Politics, and Youth Policy." In C. Williams, V. Chuprov, & V. Staroverov (Eds.), *Russian Society in Transition.* Aldershot, England: Dartmouth.

Shakhnazarov, G. 1997. "Transcript of a Presentation." *Piat Let Posle Belovezhia* [Five Years After the Belovezh Agreement]. Moscow: Aprel-85.

Shama, A. 1997. "Notes From Underground: Russia's Economy Booms." *Wall Street Journal,* December 24.

Shapiro, M. 1992. "Russia a New Loss of Control: the Yeltsin-Gorbachev 'Brawl'." *Washington Post,* October 16.

Shatalov, A. 1995. "Love, Sex and the Color of the Russian Soul." *The Moscow Times,* April 12.

Shaw, B. 1958. *The Quintessence of Ibsenism.* New York: Hill and Wang.

Sheehy, G. 1990a. "The Shaping of the Man Who Shook The World." *Vanity Fair* February.

————. 1990b. *The Man Who Changed the World.* New York: HarperCollins

Shevardnaze, E. 1991. *The Future Belongs to Freedom.* New York: The Free Press.

————. 1989, "Address to the Political Commission of the European Parliament" TaSS. December 19.

Shevtsova, L. 1997. *Polititcheskie Zigzagi Postkomunistitcheskoy Rosii* [The Political Zigzags of Post-Communist Russia}. Moscow: The Moscow Carnegie Center.

————. 1995. "Domestic Politics." In G. Lapidus, Gail. *The New Russia.* Boulder: Westview Press.

Shiraev, Eric. 1983. *The Family and Children's Attitudes to Work*. Dissertation. Leningrad: Leningrad State University.

Shiraev, E. & D. Terrio. Forthcoming. "Indifferent Public and Rumbling Elites? Russian Action Related to the Bosnia Conflict." In R.Sobel & E. Shiraev (Eds.), *International Public Opinion and the Bosnia Crisis*, University Park, PA: Pennsylvania State University Press

Shiraev, E. & A. Bastrykin. 1988. *Moda, Kumiry, i Sobstvennoye Ya* [Fashion, Idols, and the Self] Leningrad: Lenizdat.

Shlapentokh, V. 1997. "The Four Faces of Mother Russia." *Transitions* 4 (October).

———. 1996. Russia: "Privatization and Illegalization of Social and Political Life." *The Washington Quarterly* 19 (Winter).

———. 1988. "The Changeable Soviet Image of America." In T. Thornton (Ed.), *Anti-Americanism. The Annals of the American Academy of Political and Social Science*. Volume 497. Newbury Park: Sage Publications.

Shlykov, V. 1997. *The Crisis in the Russian Economy*. Monograph presented at the US Army War College's Annual Strategy Conference, April 22–24.

Shubin, A. 1997. *Istoki Perestroiki* [The Sources of Perestroika]. Moscow: Moskva.

Shultz, G. 1993. *Turmoil and Triumph: My Years as Secretary of State*. New York: Scribner's.

Shulyakovskaya, N. 1998. "Singer Pugacheva Tipped to Run for Parliament." *The Moscow Times*, July 24.

Sidorov, S. 1994. "Rossiyskaya Pozitsia Yasna: Net NATO Vozdushnum Atakam Protiv Boniiskikh Serbov." [Russian Position is Clear: No NATO Airstrikes Against the Bosnian Serbs]. *Krasnaya Zvezda*, February 19.

Sillaste, G. 1995. "Evolutsia Socialnoi Pozitsii Zhenshch v Meniaushmsia Rossiiskiom Obshestve." [Evolution of Social Positions of the Women in Changing Russian Society]. *Sotsiologicheskie Issledovaniya* 1.

———. 1994. "Social-Gender Relations in the Period of Social Transformation in Russia." *Sotsiologicheskie Issledovaniya* 3.

Silunas, A. 1997. "Hobbi Igorya Matvienko" [A Hobby of Igor Matvienko]. *Muzobo* November.

Silverman, B. & M. Yanowitch. 1997. *New Rich, New Poor, New Russia*. Armonk: M.E. Sharpe.

Simis, K. 1982. *USSR: The Corrupt Society*. New York: Simon & Schuster

Skilling, G. & F. Griffiths (Eds.). 1971. *Interest Groups in Soviet Politics*. Princeton, NJ: Princeton University Press.

Skjele, H. 1991. "The Rhetoric of Difference: On Women's Inclusion into Political Elites." *Politics and Society* 2.

Smith, R. 1989. *Negotiating with the Soviets*. Bloomington: Indiana University Press.

Smith, H. 1990. *The New Russians*. New York: Avon Books.

———. 1976. *The Russians*. New York: Quadrangle/The New York Times Book Co.

Sobchak, A. 1992. *For a New Russia*. New York: The Free Press.

Solzhenitsyn, A. 1996. "Excerpts From Telephone Conversations at *Komsomolskaya Pravda* Headquarters, April 15. *Komsomolskaya Pravda,* April 23.

Sotsiologicheskie Issledovaniya, 1 (1995).

Sotsiologicheskie Issledovaniya, 1 (1994).

Sotsiologicheskie Issledovaniya, 1 (1988).

Sotsiologitcheskie Issledovania, 4 (1976).

Specter, M. 1998. "My Boris." *The New York Times Magazine,* July 26.

———. 1997. "When Yeltsin Talks, Nobody Listens (Aides Hope)." *The New York Times,* December 5.

Stephen, P. B. 1991. "Perestroika and Property: The Law of Ownership in the Post-Socialist Soviet Union." *American Journal of Comparative Law* 39 (Winter).

Stanley, A. 1996. "The Hacks are Back." *The New York Times Magazine,* May 26.

Starovoitova, G. 1998. Interview. *Obshchaya Gazeta,* March 5–11.

———. 1996. Interview to *Argumenty i Facty* 21 (May).

Starr, F. 1988. "Soviet Union: A Civil Society." *Foreign Policy* Spring.

Stites, R. 1992. *Russian Popular Culture.* New York: Cambridge University Press.

Stroev, E. (1996). "Stanovlenie Rossii Zavtrashnei: Opasnosti i Shansy" [Formation of a Tomorrow's Russia: Dangers and Chances]. *Polis* 4.

Sullivan, H. S. 1953. *The Interpersonal Theory of Psychiatry.* New York: Norton.

1951. "Psychiatric Aspects of Morale." In Stanton, X. & X. Perry (Eds.), *Personality and Political Crisis.* Illinois: The Free Press.

Surikov, A. 1997. "Pruning of Missiles in Exchange for Handouts." *Pravda,* September 19.

Suttle, P. 1998. "Modern Markets Play Key Role in Russia, Asia Financial Meltdown." *Boston Sunday Globe,* September 6.

TASS. 1990a. May 6.

———. 1990b. November 30.

———. 1990c. September 30.

———. 1989. November 28.

———. 1986. May 27.

Tatu, M. 1987. *Gorbatchev: l' URSS va-t-elle changer?* Paris: Le Centurion.

Taubman, P. 1988. "Soviet Panel Clears Bukharin." *New York Times,* February 6.

———. 1987a. "Choice Is Offered to Soviet Voters." *New York Times,* January 29.

———. 1987b. "Gorbachev, Citing Party's Failures, Demands Changes." *New York Times,* January 28.

Tellis, A., T. Szayna, & J. Winnefeld, 1997. *Anticipating Ethnic Conflict.* Santa Monica: RAND/ Arroyo Center.

Terry, S. 1993. "Thinking About Post-Communist Transitions: How Different Are They?" *Slavic Review,* 52.

Thompson, T. 1989. *Ideology and Policy: The Political Uses of Doctrine in the Soviet Union.* Boulder: Westview Press.

Tikhomirov, V. 1997. "Capital Flight From Post-Soviet Russia." *Europe-Asia Studies* 4.

Titarenko, L. 1995. "The Post-Soviet Generation in the New Political Environment." Paper presented at the 18th Annual meeting of the International Society of Political Psychology, Washington, DC.

Transcript of the Politburo meeting of 27 December 1988. *Istochnik* 1993.

Tobacyk, J. J. 1992. "Changes in Locus of Control Beliefs in Polish University Students Before and After Democratization," *Journal of Social Psychology,* 2 (April).

Treisman, D. 1996a. "Moscow's Struggle to Control Regions Through Taxation." *Transition* 19, (September).

———. 1996b. "Why Yeltsin Won." *Foreign Affairs* 5 (September/October).

Turovskii, F. 1984. "Society Without a Present." In L. Schapiro and J. Godson (Eds.), *The Soviet Worker from Lenin to Andropov.* 2nd ed. London: Macmillan.

Umansky, L. & A. Lutoshkin. (1975). *Psychologia i Pedagogika Raboty Komsorga* [Psychology and Pedagogy in a Komsomol Secretary's Work]. Moscow: Molodaya Gvardia.

Umbach, F. 1996. "The Role and Influence of the Military Establishment in Russia's Foreign and Security Policies in the Yeltsin Era." *The Journal of Slavic Military Studies* 3.

Unger, A. L. 1981. "Political Participation in the USSR: YCL and CPSU." *Soviet Studies* 33 (January).

Urban, M. 1994. "The Politics of Identity in Russia's Postcommunist Transition: The Nation against Itself." *Slavic Review* Fall.

USIA Research Memorandum, 16 March 1992.

Vail, P. and A. Genis. 1989. *The Sixties: The World of the Soviet Man.* Ann Arbor, MI: Ardis.

Valkenier, E. 1983. *The Soviet Union and the Third World: An Economic Bind.* New York: Praeger.

Vardenga, M. 1996. Essay. *Argumenty i Facty* 8.

Verba, S., N. Nie, & J. Kim. 1978. *Participation and Political Equality.* Cambridge: Cambridge University Press.

Volkan, V. 1988. *The Need to Have Enemies and Allies.* Northvale, NJ: Jason Aronson.

Volkov, D. 1994. "Rossiyskie Otnoshenia s NATO Okhlazhdautsia." [Russia's Attitude Toward NATO Cools]. *Sevodnya,* February 26.

Volkova (Lada Dance). 1998. Interview. *Argumenty i Facty* (Moscow edition)14 (April).

Volobuev, P. and L. Tyagumenko. 1992. "Eto Rossii ne Bezrazlichno." [It Makes a Difference to Russia] *Pravda,* February 27.

World Bank Report. World Bank. 1993.

Waller, J. M. and V. Yasmann. 1995. "Russia's Great Criminal Revolution: The Role of the Security Services." *Journal of Contemporary Crimi-*

nal Justice 4 (December). www.konanykhine. com\checkmate\ yasmann.htm.

White, S., R. Rose, R. & I. McAllister. 1997. *How Russia Votes.* Chatham, NJ: Chatham House Publishers.

Whitmore, B. 1998a. "Russia's Democracy Creates Tsars, But St. Petersburg is Trying to Make a Clean Break With the National Trend." *Russia Today.* www.RussiaToday.com

——. 1998b. "Russia's Top Crime Fighter." *Transitions* 5 (March).

Who's Who in Russia Today. 1994, 1996. K. G. Saur.

Willerton, J. P. and L. Sigelman. 1992. "Perestroika and the Public: Soviet Citizens' Views of the 'Fruits' of Economic Reform." In A. Miller, W. Reisinger, & V. Templin (Eds.), *The New Soviet Citizen.* Boulder: Westview.

——. 1991. "Public Opinion Research in the USSR: Opportunities and Pitfalls." *Journal of Communist Studies* 2 (June).

Williams, C. 1966. "Economic Reform and Political Change in Russia, 1991–96." In C. Williams, V. Chuprov, & V. Staroverov (Eds.), *Russian Society in Transition.* Aldershot, England: Dartmouth.

Witt, W. 1996. "Russian Tax Law a Hodgepodge Cheaters Love." *Chicago Tribune,* December 1.

Wriggens, H. 1969. *The Ruler's Imperative.* New York: Columbia University Press.

Wyman, M. 1997. *Public Opinion in Postcommunist Russia.* London: Macmillan Press.

Yakolev, A. 1992. *Obval: Poslesloviye* [The Collapse: An Afterword]. Moscow: Novosti.

Yasmann, V. 1993. "Corruption in Russia. A Threat to Democracy?" *RFE/RL Research Report* March 5.

Yavlinsky, G. 1996a. Press Conference, Moscow, The International Press Center, June 6.

——. 1996b. Interview. Russia TV channel, Moscow, April 28.

Yeltsin, B. 1995. Press Conference with Boris Yeltsin. Official Kremlin International News Broadcast, September 8.

——. 1994. *The Struggle for Russia.* New York: Times Books.

——. 1990a. Speech in Ufa, August 13. In *Piat Let Posle* Belovezhia [Five Years After the Belovezh Agreement]. Moscow: Aprel-85.

——. 1990b. *Against The Grain.* New York: Summit Books.

Yeric, J. L. & R. T. John. 1994. *Public Opinion: The Visible Politics.* 3rd. Ed. Itasca, IL: Peacock.

Young, K. E. 1996. "Loyal Wives, Virtuous Mothers; Women's Day and Russian Women of the 90s." *Russian Life,* March.

Yuriev, A. 1992. *Vvedenie v Politicheskuyu Psikhologiyu* [Introduction to Political Psychology]. St Petersburg: St. Petersburg Press.

Zakaria, F. 1997. "The Rise of Illiberal Democracy." *Foreign Affairs,* 76.

Zaller, J. 1996. *The Nature and Origins of Mass Opinion.* New York: Cambridge University Press.

Zaslavsky, V. 1995. "From Redistribution to Marketization: Social and Attitudinal Change in Post-Soviet Russia." In Gail W. Lapidus (Ed.), *The New Russia: Troubled Transformation.* Boulder: Westview Press.

Zhirinovsky, V. 1996a. Interview. Russian Public TV, Moscow, June 10.

———. 1996b. Interview. Radio Russia, Moscow, June 4.

———. 1996c. Interview. Radio Russia, May 29.

———. 1996d. Interview. Russia TV channel, Moscow, May 29.

———. 1996e. Interview. Russian Public TV, Moscow, May 22.

———. 1996f. Interview. Radio Russia, Moscow, May 21.

———. 1996g. Interview. Radio Younost, May 14.

Zdravomyslova, O. 1998a. *The Moscow Times,* March 7.

———. 1998b. *The Moscow Times.* February 24.

Zhuravlev, G., O. Kuchmaeva, B. Melnikov, & I. Orlova. 1996. "The Socio-Demographic Situation." In C. Williams, V. Chuprov, & V. Staroverov (Eds.), *Russian Society in Transition.* Aldershot, England: Dartmouth.

Zyuganov, G. 1996a. Interview. Russia TV channel, Moscow, May 17.

———. 1996b. Interview. Russia TV channel, May 12.

———. 1996c. Press Conference. Moscow, April 9.

Index